Wakefield Press

AUSTRALIA

Friedrich Gerstäcker was born in Hamburg in 1816. Inspired by the writing of Daniel Defoe, he set off for America in 1837 intending to become a farmer, and sent his mother a diary of his adventures. He returned to Germany in 1843 to discover that his mother had been publishing his diaries in a periodical to great popularity, and so his career as a best-selling writer began.

Over the course of his adventurous life Gerstäcker travelled to both the Americas, Tahiti, Indonesia, Egypt, and Australia. His trips were funded by a fruitful relationship with his publisher, and his considerable output was devoured by a legion of devoted readers, making Gerstäcker a household name for many years.

Friedrich Gerstäcker died in 1872, suffering a stroke while preparing for a trip to Asia.

Editor Peter Monteath, a Fellow of the Alexander von Humboldt Foundation, teaches History in the School of International Studies at Flinders University, Adelaide. His recent books include *POW: Australian Prisoners of War in Hitler's Reich*, *Red Professor: The Cold War Life of Fred Rose* (with Valerie Munt), *Interned: Torrens Island 1914–1915* (with Mandy Paul and Rebecca Martin), and the edited collection *Germans: Travellers, Settlers and their Descendants in South Australia*.

Also by Peter Monteath

Encountering Terra Australis:
The Australian Voyages of Nicolas Baudin and Matthew Flinders
(with Jean Fornasiero and John West-Sooby)

Germans: Travellers, settlers and their descendants in South Australia

Interned: Torrens Island 1914–1915
(with Mandy Paul and Rebecca Martin)

Red Professor: The Cold War Life of Fred Rose
(with Valerie Munt)

AUSTRALIA

FRIEDRICH GERSTÄCKER

A German Traveller in the Age of Gold

Edited by Peter Monteath

Wakefield Press

Friedrich Gerstäcker, c. 1850
Photographic portrait by Bertha Wehnert
[Stadtgeschichtliches Museum Leipzig, F/2672/2003]

Reisen

von

Friedrich Gerstäcker.

Vierter Band.

Australien.

Stuttgart und Tübingen.

J. G. Cotta'scher Verlag.

1854.

Wakefield Press
16 Rose Street
Mile End
South Australia 5031
www.wakefieldpress.com.au

First published 2016

Translation by Peter Monteath, Aileen Ohlendorf, Harald Ohlendorf,
Lois Zweck, Judith Wilson, Storm Graham, Thomas Kruckemeyer

Copyright © Peter Monteath, 2016

All rights reserved. This book is copyright. Apart from any fair dealing for
the purposes of private study, research, criticism or review, as permitted under
the Copyright Act, no part may be reproduced without written permission.
Enquiries should be addressed to the publisher.

Designed and typeset by Wakefield Press

National Library of Australia Cataloguing-in-Publication entry

Creator:	Gerstäcker, Friedrich, 1816–1872, author.
Title:	Australia: a German traveller in the age of gold / Friedrich Gerstäcker; edited by Peter Monteath.
ISBN:	978 1 74305 419 2 (paperback).
Notes:	Includes index.
Subjects:	Gerstäcker, Friedrich, 1816–1872 – Travel. Voyages around the world. Australia – Description and travel – 1851–1900.
Other Creators/Contributors:	Monteath, Peter, editor.
Dewey Number:	910.4

Contents

A Note on the Text		ix
Preface		xi
1.	Sydney	1
2.	By Mail Coach from Sydney to Albury	31
3.	A Canoe Excursion on the Hume	49
4.	March through the Murray Valley	61
5.	March through the Murray Valley (Continued)	94
6.	The Adelaide District	121
7.	Tanunda	150
8.	The Natives of Australia	169
9.	The Manners and Customs of the South Australian Tribes	178
10.	Sydney in August 1851	199
11.	Voyage through Torres Strait	233
Afterword: Friedrich Gerstäcker's Australia		261
Notes		276
Acknowledgements		298
Index		300

A Note on the Text

Friedrich Gerstäcker's travels around the world in the years 1849 to 1852 were financed in part by the illustrious Stuttgart publishing house J.G. Cotta. The arrangement provided that after his return to Germany Gerstäcker would write a full and detailed account of his travels, which Cotta would publish. Both parties were true to their word, with the result that from 1853 Cotta published five volumes of Gerstäcker's *Reisen* (Travels). *Australien* was the fourth of those volumes, following those on his travels in South America, California and the South Sea Islands. Like the fifth and final volume in the series on Java, *Australien* appeared in 1854.

Aware of potential British and American interest in his travels, the prolific Gerstäcker also prepared an English-language manuscript based on his travels; it appeared in 1853 as a single volume titled *Narrative of a Journey Round the World*. It was not an abridged translation of the five-volume German work, but rather, it appears, Gerstäcker's own original composition in English. The section in that book dealing with Australia is much shorter than the full-length German account (some 140 pages as against 514 in the original Cotta edition of *Australien*), but it is the source of Gerstäcker's Australian travels upon which readers of English have had to rely – until now.

After Gerstäcker's death his collected works – *Gesammelte Schriften* – were published over the years 1872 to 1879 by the Jena publishing house Costenoble. A version of *Australien* was published in the sixth of altogether 43 volumes. It is, however, the original 1854 version of the text, written soon after his travels and published by Cotta, which is translated here. Because of the size of the project, the translation was undertaken by a team of translators consisting of Peter Monteath, Aileen Ohlendorf, Harald Ohlendorf, Lois Zweck, Judith Wilson, Storm Graham and Thomas Kruckemeyer. The preparation of the final version of the manuscript was coordinated by Peter Monteath, who has also added the footnotes. The over-riding goal was to balance the need for accuracy with a desire to replicate Gerstäcker's characteristically fluent and engaging style.

There were no illustrations in Gerstäcker's original 1854 work. The camera had been invented, but as early cameras were hugely cumbersome, Gerstäcker did not travel with one. He did, however, make sketches, one of which has survived and is included here. Happily, also, it has been possible to include a reproduction of the map of Australia Gerstäcker carried with him on his travels. Complete with Gerstacker's own jottings, it is an eloquent legacy of a remarkable traveller.

'The Australian Royal Mail crossing a dry billybong', by Friedrich Gerstäcker
[Stadtarchiv Braunschweig, G IX 23/25]

Preface

In late March of 1851, Friedrich Gerstäcker, the most illustrious and prolific of Germany's travel writers, set foot in Australia. Over the preceding two years Gerstäcker had gathered enough experiences to keep his pen busy for years to come. He had sailed from Hamburg to South America, crossed the Andes, made his way to California, witnessed the madness of the gold rushes, and ventured across the Pacific.

In Australia there was to be no letting up; his desire for fresh adventure could not be quenched. From Sydney he took a mail coach to Albury, where in a feat of astonishing ingenuity he fashioned his own canoe to take him down the Murray. When his canoe sank, he travelled on foot to Adelaide and the Barossa Valley, where he was eager to check on how his countrymen had made their new lives in the Antipodes. Back on the east coast, he witnessed wide-eyed the outbreak of the Australian version of gold fever. Not until his vessel picked its way through the treacherous rocks and shoals of the Torres Strait did he finally leave Australia – and with it its multiple perils, delights and curiosities. He would never return.

He did, however, devote his bountiful energies and his considerable literary talents to writing an account of his travels which would both educate and enchant his huge readership. Countless Germans came to know Australia – and indeed many other parts of the world – through the pen of Friedrich Gerstäcker. And now, for the first time, English readers, too, can learn what befell the German adventurer on his Australian travels. More than that, they can gain a strikingly vivid image of what Australia was like on the cusp of the events that would change it forever.

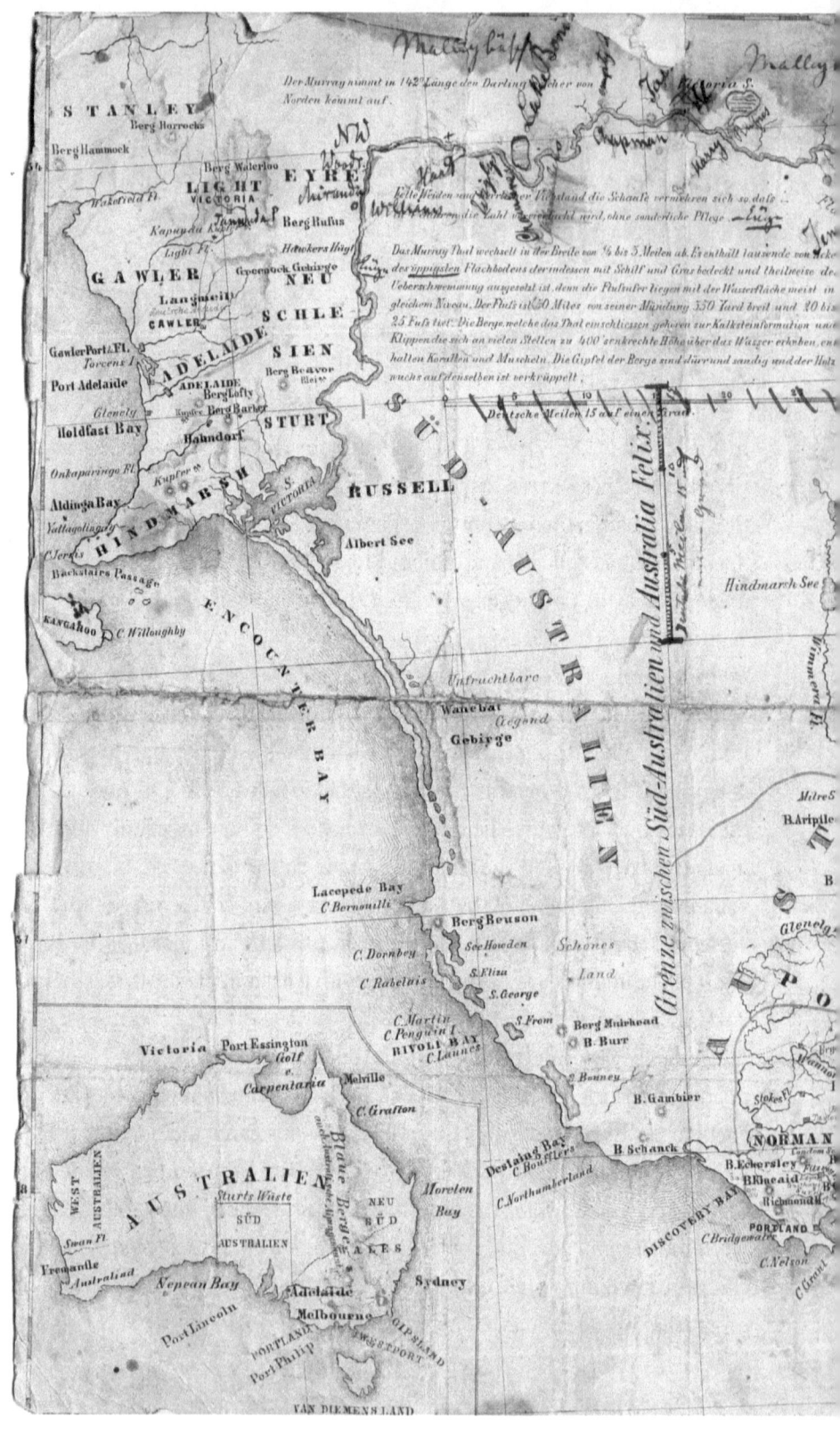

The German map Gerstäcker carried with him during his Australian travels

[Gerstäcker Museum Braunschweig]

1.

Sydney

Once again I am standing on solid ground, and as if by magic, country, climate, earth, scenery and people – in short everything that forms the actual world – have changed around me. It is no longer the rustling palms wafting above, no longer the thundering roar of the reefs and the murmuring and whispering of the wide banana leaves swaying in the wind, it is not the cheerful laughing and singing of the Tahitians, always happy and carefree, ringing in my ear. I am surrounded by this flat country, trimmed like a hedge of yew and studded with strangely symmetrical trees, by the city with its impressive rows of uniform houses, and the broad Irish brogue and English dialect are the only sounds offered to the ear as a substitute for the lost romantic magic.

It was altogether a curious feeling when I landed on Australian soil. *Australia* – everything that is upside down and strange, after the many descriptions of it from early childhood, is the first thing you associate with the very name Australia. Right away you want to look beyond the houses, which look exactly like those in every other civilised town, just to discover the curiosities surely lying beyond.

Kangaroo – even the name has a certain, magical ring to it, especially for a hunter. Platypus, cherries with their stones on the outside, trees that cast off their bark. For those coming directly from Europe, even the seasons are back to front. Those are all things that you certainly do not think about at that moment, but whose image we have in our minds as a muddled mass – and upside down, of course – the colours changing rapidly and flowing into one another like in a kaleidoscope. Merely having set foot on a foreign part of the world has its own charm. No matter how passionately people are attached to their own country, they still want to see a different one, so that they can think longingly back to their own. This is especially true as this part of the world also belongs, as it were, to the Antipodes, and the people here by rights should be standing on their heads, even if we had already found out where *up* actually is.

Australia became a sort of land of promise. I arrived hungry and was fed (for 1 shilling and sixpence). I arrived there, if not entirely naked, but in very light clothing, and was dressed (for 3 pounds, 10 shillings). In fact, the whole business of staging my arrival made such a strange impression on me right from the start, that I really do not know how better to characterise it, than if I honestly confess to the reader that it would not have taken much to make me believe that it might disappear from under my feet. So I immediately broke off a piece of stone to keep as a souvenir of this place.

I was really terribly hungry, for on board there had not been anything to eat, even if I had wanted to wait for the 'breakfast', and this made me aware that I confronted a new reality, and that an inn was what I needed first before seeking anything else. This really dealt a bit of a blow to the romantic side of things.

By the way, Sydney is anything but romantic, for if in any part of the world (even notwithstanding the Yankee States, and that certainly says a great deal) there is a perfectly genuine commercial life, it is here. Pounds and shillings are the only words which, like a magic formula, can animate the features of the indifferent faces surrounding the foreigner everywhere, and when the shillings turn to pounds for these wheelers and dealers, a completely contrary phenomenon becomes evident in the foreign traveller wandering among them. It is that, providing he is bored with the never-ending discussions about wool and shipping, he learns in a quite practical way that he is not cut out to be a businessman.

The character of Sydney is purely English, and at the same time it is strange how sharply the English spoken here differs from the American version, even though they are the same language. You find the most striking example of this in the United States, where just the narrow stretch of water of the northern lakes separates America and an English colony from each other, for never have

I found two neighbouring towns that are so unlike each other in every little detail as, for example, Buffalo and Toronto.

But to come back to Sydney, the stranger arriving here usually has to overcome a kind of prejudice that has developed in him over the years and really does not diminish during his travels, especially in California. It is the prejudice of going to a criminal colony and finding oneself suddenly among an indefinite number of murderers, thieves, burglars and other dreadful, horrible characters transported to this place in particular.

Here the new arrival finds to his astonishment that, at least visibly, there is not the slightest trace of all of that. And even if he should now and again – because he is constantly looking for them – encounter suspicious-looking faces perhaps more often than anywhere else, these in no way justify the terrible expectations that he might have had of the whole population based on what has been written. The 'Government people' (convicts), as they are called here, have now really merged with the immigrants, so that it takes someone in the know to recognise them. One would hope that the easy access to food here has turned most of them into honest people, whatever their former crimes may have been, and that it will no longer be necessary to differentiate between them. Who knows, perhaps in future centuries this kind of deportation could lead to a mark of distinction, a type of nobility of the colony. The children of the convicts sent here in former years now in part form a considerable and respected section of the population (here and there even former convicts themselves); after centuries their children and children's children will make up large numbers of descendants. Our European aristocracy, after all, sprang from even stranger origins.

At the beginning in Sydney I had a few problems finding a good establishment where I could live; I passed by most of them, since the bars downstairs did not look very inviting. Following the principle that in a strange city, the best thing to do is choose the best hotel – at least until one knows one's way around better – I decided on the Royal Hotel, a large, imposing, but somewhat rambling building, and moved in. The next thing was a warm bath and then a good breakfast. After that I had to get a completely new outfit, for during my travels I had become rather dishevelled. Here in Sydney there are lots of opportunities, because there are plenty of clothes shops, and clothes are relatively inexpensive.

On Saturday the 29th I wrote my letters, which at that time had to be dispatched to England by sailing ship. As I was sitting in my room in the evening, I suddenly heard a dull noise from one of the lower rooms, shouts of bravo, stamping of feet, drumming and the loud booming voice of a speaker in between. In any event there was a meeting going on, and when I enquired about it, I was told that it was an anti-transportation meeting.[1]

The meeting was being held in the large ballroom below in the Royal Hotel, and there was a lively discussion among the numerous participants. By the way, the meeting was concerned, as I soon found out, only indirectly with the transportation of convicts at this time, and more directly with a bill proposed by the government. If passed, according to the speakers the bill would unfairly reorganise the electorates of New South Wales to favour the squatters or settlers in the interior over the people of Sydney: 'The most infamous, unjust, treacherous and diabolical measure', as one of the speakers remarked in the heat of the debate. The squatters, especially those in the north, it seems, are not so opposed to the transportation of convicts to these colonies, because in this way they get cheap labourers, while now sometimes there are none to be had. The inhabitants of Sydney, on the other hand, are vehemently trying to prevent a new shipment of these subjects. Sydney has also of course continually received a bad name from this practice, as was particularly evident a little while ago in California, where the very words 'from Sydney' had a completely abhorrent effect.[2]

In order to deal with this jointly with the inhabitants of Sydney, delegates from Melbourne, Adelaide and Van Diemen's Land arrived here and were treated to a sumptuous meal a few days later. In order to prove to the government that the people were serious in their opinion, they called a public meeting for the purposes of a demonstration for the following Monday. At this they intended to voice their opinion about the proposed bill and thereby express their thoughts about transportation or non-transportation.

The meeting proceeded calmly, although matters of considerable controversy for a *royal* colony were discussed. Our German police would certainly have intervened as much as possible and would have stirred up as much trouble as they could. The local police knew better how to react – people governed by a monarch would, of course, not have allowed them to interfere.

I did not attend a later meeting, but I heard that it took place and decisions were made in the same fashion as at the preliminary meeting.

In Germany I had been recommended to a Mr A. Dreutler, quite an important German who has a business in Sydney, and I was welcomed by him most warmly.[3] The following Sunday, the 30th of March, we went to the lighthouse together, one of the most popular amusement parks in Sydney, and found most of the population there. For Sydney, the lighthouse is indeed a quite romantic spot. The lighthouse is at the southern side of the harbour entrance; the coastline facing the sea is formed by rugged cliffs, two to three hundred feet high. A quarter of a mile away there is a hotel, and some Sydney-siders out for a jaunt commonly come out here on a Sunday, while others regularly visit the more interesting Botany Bay and Cook's River.

The lighthouse itself is magnificent and consists of a revolving light, formed by nine lamps with metal mirrors. The rock on which it stands may be about 120 feet above sea level, and the lighthouse is some 60 to 80 feet high. Its light can be seen from the sea at a distance of 30 and sometimes even 40 English miles, if the weather is clear.

The view from here over the calm sea is truly delightful, and from this height the background of the deep blue sea shows ships approaching from a great distance with their white, shimmering sails. Strangely enough, all the beauty of the scenery is restricted to the sea and to the nearby coast of Port Jackson. Immediately behind begin the dry, sandy plains, dotted with woody bushes, 'grass trees' and a kind of reed-like plant. Every little shrub very often has attractive flowers, and a lovely little creeper (the Kennedia) with its fragrant, violet flowers often fills entire bushes. Small, individual groups really look very inviting, but the entire landscape toward the interior looked desolate and sad, and the harbour with its delightful coastline lay there like an oasis in the wilderness.

I must say the pleasant company together with the exotic impressions all around me, made my day pass very quickly. It made for a refreshing change from my hitherto sometimes really dreary wandering around the world.

Having not returned from the lighthouse until late, the next day I endeavoured to find out something about the interior and the possibility of travelling by land to Adelaide. In any case, I wanted to visit the Adelaide area particularly because of emigration there, but I did not want to go there by sea.[4] On the one hand, lately I had spent enough time sailing around on salt water, and on board I had seen nothing of the interior other than the harbour ports, which are the same the world over. On a journey through those parts of the interior hitherto explored, on the other hand, I would get to know everything, or at least a great deal of this part of the world that might be useful to me in the future, and for this reason I decided to explore it all in detail.

In fact, in the beginning, I heard barely anything positive about it all. First came the most horrific accounts of native Indians,[5] and then followed not only a thousand other difficulties, but even the most impossible obstacles for the individual. However I was accustomed to that by now and knew what I needed to do. Above all, I thought it most important to talk to somebody who had first-hand knowledge of those areas or at least a part thereof. For this purpose I was introduced to a Mr Shepherd, who was said to have made the trip once in the past with a herd of cattle and a small caravan.

In a most friendly manner he told me everything he knew about it, but even his account was in no way encouraging. Apparently this time of year was normally the least suitable for an overland journey, but particularly so in this year, because it had not rained at all along the River Murray for the past year and probably even longer than that. So there was no grass at all – one could only make the trip on horseback, and under such circumstances the animals would find little or no fodder on the way. At night one would of course have to hobble the horses and let them roam free, because fodder in those areas is not available everywhere, in fact probably very seldom. In the mornings it was likely that one would have to spend hours or indeed half the day looking for them. Furthermore, nothing exhausts a rider more than the knowledge of a hungry, tired and worn-out animal underneath him. The continual worry about all of this ruins the whole trip for him, so that in the end he prefers to walk rather than being dragged along by a constantly weary animal.

In view of this, Mr Shepherd thought that I could hardly expect to reach Adelaide in less than three months. I could possibly do it in slightly less time, but all in all it would end up taking three months. On top of that, I would have the pleasure of meeting almost all those tribes of often very hostile and treacherous natives along the Murray itself, where I would have to travel because of the water.

Three months in the saddle, and on top of that in such a manner, was an awfully long time, and the whole business went round in my head all day long.

That same morning I was strolling through the city streets, when suddenly an elderly gentleman addressed me in the warmest manner, but by a different name. He was taking a walk on the sunny side of the street, under an open umbrella. He was dressed in a slightly worn, but otherwise clean and proper coat and was wearing a heavy gold (perhaps gold plated) watch-chain and signet-ring of the same material. I attributed his use of the wrong name to him having mistaken me for someone else, which I would be able to rectify in a few words and then be able to go on my way; but I was not to get away so easily. The stranger of course apologised most profusely, but then indicated that because he had mistaken me for someone else, he now wished to make up for it as best he could. Fortunately, by a very great stroke of luck, he had received just a few days previously, sadly, just a very small amount of 'galvanic – ' (the reader will have to forgive me, I have totally forgotten that most terrible Chaldean name), and it would indeed afford him great pleasure to let me have one of them. The price was not even worth talking about, but the item would speak for itself, and I needed merely to permit him to show me a sample and hand it over. With that he grabbed me by a button and pulled me, without any resistance on my part, into the nearest hallway.

The good man thought he had convinced me, and I let him believe this, for obviously this was something that would have to run its course before the two of us parted company. Foremost I had him show me the galvanised monstrosity of a name, which consisted of no less than a small bottle in a Morocco leather case, which he now urged me to smell.

At first glance I had in no way done the little bottle an injustice when I took it for ammonium chloride. So I only sniffed it very carefully from the side and then, fully satisfied, was about to hand it back to the obliging stranger. He, however, urged me to take a hearty sniff, and for the first time I now viewed the man with some suspicion. Had I really taken a hearty sniff, within a few seconds I would not have been able to breathe and would have lost consciousness. He, in turn, would easily have been able ... But no, I was doing the man an injustice, that was not his business. He also looked too fragile, and I simply handed the bottle back to him and then asked him all about its use and benefits. At this very moment in time, there really was no known condition (not even shattered bones) that could resist this galvanic monstrosity of a name. It cured them all, and its effect on various ailments such as gout, toothache, inflammation of the abdomen, sprains etc., was as interesting as the means by which it was ministered – it was simply a matter of smelling it, either intensively or more lightly, depending on the severity of the illness. The price was also very low, only 3s and 6d (not quite a German *Speziestaler*).[6]

The little man finally started to get impatient, I was too gullible for him, because probably none of his victims had asked him so many questions – we would have been in the hallway for three quarters of an hour. He also told me very quickly that that very morning the English bishop had bought two samples from him and had voluntarily given him a guinea for them; it would be possible for me to do likewise. And, with a friendly nod of the head, he handed me the bottle, now closed, for the second time.

The end of the story is brief. I expressed my regret that at that moment I did not have the slightest physical pain, neither tooth- nor ear-ache, neither gout nor podagra,[7] and no inflammation of the abdomen etc., but I gave him my firm assurance that I would approach him at the first sign of any of these symptoms. For the first time he looked surprised, glanced at me from head to toe and then amicably gave up.

He said that since he had at first only approached me by mistake as a complete stranger, he felt obliged to offer me his invaluable galvanic medicine at a lower price than to others and was going to let me have it for half a crown. To no avail – I did not have any pain. Two shillings? Not even that. Eighteen pence? His face alone as he made this last remark said as much as: 'I am really sorry I have to utter this miserly sum and trust you will not be so miserly.' But I was so miserly, thanked him a thousand times that he had taken such interest in my health and left him, just as he was taking his large gold watch out from his pocket to check the time.

Regardless of how well that man knew me from the first time we met in our lives, I was a total stranger to him when I encountered him a second time.

On 3 April there was, in the Botanic Gardens, an exhibition of work by women for the benefit of the poor, and since almost the whole of Sydney flocked there, I of course headed there as well. The exhibition was held in a large tent pitched on the lawn and contained, from what I could gather, nothing special. The better articles had, I think, already been sold or raffled off, but even around the rest there was such a crowd beside the two long tables that one could only push in at one's own peril.

All of Sydney's fine society seemed to be here, and it was a pleasure to behold such a crowd of charming figures gathered in one place. To me it was again something quite new, and it almost reminded me of home. A strange, colourful mixture of people mingled under the fragrant flowering bushes and trees collected from all over the world; the fair sex was of course most prominent, because charity was the main reason for this event. And it had been a long time since the Botanic Gardens displayed such a magnificent array of colours and resplendent floral arrangements as seen today. Neither was there a shortage of interesting groups of people making the scene so much more lively and exotic. Here and there a young officer, in a close-fitting red uniform with tight sleeves, a happy young and beautiful lady on his arm, strolled through the crowd and tried, albeit in vain for a while, to reach one of the crowded tables. In one spot, a happy father, by the sweat of his brow, was pulling four or five of his offspring, hanging on to his hands and coat-tails, and on his arm his other half – carrying food and dressed, it seemed, in clean clothes – along the gravel paths. In another spot a family was resting on its laurels, looking at a small cardboard cigar lighter and cigar case that they had just won for three half crowns in one of the small raffles. In yet another place, the faces of a few wild, rosy-cheeked girls flashed across the soft green grass, laughing and joking and apparently engrossed in their own company. A pious, somewhat bent figure, in a white waistcoat and necktie, respectably buttoned into a black dress-coat and shaded by a wide-brimmed hat, was slinking along the row of bushes. He seemed to be completely absorbed in godly devotions, glancing neither right nor left and appearing mildly irritated, when, again and again, he ran into the lively, jolly and happy girls.

In the meantime, the sky had become overcast; grey clouds were rising in the south-west, and pale yellow streaks of lightning flashed across the dark backdrop. Unfortunately the clouds did not seem heavy enough to fear a real downpour, for I was feeling mischievous enough to look forward to the chaos that would most certainly ensue. Notwithstanding this fact, some rain was bound to come, and so I dashed under one of the trees in order to wait for the impending moment.

Dear God, the tree was an old friend from Louisiana, a kind of acacia, with truly dagger-like thorns protruding from the trunk; once in the pursuit of a bear in the swamps of the Red River my horse, with a wild and dangerous jump, carried me between two such trees, just far enough apart to let us pass through. I still remember exactly how I shuddered with terror when I thought of what I would have looked like if, to the right or left, those dreadful thorns had caught me. In this moment I was on the banks of the Mississippi under the shady palms and cypresses, the rampant grey Spanish moss and the fragrant magnolias of that beautiful country, when I was suddenly rudely awakened from my dreams by a well-dressed gentleman, who was carrying the crudest looking piece of furniture under his arm and asked me in a low, ingratiating voice, whether I would not like to buy a raffle ticket for this 'extraordinarily beautiful object'. The ticket was only half a crown, 2s 6d, about 25 *Reichsgroschen*.[8] But what was this 'extraordinarily beautiful object'? God knows. The reader may imagine a rectangular box, 2¼ ft. high and 1 ft.

across, slightly narrower at the bottom than at the top, with a standard lid. The box itself was covered in red Morocco paper, the lid decorated with mediocre embroidery. What could the box be used for? I straightened up and, very excited, asked the man that question. Smiling, he just shrugged his shoulders and told me that one would be able to use it for anything. His main interest, however, seemed to be to persuade me to buy a ticket, and he assured me, when I did not show any particular interest, that this was the first prize. I should just let him draw the ticket for me, because he was a very lucky person and had often won for ladies and gentlemen. At first I really did have the intention to buy a ticket, but now the danger of winning this awful object was too great, and I refused obstinately. The man gave me a pitying look and went his way.

The rain cloud, meanwhile, was approaching ever closer. Far in the distance I could already hear the wind rustling in the treetops, and what was about to come had to come soon. Here and there a few anxious couples and even whole families were already fleeing across the field, the children as light infantry, and the father following with heavy artillery. Young men flew in busy haste ahead of smaller groups of young ladies, supposedly in the hope of finding and hailing a carriage, but inwardly with the firm conviction that they would not find one at this moment. The whole scene looked like a dovecote that, with the sudden appearance of a large bird of prey, descended into total disarray. However, the largest number fled into the marquee, where people were standing side-by-side like the front of a tightly packed phalanx; it seemed to me that not even a mosquito could have penetrated it.

The rain now started to pour down. It approached over a dense group of Norfolk pines, and everybody, it seemed, had found protection and shelter, when suddenly in wild leaps the man with the 'mysterious object' came running up. The red Morocco paper was in the most serious danger, and holding the upholstered lid like a kind of battering ram in front of him, and seemingly also using it, he forced a gap in the dense throngs, until in the blink of an eye he was gone, as if the ground had opened up and swallowed him. Like the waves on the sea, the swaying crowd of people closed behind the fugitive.

The rain did not last long, and very soon the sun in all it glory was again shining in the sky. The raffle of some of the diverse objects took place very soon after that. I was only interested in the main prize, and indeed if I had been the one to hand it out, I could not have given it to a better winner, at least not to someone who could have made less use of it. Fortune is really a jester – the lucky person was the helmsman of a whaling boat.

I wandered slowly back into the city, wrote a few letters and retired to bed early. Thoughts of the journey overland to Adelaide swirled around in my head. Again I had talked to people who advised against undertaking the journey at the present time, as the horses would hardly find anything to eat. Apparently it had not even rained once along the Murray this past winter and the drought was extreme. The old familiar thorn bush from the Red River swamps had in this connection re-awakened fond old memories. It really was a fine wild time, when I hunted deer and bears in the magnificent forests of the West, and I glided along the calm, fast-flowing waters of the mighty Red River in my sleek, light canoe. Canoe? At the very thought I sat bolt upright in bed. And what would prevent me from likewise paddling down the Murray in a canoe? The distance? If I had managed the 500 miles on the Red River back then, 2000 miles along the Murray were not impossible. The native Indians? I was carrying an excellent shotgun, and the native Indians are only too often made out to be bogeymen, and quite often very unjustly.

I knew already that from here to the Murray itself I could travel by mail coach. Once there I would be able to buy a canoe, or, if that did not work, there were enough trees along the river to cut one out myself, something that I felt I could do in a few days on my own. And the Murray? Well, there were enough people in the city who could tell me whether at this time of year there was enough water in it for me to go down it by canoe, and I only needed six to eight inches of water; I could then navigate round individual rapids and shallows. I had found a way – a journey by canoe down the Murray of a kind that no one before me had ever made, at least not as far as Adelaide. And there would be the hunting along the river itself: kangaroos and cassowaries, wild dogs and black swans. God knows what dark dreams I had during the night. The next morning I was still as enthusiastic about my plan as I had been the night before. Enquiries I made about the river that day left me in no doubt that I would be able to make the trip – my mind was made up.

During this time I also had the pleasure of making the acquaintance of another German family (from Frankfurt), the photographer Hötzer with his charming wife.[9] Herr Hötzer has really established photography here and was extremely busy; Frau Hötzer plays the pianoforte expertly – she also teaches it – and was kind enough to play for us. Oh it is such a special, wonderful, indeed powerful feeling to hear suddenly once again after so many years the dear, familiar tunes of home. I know of nothing else in the world that pulls at the heart stings so strongly and profoundly. How I would have liked to retreat to a quiet, private corner, where I could listen to the tunes that I had missed and yearned for so long.

The next evening I was with Consul Kirchner, a local businessman and landowner, who was particularly interested in the immigration of Germans to this country and has done a lot for this cause.[10] He welcomed me most warmly, and I had the pleasure of listening to German music again at his house. Although Frau Kirchner was born of English parents in Australia, she was completely familiar with the German language and music, having lived in Germany for a few years.

The following day, a Sunday, I went out to Botany Bay, Sydney's most interesting spot, with Herr Dreutler, his niece, the captain of the *Dockenhuden*, a ship that had only just arrived a few days ago and was due to return to Hamburg, and a passenger from the same ship; and we spent a very pleasant day at Botany Bay. With its charming location on the beach of the small but friendly bay, a really excellent tourist destination has been created. Apart from its very attractive garden, this spot is particularly interesting, since the owner has a large collection of native animals, at least the most important ones, and thereby has, as it were, transformed his little spot into a zoological garden. Apart from the cassowaries or emus there are three wild dogs, quite sturdy fellows of a reddish yellow colour with heads just like German shepherds and foxes' tails, which look as if they could do considerable damage to flocks of sheep. You can also see many very beautiful large birds of prey, together with the strangest kinds of local doves, parrots and cockatoos; furthermore there is the possum, which incidentally is quite different to the American opossum. This one is a much friendlier animal, does not have the evil appearance and bare tail of a rat, like the American one, but looks more like a fat, ponderous, retired grey squirrel. Then there are also two black swans, magnificent birds with their dark brown feathers and red beaks, Muscovite ducks, also native, and, the main attraction, five kangaroos, which live in a small enclosure with two roe deer (recently imported from Manila). Their leaps are truly comical, and they knew how to use their short front paws most skilfully to fend off the more than obliging roe deer, that usually refused to budge, when we fed them with bread on our way back. By the way, the climate did not particularly agree with the deer, because when I returned later, the buck was already dead.

But soon I would be able to observe Australian wildlife myself in its own native and much more interesting habitat and will save this description until then.

In the same enclosure there were also the following non-native animals: a young Bengal tiger, a magnificent, sleek, smooth animal, and a small black bear from the Himalayas, a small, ugly, scruffy chap, lazy and morose looking, who incidentally seemed to be quite ashamed of his ugliness, because he kept his front paw in front of his face almost all the time.

The next time I visited Botany Bay, we also crossed by boat to the other side of the bay, which is noteworthy, because Captain Cook, as well as La Perouse, the famous French navigator, set foot on Australian soil here for the first time. The beach there consists of very soft, yellow sandstone, which rises steeply into a low cliff. In memory of this event, a small copper plaque with the exact details has been inserted into the rock here.

For La Perouse, on the other hand, a small sandstone column has been erected on the left-hand side of the bay in order to commemorate him. After he had left the coast of Australia, he was never heard of again and, if I am not mistaken, only after a long time traces of him were found on the coast of New Guinea, indicating that his ship had run aground there and that the crew must have been lost or killed.[11]

Botany Bay, by the way, offers nothing in the way of scenery and can in no way be compared to the neighbouring Sydney Bay or Port Jackson, as it is usually called. With the exception of the immediate beaches of the bay and some small, low valleys, the area consists of sand covered in bush, which literally in many places becomes dried-out stretches of white sand. Port Jackson, which is situated so picturesquely in the middle of this barren area, truly seemed to me like a small trader who puts all his polished wares on show in the shop window, and to this end empties the rest of his shop. Botany Bay, however, is famous for the many new plants that have been discovered there, and I have to admit that if one looks closely, one can find various shrubs covered in flowers, numerous species of banksias and other extremely beautiful and interesting plants. That, however, does not change the character of the whole scene, which is definitely sad, once you leave the sea level.

Botany Bay is also an extremely harmless place and quite innocent of the bad name it has earned in the civilised world. Along its beaches there has never been a convict colony, indeed people have not even been forced to work there, as there was nothing for them to do, and yet the name Botany Bay is now associated with almost all the horrors of that period. This is what happens when one has bad neighbours.

Of course I went to the theatre in Sydney, but I have to admit that I was not overly impressed by the taste of the Sydney audience. I had been under the impression that an audience coming directly from England would have had a little more artistic sensibility than Brother Jonathan in the United States. But heaven forbid, I found the same bombast, the same raucous tones of a market-place. The actors, with only a few exceptions, were of the kind that would have received the same response on a mediocre stage in Germany as they did here, only with a quite different meaning. Here the stamping of feet and whistling signify unlimited approval, and it warmed my heart to be able to join in as I would in Germany, without being impolite.

The whole programme was in fact American: first of all a drama with a detailed list of the various scenes and horrific events, just like in a cops and robbers novel, then comical songs, for all of which the audience, in the roughest manner, demanded an encore and extremely mediocre – yet enthusiastically applauded – dances in between. The story I think was supposed to depict a Moorish dance, and among the dancers, all of them females, were two young ladies painted black, who reminded me vividly of our blackened fake Moors in German show booths.

Perhaps it was by mere chance that evening, but there were lots of ladies in tight leotards, who frequently said things that were by no means delicate but were always met with hearty applause. The audience did not seem at all odd, as I thought I discerned from a little comedy performed after the drama, and after which I owed the actors an apology, because they were excellent. The topic was very simple: a sulking young married couple are reconciled by the woman's unknown brother, an officer of course, who upon his sudden appearance is taken for a rival. As the plot develops, the husband states that the officer, who refuses to duel with him after kissing his wife, deserves to be stripped of his uniform. The officer replies, 'If you so wish.' Then, quite calmly, he takes off his jacket. 'Perhaps my waistcoat as well?' he adds, and divests himself of this too. The married couple and their servants – an elderly manservant and the young maid – stand there in disgust, jacket and waistcoat draped over the chair. The audience listens with breathless suspense. 'Would you like anything else?' asks the dreadful officer calmly, with an unambiguous gesture, as if about to drop his unmentionables, which is prevented only by the husband anxiously holding up his hands, the joint shriek of horror from the wife and the maid, and the enthusiastic jubilation of the audience. A single young man in the stalls also seemed to want it, because he yelled at the top of his voice 'Down with them!', but he was shouted down.

The audience was almost more interesting to me than the play itself. I have hardly ever seen a more colourful and mixed crowd in one place. The dress circle is exclusively for fine society; the very name *dress circle* indicates what it stands for, and black coats and tails and white kid gloves are indisputably in the majority here. The ladies are also decked out in their finery, just as in other dress circles, and only very rarely is displeasure or criticism expressed; a noble, dignified stiffness is the rule. The upper circle is for the middle classes, but it is only half respectable, for one should not be surprised if suddenly a young lady puts her hands on someone's shoulders and, over the head of the unsuspecting person in front, watches the play unselfconsciously and most intently. The balcony has the cheapest seats, the home of the righteous and a kind of paradise which is all the more crowded if the programme is dreadful. The most interesting place, however, is the stalls, for if the former deserves to be called paradise, in the stalls it looks as though the sheep have not been separated from the goats, and as if they were constantly and impatiently awaiting the command to direct them to the extreme right or left. As if they had been shaken out of Noah's Ark, a small man and a small woman are sitting together cosily, along with sailors and housemaids, grey old ladies and shop boys, tradesmen and water-men, in brief, both sexes in the most colourful array, with straw hats, caps, flowered bonnets, red shawls, shirt sleeves, lace collars, coats and tails. During the performance this crowd has a lot of fun, laughing, shouting bravo and encore, with stamping of feet and whistling and all of this with gusto. Both, as mentioned before, are expressions of approval. In the short intervals the enthusiasm gets even noisier, so that a theatrical evening of this kind is like a continuous sequence of entertainment for the crowd. Then comes the time when here and there a member of the audience gets up on a bench and gives an oratory or musical performance to the surrounding crowd who listen with delight. Here two sailors perform a mock sword fight with sticks, much to the discomfort of a quiet gentleman in a brown coat, who receives all the strokes that one of the sailors parries; there another fellow has, like a wily robber, taken the seat of someone who has just got up, and the heated discussion threatens to end in a brawl. One of them rips off his jacket in order to free up his elbows in the upcoming fight, when suddenly a vendor intervenes quite literally with his body and his basket, quite unwillingly, but just as fortunately for keeping peace in the establishment. For, with his basket fully laden with oranges, apples, pears and figs, he was stepping calmly across the benches in the usual manner, offering his fruit for sale. His unfortunate curiosity took him straight towards the incipient brawl, where he could not have expected any customers at all – from there he had an excellent view of the arena – but as he takes just one more step, he suddenly gets caught in something. Was it a treacherous stick, or did his normally safe foot slip? He sways for one moment, but the heavy basket with its terrible velocity decides his fate. Like a hailstorm the apples and oranges rain down on the brawlers, while the previous onlookers suddenly get involved and recklessly make a grab for the loot of fruit, leaving the vendor lying there with his basket.

But there is no time for those in the circles to watch even this, because in another part of the stalls there is an almost louder noise. Here a bottle of soda water has exploded in the midst of a gathering of women and children, and amid the children's screams, the ladies' screeching and the men's laughing and pushing out of the way, the curtain rises again. After a brief shouting of 'hats down', which is only sporadically obeyed with a disgruntled sideways glance, there is, broken once again by the screams of small, naughty children, more stillness than you would expect from such a crowd.

The orchestra is very weak, some of the scenery so mediocre that it appears to comprise caricatures, while other parts are quite good. On the whole everything that I saw of the theatre, which I later visited quite frequently, I found quite convincing. The artists were suited to light, conversational pieces about everyday life, but as soon as they went beyond that they were flops, and more often than not in Europe that would be the case even with our best artists.

To my utmost surprise I saw the actors here in so many different roles that we could not imagine at half-decent theatres in Germany. Have any of my readers seen, on board a ship, a sofa which before one's very eyes turns from a seat into a wardrobe, chest of drawers, bed, washbasin and God knows what else? That's what happens with actors and actresses here. Madame Magnus, who played Kilian and Agathe in *The Marksman* at the same time, was nothing in comparison. I saw the leading female lover as the supporting youthful male lover, as a soubrette, as a member of the chorus and as a dancer, and from then on nothing surprised me anymore. Most of all, however, I was amazed by a small corpulent figure, who played maids and mothers, second and third supporting female lovers, gentle fathers, was a member of the chorus and did other small parts as well. This figure was perhaps 4 foot tall and 3½ in diameter, always respectably dressed, and without any exterior features of extravagance. This figure suddenly appeared on stage as a ballet dancer with a magic wand, in the shortest possible skirt, sticking out cheekily in all directions, in skin-coloured tights with bare arms and neck, then began to hover in the air, waving her little fat legs around in such a strange and careless manner, that I was quite convinced on several occasions that she would never be able to sort them out for the rest of her life. I sat there transfixed and could not even applaud. As far as the seats in the theatre are concerned, I had heard, after visiting it once, that the second circle was in no way respectable, and so the next time I went to the stalls in order that this time I could view the interior from below. But here I found out for myself what I had been told about the second circle, for the ladies of pleasure, who probably, like in America, are given free admission, wandered around in a truly scandalous manner. In other words, there really are no reputable seats in the theatre other than the so-called dress circle, where one is obliged to appear in formal dress and to pay five shillings (about 1 Thaler 20 sgr). Furthermore, it does not say much for the people of Sydney that such a confined space as the dress circle seems totally sufficient to hold the reputable members of the audience.

I would like to add a word of warning for all those coming here after me: not to move from one's seat in the theatre during the Australian expressions of approval. A man from the country came into the stalls with his wooden riding crop, just as a *pas de deux* had ended, and vehemently demanded an encore, as he probably had not seen the dance. He made this clear by violently hitting the wooden bench in front of him with the heavy wooden handle of his whip. A corpulent gentleman, who came in at this very moment and was gazing at the stage while he was striding across the bench, unfortunately came close to the applauding fellow and cleverly managed, albeit unwittingly, to get one of his corns caught right between the handle of the whip and the bench just at the crucial moment. One can imagine the result.

Incidentally, my sojourn in Sydney itself lasted longer than I really had initially intended; in fact I needed a short break, not just to recover from previous strenuous challenges but also to prepare for new ones. And I therefore indulged myself without having a bad conscience in an extremely beneficial brief idleness. I stayed in Sydney so to speak 'to enjoy myself', which in certain German cities would have been considered suspicious, as is well known, but here no one even raised an eyebrow. Of course I never felt quite at ease in cities when I was travelling. Indeed cities rarely offer anything new or interesting, given the amount of money it costs to be there. At the same time, however, it was also important to me to learn as much as possible about the Murray and my inland tour, before setting off on my expensive journey, in order to avoid perhaps being forced to return later, and this was a twofold reason not to be in too much of a hurry.

Life in Sydney is both expensive and cheap just like in all larger cities, depending on how one organises oneself. The hotels have the most varied prices, and the worst thing is that as regards the larger ones, board and lodging do not correspond to the vastly inflated prices. In the Royal Hotel you pay 49 shillings a week for only mediocre and very basic cuisine, for poor service and a sparsely furnished room, while you can, if you hit the right spot, get almost as good accommodation for 12 shillings and in most places the same for 16 and 20 shillings. As soon as I became a little more familiar with Sydney I of course moved to a cheaper and indeed better guesthouse than the Royal Hotel.

The city has a decidedly English character and is quite lively during the day until 10 o'clock in the evening. Numerous omnibuses cross it from one end to the other, up and down George Street, the main thoroughfare. In addition there are elegant hackney carriages standing at various points around the city. The streets are lit by gas lamps, with good pavements, and the shops are elegant and tastefully decorated. Sydney, in any case, measures perfectly well to a third-rate city in England.

Public life is particularly lively here, the numerous bread and vegetable carts hurry past each other everywhere, fish vendors tirelessly hawk their wares displayed on wheelbarrows, and on almost every corner cake sellers proffer their hot pies, 'penny a piece'. Stalls and fruit shops can also be found in large numbers, and one can easily imagine that the visitor has an excellent opportunity to spend his money.

However, the truly astonishing number of public houses, according to their signs 'licensed to sell spirituous and fermented liquors', surely has a most unfavourable influence. Their number is legendary, and drunken men and women are part of daily life. Among these I also saw a few specimens of the genus *homo australiensis* or of the so-called black fellows – dreadful types with revolting, wild, dissipated features.[12] What is more, the Australian savages have little to contribute on the subject of beauty, but drink has made them into real monsters, and they could indeed without any preparation serve as deterrents for any temperance society with modest requirements. The 'fairer sex' looks even more dreadful than the 'ugly one', and the glassy eyes staring blankly ahead sometimes resemble those of the mad.

In Botany Bay a few of those black ladies accosted us; that is, they approached us, curtsied most gracefully, which, however, looked quite comical, and begged the group in the politest, most carefully turned phrases for some 'white money', because they know very well the difference between this and the red money.

'Black fellows' or just 'blacks' is the name used exclusively for the wild native tribes, whereas the whites born here, who in Louisiana would call themselves Creoles, for example, have taken on the name of 'natives'. People are also very polite towards the transported or deported, who are always called 'government people'. Here, however, this politeness is, so to speak, a logical consequence of a most unpleasant relationship for the stranger, who has a limited knowledge of the people he is dealing with and their family relationships. For one can never be quite sure, even in the city's best circles, that one is not with someone who was deported himself or is a descendant of such a person, albeit now in totally different circumstances. If one does not want to offend deeply and irreversibly people who have caused no offence, one always has to be extremely careful, especially when talking about deportation and deported persons themselves: 'Politeness never hurt anyone.'

By the way, the criminal elements of the city certainly do not pretend to be anything else here in Sydney. I have never in my whole life heard so much about break-ins, murders, theft and other robberies as I have here, not even in California. Each daily paper reports new crimes, and again at this very moment, apart from a mass of wrong-doers getting away with minor punishment, a dreadful murderer, who seems to have almost made a career out of it, has been sentenced to death and was to be hanged on 25 April. The mail coach is regularly attacked, and it would not have surprised me if on my journey to the Murray I was to experience a minor Apennine incident. To reach the Murray I had to travel 400 miles by mail coach through the very part of the country where such attacks occurred most frequently.

One charitable institute here is the Mechanics School of Art, a kind of reading circle which keeps the latest English and Australian newspapers, and which is also a type of library that belongs to the institute itself and lends its books to its members. Among its newspapers one can find *The Times*, *London Illustrated News*, *Scotsman*, *Art Union*, *Athenaeum*, *Calcutta Englishman*, *Punch* and most of the quarterly reviews and magazines, together with the better Australian newspapers. But the fact that not one French or German newspaper is kept here, indicates how little attention is paid to strangers or foreigners, some of whom, after all, are members. The Germans here on the whole seem to stick together less than in North America and are therefore also totally isolated in the otherwise English population.

Not a single German newspaper, not even one in private hands, can be found in Sydney, and they get all their news from home only from *The Times*, which, as is well known, is always hostile to German affairs; one can imagine how incomplete and in most cases distorted this news must be.

As far as the land is concerned, particularly close to Sydney itself, it is not particularly suited to agriculture. New South Wales has, in fact, been recognised as being far more suited to livestock, but only recently individual farmers, especially up on the Hunter River, have tried viticulture and indeed with very good success. I was, in fact, advised by several parties to visit the Hunter River, since that was undoubtedly the best land for both agriculture and viticulture, and that it was also the most suitable spot for Germans who wanted to emigrate to Sydney.[13]

I would get to see enough of 'The West' fairly soon. So I decided not to miss the opportunity, as I only had short time left, to make a little detour to the north to get to know the Hunter River and surrounding area, at least en passant.

On Saturday 12 April at 10 pm I went aboard the beautiful iron steamship *Rose*, and at about 9 o'clock the next morning I arrived at Newcastle after a somewhat rough voyage, for we had a head wind, and the waves were fairly high. Newcastle is a small town in the most desolate sandy desert, but it has a fairly good harbour and excellent coalmines, which will surely soon lend the town, in spite of its desolate appearance, some importance. There used to be a convict colony here.

From here we left the open sea and travelled up the Hunter River, which is quite wide here. The countryside was fairly monotonous as long as we stayed within the low swampy area. On either side of the river the banks were covered with low shrubs and flowers. Often these banks were hardly visible above the water, submerged by frequent floods and only sometimes brought to life by garrulous cockatoos or swooping seagulls. Here and there the land formed proper islands, and the overall impression it gave was sad and desolate, similar to the mouth of the Mississippi. Further upstream, however, the landscape took on a more pleasant character; now and then small country houses emerged from the scrub, and cultivated fields came into view. One spot, on the right bank, was located almost romantically in a thicket of orange trees and Norfolk pines, between which, half hidden, the broad tropical leaves of banana trees were visible.

The further we sailed upstream, the more cultivated I found the land; the withered trees left standing in the fields, the forest behind and the low banks all made the whole area look uncommonly like the Mississippi, though of course on a much smaller scale. For the river itself is quite insignificant, and only in summer does the water flow up to here, where the tide reaches, while the valley itself is narrow and clearly must not be compared to the lower reaches of the Mississippi. The similarity was only superficial, and it could even be seen again in the fenced-in fields and the many fields of maize. The Australian farmers do not grow the latter for their own consumption like the Americans, but only for their livestock. The Australian does not eat anything but wheaten bread.

As it was autumn now, the corn, of course, was still in the fields, but the wheat fields had been ploughed, and here and there I saw ploughs pulled by four or six oxen.

Raymond Terrace, a flourishing small town, was my first stop. From here I intended to travel to the farm of a certain Mr James King in Irrawang, about three miles from Raymond Terrace, who had been recommended to me by Messrs Dreutler and Kirchner in Sydney.[14]

For the first time I was now striding through Australian forest. It is always a singular, wondrously uplifting feeling for me when I enter the forest of a foreign part of the world, and I rushed as fast as I could to escape from the feeling of being hemmed-in by the houses of the little town. The impression that the real forest, or bush as it is rather aptly called here in Australia, made on me, was, however, not at all of the kind that I had initially expected. I found only very few really tall and beautiful trees, and while most of them were slender and straight enough, they were not such that they could be compared to an American or even a Tahitian jungle. Van Diemen's Land and New Zealand are, incidentally, supposed to have much more significant forests than New Holland. The trees themselves all look almost the same, and most of them also belong to the species of the gum trees with tough, lanceolate, elongated leaves, and are divided into 'stringy barks', common gums and 'black-butts', distinguishable only by their different types of bark. I did not, however, get to see a single proper stringy bark here; the settlers use their tough, strong bark for the roofs of their houses and other purposes, and the trees themselves, once they have been stripped of their protective bark, then of course die off. Other gum trees shed their bark voluntarily in winter and now stand, albeit with green leaves, but otherwise as bare and ugly as the wild stubborn natives of the country, between their brothers who have a greater sense of decency.

Australia has almost always been described to us as the land of contradictions, and the European very often thinks that even the most trivial details must stand in contrast to the old world. But when you come here yourself, these seemingly extraordinary differences recede far into the background, and at first sight the surroundings seem quite ordinary. Peculiarities, however, on closer inspection emerge soon enough, and apart from the trees denuded of their bark, the casuarina tree among others, with its oak-like trunk and fir needles, also fits in here perfectly. The timber of the casuarina is almost identical with the timber of an oak, as regards hardness and appearance. The needles, however, are similar to those of the fir only from a distance and up close look just like horsetail,[15] with the one difference that they do not have the same qualities.

The timber of all gum trees is hard and so heavy that it sinks in water like lead, even though the core of almost all of the larger trees is said to be rotten. But along the coast in a small number of valleys a type of cedar grows which yields excellent timber, and in the interior one can find a very attractive species of fir. Only a few types of gum trees can be split easily.

After walking the few miles, I arrived at Mr King's farm toward mid-day, and even though I did not find the man himself at home, I was told that he was expected any minute, and in the meantime I was welcomed most cordially by Mrs King. There is still hospitality here in Australia in the real patriarchal sense, and the further into the bush one goes, the more welcome the stranger is to the settlers, and they are loath to let him go again.

Mr King is particularly involved in viticulture, and he works the land really just for this purpose. The remainder of the land he has leased to tenants, as I will explain later, and he receives a certain income from it according to certain agreements and numbers of years. Here I tasted the *Irrawang 47*, a white wine that had been bottled for a while, and thought it was excellent. It has a most pleasant taste, quite similar to that of the *Hochheimer*, and it is almost more fiery than the *Hochheimer*. A red wine from the same farm is, in my opinion, absolutely up to the standard of the *Aßmannshäuser*. Mr King is considering sending samples of this wine to Germany, but I fear that they might lose some of their taste during the long voyage, just like the Rhine wine, which does not cope well with long sea crossings either. Mr King did not return home until evening, and the following day we rode around all his fairly extensive properties. The land is quite good, and the pastures are excellent, but the land close to the river is said to be much better, as might be expected, as in some years it is particularly exposed to flooding, which leaves behind excellent mud, without being dangerous on account of too strong currents. Here he had about 4000 acres in one stretch, and even though a small part of it was stony, hilly land, a large section of it, on the other hand, seemed to be suitable for growing maize and wheat, and the remainder was almost entirely usable for vineyards or pastures.

By leasing the land to immigrants or poorer people who are about to make a start in agriculture, his land is gradually being made arable for him. The tenants themselves profit from this extremely well, since they do not have many expenses and in the first two years do not have to pay for the leased land, which of course they have to make arable first. The further lease is also moderate, and the settler is always able to earn enough money for himself bit by bit and to start on land of his own. One area, however, where Australia is not as generous to the immigrant as, for instance, the United States, is the relatively high price of the land here. One guinea an acre is the government price, and at the auctions, where all land is auctioned off, it is usually even higher, if it is at all in a good location. Australia does not have the preemption rights that the Americans have. Nonetheless, in earlier times the ordinary poor worker, even if penniless when stepping onto Australian soil, never had to worry about lack of work. On the contrary, it was workers they needed, and without exception everyone found work – some more successfully than others. That was, of course, before the discovery of gold, and circumstances have changed considerably in that respect, but I will return to that later.

I met here two German families, who, with many others at the same time, had been enticed to Australia by government money, and who had now had to work here to pay back their fare by means of a two-year contract with the settlers. They talked very favourably about the land and assured me that whoever wanted to work would get by and do very well by it. On the other hand, they did not particularly like the 'life in the bush'. Whoever in Germany was used to the noise or even just the more social aspect of life in the major or minor cities, and was perhaps a little too emotionally attached to the local places of amusement, will always miss those things, no matter to which country he immigrates. It is for this very reason that his personal circumstances are so much better than in the old country, because workers are in short supply, and consequently there is a dearth of the social life that the presence of people provides. Life in the bush has a character of its own, and like every other life has to be learned or at least to be understood, and whoever is not self-reliant will not be able to feel at home there. The immigrant only needs to look on it as preparation for a better future, for his own hard work attracts neighbours, and in time 'society' forms itself.

'Shortage of workers', but not of work, was the slogan I heard everywhere, and all the farmers complained that they could not get anybody to work for them. This is the sole reason why in certain districts they are calling for a return of the deportation system, as for example in Moreton Bay to the north, where most people support the return of deportation, and where meetings have even been held for this purpose. The reason, however, is easily found: when immigrants arrived here, they were immediately snapped up by the local farmers, and if any of them expressed the wish to go north, they were told such terrible stories about the atrocities committed there by the native Indians, that they readily gave up their initial intention. The inevitable consequence of this was that the farmers in Moreton Bay could hardly get any decent workers at all, even when they offered higher wages, and consequently they on the one hand were for a new transportation law, while on the other hand those in the more southern and more pro-immigration areas of Australia were against it.

Attempts have been made to bring in workers from China, and in some areas, for example along the Clarence River and a few other places, farmers actually have Chinese people in the bush working as shepherds and doing other work. The farmers seem to be quite satisfied with some of them, but on the whole I do not think that they like the Chinese – because of a few peculiarities or even vices – and everybody is longing for immigrants from Europe. Germans in particular are the most sought after.

The settlers in Irrawang were just in the process of founding a 'national school' in the midst of their settlements. It was too far to send the children to Raymond Terrace, and donations have been widely collected for this purpose. The government is also very liberal and appears to be in favour of fully supporting the school. It contributes two thirds of the cost of the school building, that is, if 30 students can be found, only a third of the cost has to be carried by the parents, and the government pays a teacher 40 pounds sterling per year. The people of Irrawang, however, much to the disapproval of the district's clergy, are proud of getting a national school, that is, a school that does not depend on the clergy and allows them to provide religious education only at the time when the children are at home and on Sundays. The enthusiasm of the valiant Richard Cobden[16] for the reformation of schools is beginning to take hold here, and God knows a reformation of the schools would be necessary in Germany, albeit not in the manner it is being carried out at present. The English in their national schools do not intend to take religion away from the people. No reasonable person, no one who genuinely has the interest of the people at heart, will ever demand that; they just want to include it in a sensible way. But it will take more effort before we obtain permission for this in the future – or before we seize it ourselves.

I also intended to visit Maitland further up river and a few farmers in the vicinity, for which Mr King very kindly gave me a letter of recommendation. Unfortunately I missed the steamboat up river, which on this morning had been unusually favoured by a strong breeze, and as my time was a little short, and the weather was clearly turning to rain, I decided to return to Sydney instead on the boat which came down river immediately afterwards.

It turned out as I had expected. During the day it already rained a few times, there was a fresh southerly wind and in the evening there was shower after shower. On board the steamboat things looked terrible; we were carrying a large number of passengers, the ladies' cabin was crowded, furthermore there were 12 or 16 cabin-passengers and 20 or 30 steerage passengers, and they were all seasick. In the ladies' case it was really heartbreaking. In the dining room we were only two, and even he, my last companion, displayed the most alarming symptoms after the meal. Until evening he managed to remain on deck with me, but he became extremely monosyllabic and even expressed his distaste for brandy, which the captain, who had known him for a while, at first did not want to believe. As it got dark, and the sea became rougher and rougher, he also disappeared, and I remained the 'last of the Mohicans'. At 11.30 we reached Sydney, and I entered this harbour in the dark for the second time.

Of particular interest at that time was the fate of our compatriot, Dr Leichhardt.[17] On his second expedition – he made the first, as is well-known, from Moreton Bay to Port Essington in the face of unspeakable danger – he travelled west from the same spot in order to find a land route for communication to the western part of Australia. The date of his return was already so overdue, it was almost feared that he had met with disaster in the desolate interior of the country. Leichhardt, however, was far too well-known and too popular in Sydney for him to be just abandoned to his fate. Several meetings were held in which citizens adamantly voiced their opinion that a petition should be sent to the government, urging them to take the matter in hand. His Excellency, the Governor-General of Australia, Mr FitzRoy[18] granted 2000 Fr.[19] to launch a new expedition, to either find him or gather some information about his death. Of course, only volunteers were to be recruited, and I would very much have liked to join such a party, if I had been at all able to spend such a long time travelling. The expedition could hardly be completed within eighteen months, as enough people had to be recruited for it, and the party had to wait for a more favourable time of year, because the continuing drought in the interior would definitely have been detrimental to the animals. After the advent and the actual onset of the wet season – for the previous year had proved that in the interior the two do not always coincide – better fodder could be expected.

On the whole, this part of Australia has suffered badly from drought in the last few years, which has not only been extremely detrimental to farming and pastoral land, but has also led to an outbreak of a bovine disease, which killed thousands of cattle and was even harmful to humans.

Furthermore, the Port Phillip district was also affected by a bushfire, which burned I do not know how many thousands of acres of bush and fields, as well as fences and houses and even cost a few human lives. A large number of cattle were thus lost, together with this year's entire harvest. Crops which normally would have been transported to Sydney, now had to be sent from here to those affected areas.

In Sydney, by the way, I found the time beginning to drag, because everything revolved solely around business activities, and so I decided not to delay my journey through the interior any longer. I took my trunk to Consul Kirchner, who had kindly offered to send it on ahead by a schooner, which was due to leave for Adelaide in a few days, and I did not ask anyone else about the journey on foot and the local native Indians. I was fed up with the horror stories with which people tried to dissuade me from my trip. It was all death and mayhem and other barbaric atrocities, and when one later arrives in those places, it turns out the actual dangers have been grossly exaggerated. It had been like that on all the somewhat unusual journeys on foot that I had made so far.

I was actually well equipped with weapons, in order not to overlook anything on my part, and I was fully determined to have as little as possible to do with the savage tribes, who might be quite treacherous, as I was rather inclined to believe. The rest would sort itself out when I got there.

2.

By Mail Coach from Sydney to Albury

Here in Australia the transport of passengers and letters is totally in the hands of private persons, who are contracted to deliver the mail, that is, bags of letters, to their destination at a certain time, and they consider the passengers, who are at their mercy, as an irritating addition, but necessary because of the profit they bring. For this purpose and on this principle the entire postal system has been established, and a passenger who embarks on a journey on the 'Royal Mail', as the coaches are bombastically called, may just as well commit his soul into God's hands and concentrate totally on his body, for its mistreatment will surely take up all his time and attention. But let me come to the point.

On Tuesday 22 April, at 4 o'clock in the afternoon, the mail coach set off. The day before I had purchased my ticket, or at least I had paid my money, because a ticket was not issued, and in response to my question whether there would be many passengers, I received the laconic and somewhat peculiar reply: 'Only a lady, and you will have to look after her.'

That was short and sweet, and at first I did not know what to make of it. But the man looked so serious and was dreadfully busy – not with the transport of mail, but on the side he was also a barman in a spirits shop and was constantly serving his customers. While that was going on, he was also sizing me up from top to toe, and so I patiently paid my 'Three Pounds Sterling' as far as Yass, a staging post on the way. I then did not worry about the mysterious lady any longer, but made preparations for my departure the next day and calmly let fate run its course.

Four o'clock in the afternoon arrived, and with it the mail coach, a very comfortable and elegant vehicle and not unlike our mail carriages, but without front and back compartments, a simple coach with excellent upholstery. Prudently I waited in the right spot in good time, got on and settled comfortably in a corner on the back seat. Right, I had got my seat.

I had hardly sat down properly, when the door opened again, and a lady was ushered in by the chivalrous coachman. Ah, my charge, I thought to myself, and slid a bit further into my corner. She was a lovely little lady of 20 to 21 years, carrying a small, red-cheeked infant. The seat was wide enough, so that we were able to sit quite comfortably beside each other, and the lady sat on the other side of the seat after a short greeting.

So, now we can set off, I thought, but I was wrong. Rapidly a second door opened and not, as one might have thought, to let someone out, but a lady was now pushed in, as it seemed by the 'recoil' of two vermilion male faces. The said lady by herself would have completely filled the shell of a regular sleigh and now looked at both of us, two astonished passengers, as if to ask: So which of you should I first squash to death?

My precious back seat! Chivalry demanded that I give it up, and this behemoth could have demanded enough chivalry for two ladies. I slid onto a seat in the front, Pumpkin squashed herself in beside my charge, and, once there, also produced to my utter amazement at the unfolding of her wide, reddish-coloured shawl a tiny citizen, who now began to scream at the top of his voice. Until that point she had kept him hidden under the wide folds of her shawl. We had not yet even settled down, however, when the door opened for a third time. It was not, dear reader, to let in just one, but *three* 'ladies' at once. One of them was also carrying a child, and the other two similarly looked around once they were in, as if they too were expecting to be handed a few little squalling babies. Ladies here seemed to carry babies, like we do umbrellas or parasols.

'For God's sake, how many more are meant to be getting in?' I now enquired of the coachman in despair. 'Six,' was the laconic answer, and the door slammed shut.

We were already six, 'not counting the women and children', as they would say in war correspondents' reports; in this case, at any rate, it was without the latter. I had to watch helplessly and grief-stricken as the last passenger – some rude, red-cheeked young woman from the country – climbed in. With difficulty but with determination she squeezed in beside my poor little charge. Well, for God's sake, which of all these ladies was I supposed to be looking after?

'Is your gun loaded?' suddenly shrieked the fat lady, who only now had noticed my shotgun, jammed in between my knee and the door.

'No, Madam,' was my polite, if very terse reply.

'But if it were to ...'

"There is not a grain of gunpowder in it.'

'But if it explodes ...'

'Explodes?' I asked in amazement and looked at the corpulent woman, who really made a face as if she expected the dreadful weapon to explode at any moment.

Our conversation was interrupted at this moment by the door opening again.

'Only one more!' shouted the coachman, and was actually going to usher in a lady with a child, but that was too much. I enjoy the company of ladies, but enough is enough. Luckily I was sitting right next to the door. However, I had jammed my right knee between my beautiful and ugly neighbours, who could not move an inch to the side either, so that it really required a major effort to get free. Pumpkin, who was sitting opposite me, sat up as straight as possible, but shouted murder (pressing her child up against the carriage roof with both hands, in order to have room to move), when the coachman, to whom, of course, I had handed over my gun, held the nozzle directly under her nose. I did not wait around any longer. Grasping the hand of the coachman, who held me by the arm and pulled me out into the open with the help of a sympathetic bystander, I reached fresh air, happy and breathing a deep sigh of relief. Leaving my Californian serape and a few other trifles behind, I worked my way up 'on deck', that is, to the top of the coach, where I found a group of six people.

When the coachman finally climbed up, and with his whip invited the four sturdy and well-fed horses to move along with us, we were almost one and a half dozen souls on the one axle.

It was the first time that I travelled on top of a coach. The wild gallop with which our coachman was probably trying to make up for lost time did not exactly serve to calm the somewhat uneasy feeling that overcame me at the idea of the coach being overturned. The roads there, however, are excellent, the coachmen very safe and very familiar with their animals, and we travelled about seven English miles in a relatively short time. Fortunately I heard only later that, not too long before, such a coach had overturned on the very same road between Parramatta and Sydney in a wild race, and that seven people had been killed immediately and others seriously injured.

We rattled down the road at full gallop toward our next staging post, which we would not reach until after dark. Several of the 'top deck' passengers had, in the meantime, got off here and there. In most cases they came from small places or individual farms along the way and were 'delivered' to their homes, or at least as close as possible to them. A few times I also saw light-coloured garments disappearing from the interior of the coach in the approaching dusk. Even Pumpkin got off at a small, single farmhouse, at the door of which a small, thin man was looking out, perhaps awaiting her tenderly, but at any rate holding aloft a large stable lantern, in order to see below it.

The weather looked like rain, and I was already planning a strategy that would get me back inside the coach, where I now hoped there would be a seat for me, when the coach suddenly stopped in front of a long, low building, and we were told that 'the horses and carriage' would be changed here.

Reality was soon to overtake our saddest expectations or indeed fears. Instead of the closed calèche, we got an open phaeton, which had good springs, but hard seats and was relentlessly exposed to the elements. Granted only a short respite for an evening meal, we continued our journey into the pitch-dark night, rain looming.

Thus we covered perhaps 20 to 25 miles, not exactly in the best of spirits and loaded to the hilt, and even if we had hitherto been sitting reasonably comfortably, we were now to experience what it really meant to travel by Royal Mail coach.

Then the horses and carriage were changed again, and we got a really special, indeed a peculiar kind of transport. Now our mail coach, also open like the previous one, resembled a common hearse. The seats were along the sides and consisted of two very narrow and only scantily upholstered benches, so narrow in fact that they looked more like utterly useless ornamentation rather than being meant for any real use. This box differs from a hearse only insofar as one person lies comfortably inside, whereas on the Royal Mail an undefined number of passengers are literally crammed in. All travellers, men, women and children, travelled in this way, without anybody in the least concerned whether they had enough room or not. Indeed, the very concept of 'room' implies the notion of existence on an Australian mail coach, or indeed managing to exist on it at all. Shortly afterwards, to our utmost astonishment we found ten people accommodated in a space that previously I would not have deemed possible to receive and to hold six properly. Sitting down was inconceivable, our legs – and five of the ten sets of legs belonged to women – were all tangled up. Mine were so tightly squeezed in that I could not have moved them one inch if my life had depended on it. It had also got to the point that within an hour we would not have finished shouting and looking for space where none was available, when suddenly the coachman put a violent but also complete end to our concerns.

As he whipped the horses on, the coach – if I may stoop to such crude flattery in calling such a vehicle a coach – shot ahead. With a sudden jolt, or I should say a series of jolts, we were shaken about so mercilessly that some of the passengers sat down, and not in a civilised and socially approved manner, but as if turned into dregs by some chemical process, while the other, lighter passengers landed on top of them. I sat – or 'sit' should be a passive verb here – therefore I was sat down.

To make matters worse, it started to rain at about 10 o'clock at night, and at 12 o'clock it poured. We had every reason to feel miserable, and we would have been totally excused if we had given vent to our anger by cursing and voicing a fierce wrath. But perish the thought! Extremes were not so far apart here either. I cannot remember having laughed and enjoyed myself more, even in the most pleasant company and in the happiest circumstances, than in this flying torture chamber. We had hardly seen one another's faces, except when we got in, when one does not take much notice of each other, and perhaps for a few moments at dinner. What is more, so many got off along the way that one could not even know who was still seated. Nevertheless, we all laughed and talked so easily, as if we had already been on the longest journeys together. We told anecdotes and stories and sang songs all night long. We also had to climb a steep hill, the so-called Razorback. At the same time the rain was bucketing down, the horses where hardly able to pull up the empty coach, the poor women could hardly drag themselves up, and I carried not only my shotgun, of which I did not let go, but also little children up and down the Razorback – a very nice activity for a travelling writer. But nothing could spoil our good mood, and the coachman kept shaking his head in amazement, saying he had never come across 'such odd people' in his working life, and he had transported heavier loads in even more dreadful weather up and down this hill.

Looking like drowned rats and completely covered in mud, we got back on the coach, but our good mood did not change, and only toward dawn, when it stopped raining, and the cold, shivering morning wind swept across the hilltops, did our conversation start to get more monosyllabic and our laughter shorter and more sporadic.

Here and there one or the other started to fall asleep and buttoned himself more tightly in his coat when stirred by the jolt of the coach, which had no back support at all. Shivering with cold, he realised that he was not by any stretch of the imagination in his bed – which he might have envisioned fleetingly in his dreams – but rather on board an Australian Royal Mail coach.

When morning finally broke, I wished I was able to draw, for never in my life had I seen such a group of miserable souls; indeed, we all had to laugh out loud when we looked at each other. The funniest image was that of a colleague sitting opposite me, a Mr Johnson, the editor of *The Goulbourn Herald*, who had gone on a jaunt to Sydney in the best of weather and who now, in the cold rain, clad only in a summer coat, was shivering in his seat with his hands folded and pressed between his knees, his sopping wet silk hat pushed down low over his forehead. He was the picture of suffering and resignation and was using the collar of his coat as a two-fold gutter, patiently catching the rainwater that was again dripping from a light blue cotton umbrella on the right and from a green parasol on the left. He not only channelled the water further on to his shirt-front, but also transferred the respective light blue and green colours, faithfully and neutrally.

At one of the staging posts, the name of which I have forgotten, we dropped off some of the passengers and now had sufficient room. In Goulbourn we also dropped off the editor of the *Herald* at his own door, where the good, but somewhat damp man was welcomed most heartily by his wife, children and dogs. He also promised most faithfully to describe our journey in every detail. In Goulbourn we also had our first rest stop of three hours since leaving Sydney, but were already called out again at 2 o'clock and, in complete darkness on truly dreadful roads, galloped towards our destination, sadly still so far away.

The journey became rather interesting because of the rumour of bushrangers, who lately had turned up on the roads again and had held up the mail a few times. For that reason I also kept my shotgun continuously loaded; the most dangerous spot was said to be just here past Goulbourn. As for the passengers, there was a man in a blue blouse, a so-called bush shirt, and one of the ladies, 'the last rose' and most likely my charge, a woman perhaps 28 to 30 years old with a small child – I have seen very few women without one. The poor woman actually wanted to get to Gundagai and had to endure a great deal from the elements. Indeed, I do not know how the child could have survived day and night on this open coach in this dreadful weather, if I had not fortunately had with me my woollen blankets for my overland journey, which at least sheltered mother and child from the worst.

We might have travelled about four to five miles in this fashion, our road leading through a dense forest of gum trees. The reader should not imagine in any way that we were travelling on a properly graded mail road. On the contrary, as far as the hilly ground and the dense trees allowed, carriages over time had made tracks and others had followed in them. In this way, mail roads were gradually formed, on which, however, one was totally safe and only exposed to the danger either of being held up, shot dead by bushrangers or, more likely, of breaking one's neck or some otherwise vital limbs because of the coachman's mad driving. I had already tried in vain a number of times to steal a few minutes of sleep on the shaky seat with a back scarcely four inches high; the danger of falling down between the wheels was too great. Finally I was trying to force myself to stay awake, when suddenly the woman who had been fearfully looking around seized my arm and whispered to me that she had seen a figure sneaking across the road a little way behind us. After watching carefully for a short while, I was convinced that a rider was galloping through the forest, now to our left and no longer on the road. He seemed to be overtaking us, but he kept more to his left, and a small clump of bushes soon hid him from our sight. When I informed the coachman of what we had seen, he cursed quietly and said that the damned fellows had only recently held up his mate. He added that when his mate and his mail horses were too fast for them, they had fired a pistol randomly at the coach from behind, but without injuring anyone.

Of course, in the meantime I had thrown my poncho off my arm and had put my loaded shotgun on my knee. Luckily I did not have to use it. Had the fellows found out in Goulbourn that we were armed, or had we done the perhaps most honourable night-rider an injustice by mistaking him for a highwayman? Enough of that; we never saw him again and only once did we think we heard rapid hoof beats on the road in front.

For a long time I had been looking forward to seeing the real Australian landscape and the bush with all its peculiarities. For up there on the Hunter River it had appeared to me as if nature had been tamed too much by man. At any rate, I could not find any great trees to speak of, as has often been mentioned before. Instead of a change in the trees, it was simply one gum after another, again and again. People there assured me that it would improve along the Murray, and I began to reassure myself of that, because here in the interior the scenery was becoming more and more dreary. As far as Goulbourn it seemed to have rained quite heavily in the last few weeks. The grass was growing high and lush, the cattle looked well fed, and green bushes in the fairly heavy undergrowth lent the whole landscape a rather friendly appearance, albeit monotonous because of the sameness of the foliage. However, the further west we travelled, the drier the soil, the sparser the vegetation, the thinner the cattle along the road, and when we reached the small town of Yass, everything came to an end.

In Yass something else awaited us. For, as bad as the coaches had been so far, one had at least been able to sit on them, without being in constant danger of falling off, but here in Yass even that was about to change. From Yass we got a two-wheeled cart, on which two passengers were able to sit facing forward and two on the back seat with their backs to the horses. However, three in the front and three in the back are permitted, providing enough victims can be found. Those in front had no cause to complain. The cart was reasonably well sprung, and the front seat, although not comfortable, was acceptable. It was like sitting beside the coachman on a normal coach. The back seats, however, did indeed prove to be life-threatening. And, as I heard later, there have reputedly been a number of accidents, especially involving ladies, who, as a result of the terrible jarring of the box and with hardly any footrest either, were not able to hold on to the low iron railing and were flung off, unable to be caught. They could thank God, however, if they did not fall unto the turning wheel.

The tracks leading up and down hills and through dry lagoons and gorges are truly perilous, which somehow explains the two wheels; a four-wheel carriage would be in greater danger of overturning. On it goes, galloping up or down steep slopes, so that, when going up-hill, those sitting at the back have to bear the entire brunt of their bodies solely with their hands or with their arms, which they have wound around the narrow iron bar.

The scenery here was getting even more desolate, if that was at all possible, these last few miles. There was not a single blade of grass as far as the eye could see, not a bush except for low eucalyptus trees, and everywhere the same type of foliage; indeed even the leaves are so identical in shape that one cannot determine which is their upper and which is their lower side without having pulled them from a branch.

Those sitting with their backs to the front of the coach have the pleasure of not only having low-hanging branches often whip off their hats, but sometimes the branches even want to take off their heads as well. Through all this the coach rattles on, until the coachman or the horses can be persuaded to stop, and the passenger, still half stunned by the blow, may have to run back one to two hundred paces in order to retrieve his lost headgear.

'Do you sometimes lose passengers off the cart?' I asked the coachman, when we were first shown the instrument of torture.

'Rarely!' was his laconic reply.

On Friday night, the 25th April, we arrived safely in Gundagai, a small town on the Murrumbidgee. Here we dropped off our last lady, and the poor woman really was more dead than alive after the strenuous journey.

We stayed for about an hour in Gundagai, which we reached during the night. The little town was still in uproar because of an attack that a neighbouring Murrumbidgee tribe had made on the peaceful native Indians or blacks, who usually lived in Gundagai itself. They had suddenly attacked the latter in the middle of the town, had wounded several and killed one, without injuring a single white person, several of whom were just crossing their paths. People here were again full of dreadful tales of the 'treacherous devils', as they were called everywhere.

Here we had to cross the Murrumbidgee, which I can hardly call a river, even though it does have quite a sizeable bed. For it consisted, albeit at this very dry time of year, of only a chain of waterholes without any flow, indeed without any connection between them, and each summer it was the same. In this very spot, however, there was enough water, and we crossed it on a large, wide ferry.

The following day we received another passenger to join us in our misery, replacing the lady we had dropped off. The passenger was a young man, who from his white necktie and the somewhat broad-brimmed hat, clearly had to be a clergyman, and who, as I very soon learned, exposed his limbs to the Australian torture instrument known as the Royal Mail every month, in order to fulfil his clerical duties in Albury. With a degree of awe I looked upon him as a kind of martyr. After happily arriving in Albury without broken bones, he gives his regular sermons every Sunday, baptises and marries whatever is brought to him and has accumulated during his absence.

His entry was interesting. Of course, he sat next to me on the back seat; ascending with a gentle, engaging greeting, he took his seat and from his pocket pulled a small prayer book, in which he started to read. He had, however, been on this coach before and had every reason to commend his body to the Lord of Hosts in particular and to the powers that be in general. However, he also provided a fitting example that in times of need you must not fold your hands when you wish to pray. On the contrary, you have to hold on with both hands, for he could hardly have read 10 words when the coachman whipped the horses, and with the first jolt, both the book and the hat of the man of the church, who used both hands to save himself from his own fall, flew overboard. We had to stop again to retrieve both, and the travelling preacher from now on sensibly put his book in his pocket.

The following evening we got about two-and-a-half hours of sleep, but when we wanted to leave the next morning, it transpired that the holy man did not have any 'small' change on him to pay his bill. Upon his request to lend him the money until we arrived in Albury, I was pleased to comply, but on our arrival I was a little surprised at his bad memory. He said not a word of the three shillings, and I have to presume that he used me as an 'instrument of God'.

That morning I also met a few German families, who were tenants of English people and had set up their new homes in the grass-less, dry eucalyptus forest. They nevertheless felt very happy, because they were doing very well here, unlike in Germany. Their needs were very modest with their family around them, and they needed no further compensation for what they had left behind in the old country.

By the way, the area here was so lacking in water that people assured me that in the forest not far from here there was a waterhole, and its lucky owner had put a man with a loaded gun beside it to keep away cattle and stockmen that did not belong there.

At present, butter and milk are considered curiosities of nature in this area.

On Saturday at 12 o'clock, on a better track leading across the plains which separate the waters of the Murrumbidgee and the Murray, we finally arrived in the small town of Albury, on the banks of the latter. Stiff in all my limbs, hardly able to move my arms because of constantly having to hold on, I climbed down from the torture cart in front of one of the public houses in Albury and was really amazed again to find myself in one piece, with only a few really minor bruises in comparison with the knocks I had received. Here I left the so-called Melbourne Mail Coach in order to sail down the Murray or Hume, as the Murray up here is mainly called.[1]

Albury is a small, growing town right in the centre of the country, and until now has been connected to Melbourne, only about two hundred miles from here, by this passenger coach and otherwise by goods carts.

At the present time this connection is, however, restricted to the mail coach, because the complete lack of grass in the vicinity, and the very high prices for any fodder, have made it almost impossible to run goods carts as in previous months, as the animals could not be fed. As a result, the prices, particularly of victuals, had risen considerably. Trade and traffic for this reason were also somewhat slow in Albury, since there had not been any rain to speak of in sixteen months. At this point in time the Murray was so slow that even the proverbial oldest man with a bad memory could not remember having seen it so low.

Albury, incidentally, prides itself in having as a sign of progress in the civilisation of Australia's interior a steam mill, built by an enterprising Englishman, a Mr R. Heaver. The town also has three shops, a blacksmith, a tinsmith and the promise of a church. It also suffers the pleasure of three public houses, licensed to sell 'spirituous and fermented liquors'. The church for the time being is restricted to that peripatetic preacher, but the inhabitants stressed that they wanted to have a regular and permanent church there. They did not want to run the risk every month that the provider of their monthly spiritual solace would one day break his neck on the way – who could offer words of solace then? Their children would not be baptised for another four weeks, and their young people would not be wed.

I was most heartily welcomed by Mr and Mrs Heaver in Albury, for whom I had brought letters from Sydney. During my short stay they treated me not as a total stranger but rather as a family member, and it was here that I experienced the almost unlimited hospitality of the Murray for the first time, and indeed in all its forms. I will never forget the most pleasant week that I spent in their home. My first concern in Albury was now, of course, to look for a canoe or other means of transport with which to commence my journey. Alternatively, as there was no canoe available, I would seek suitable wood, from which I could hollow out my own. Unfortunately everything that I had previously been told by friends in Albury was now confirmed. There were eucalyptus trees as far as the eye could see, eucalyptus trees wherever I went up and down the banks of the river, indestructible, unavoidable, unbearable gum trees everywhere, their wood so heavy that the smallest chip sank like lead, and I was supposed to cut out a canoe from that? But one hope remained: I had heard that in the hills near Albury there were stringy barks with somewhat lighter wood that was easier to work with, and in order to find these trees I took with me one of the native Indians or 'blacks' wandering around in the area.

A small tribe was camped near Albury, and for the first time I set eyes on the sons of the Australian wilderness in their original, largely uncivilised state. Oh my beautiful Imeo,[2] with your palms and guava shade, your oranges and breadfruit, and your kind, friendly, slender and well-kempt inhabitants – the men with their open faces and sturdy bodies, the women with their clear, liquid eyes, the full, sleekly oiled and combed hair and their friendly smile and swept from there to here as if by one stroke of magic, in amongst the eternal, dreary gum trees and amongst the black, dirty, treacherous, murderous people of these forests – the contrast was too awful. And in order to get here I had exposed myself to the danger of travelling on an Australian Royal Mail coach! But it served me right. From early childhood I have exposed myself to all kinds of awkward situations; with the greatest difficulty and often with no little sacrifice, and frequently to my amazement, I have managed to escape them, though not always unscathed. This time I seemed to have landed in a right pickle, and I began to wonder how I would manage to get myself out of it.

The stories I heard here about the native Indians or blacks, as the English call them, were not at all comforting; it was said that particularly in recent times several murders had taken place. While a few people still doubted whether I would be able to navigate my canoe down the river successfully, they all agreed that I would probably be 'speared' by the blacks on the way. A pleasant thought, considering that the spears are made of very hard wood and have very sharp points; and these careless wild men always throw these spears with the sharp points at the front. People took the greatest possible care to tell me the precise details of what must surely be of interest to me, namely with what certainty the blacks could hit their target, even at a distance of 80 to 100 paces. And the middle of the river, to which I could not always keep, was at no point more than 40 to 50 paces from the banks.

I was also informed in the most long-winded way what they do with those they either attack or get their hands on by other means. They are in fact not particularly interested in killing their victims (except if they require human flesh for a special sacred ceremony, such as the initiation of a witch-doctor), and they extract the fat only from the kidneys – nowhere else – and then abandon the victim kindly to his fate.[3] Subsequently they cover themselves in this fat and foolishly believe that in so doing they acquire the victim's strength. And one is supposed to allow oneself to be cut up because of such a foolish superstition? It is outrageous.

What I discovered about the blacks around me was not conducive to having a great deal of trust in them. On the very evening I was passing through the small town of Gundagai, one tribe had attacked another there and in the middle of town had killed one of the blacks with a spear. And in Albury a villain painted with white clay (a sign of mourning) and red earth was wandering around. This man two days earlier had smashed in his own wife's skull without any provocation at all and was known to have already murdered seven white people, partly on his own, and partly by joining in with others. And yet the courts calmly allowed him to roam about freely, and even prevented him from being punished by his own tribe on account of the murder of his wife. The eminently wise court held him in a police cell for one night – what sort of a moral impression would that have made on the rogue!

While I was still there, a horse stepped on his foot, severing his middle toe, but he was still running around with the bloody stump on this quite frosty morning, as unconcerned as if there was nothing wrong with his foot at all.

On Sunday the 27th I set off in to the hills with one of these black souls, but we found only very few stringy barks large enough from which to cut a canoe. Only half a mile from the river, however, there were several, and I decided to give it a go with the best of these.

On Monday I engaged the help of a worker, a young Australian, to saw down a tree and help me with hollowing it out. But the best stringy bark that we felled was hollow and rotten and broke when it fell, and my helper assured me that we would not find a single healthy stringy bark near the river. In order not to lose any more valuable time, our only alternative was to fell one of the heavy gum trees, which were hard to work, and to try as best we could to hollow it out and make its walls as thin as possible.

No sooner said than done – we vigorously set to work, and two hours later we had found and felled a suitable tree. The same evening we scraped off the bark, and the next morning we began the tough job of hollowing it out.

Meanwhile I made the acquaintance of a few interesting people in Albury, among them a Mr Roper, who had taken part in Dr Leichhardt's first expedition to Port Essington, on which he had lost an eye as a result of a spear thrown by the blacks.[4] But the inhabitants of Albury were also interested in the journey I was about to make, as it was going to revive a long-time favourite project, the potential navigability of the Murray and Hume rivers, which had to be of inestimable benefit for their small town. Consequently, the decision was made to christen the canoe officially on my departure, and a few people declared that it was a real shame that they would never hear about the outcome of the adventure, because, of course, the blacks would 'spear' me somewhere along the way.

On Saturday 3 May my canoe was ready for launching, and I took it down the river, which at this point was full of dreadful bends, for about seven miles, as far as the landing stage at Albury. From here I planned to set off on Monday, very well equipped with supplies and other essential items.

Even now many people tried to dissuade me from embarking on this long, difficult journey on my own, but I had made up my mind. Clearly I could not turn back, for all my belongings had been sent from Sydney to Adelaide, my money, dear God, had already dwindled away severely, and I had a long, long journey ahead of me. But I had enough ammunition and did not fear anything except, perhaps, the considerable problems that might arise in those areas where the native Indians were a danger, and where I would have no one with whom to take turns in keeping watch during the night.

I was in God's hands. I had escaped from so many tight spots and would not get stuck in this one either. Moreover, in my many adventures I had learned that dangers are usually greatly exaggerated from afar and lose much of their terror if one meets them head on. This had also been the case in South America, where only a single old Spaniard conceded to me that it might be possible to cross the Pampas with their insurgent tribes and the snow-covered Cordilleras, and yet I still arrived safe and sound in Chile.

On Sunday I suddenly had a visit from a young German, who, having just arrived in Albury, had heard of my somewhat adventurous journey and now offered to accompany me, as he was penniless and really unsure what to do.[5] He was a young sailor and assured me that he also knew quite well how to handle a canoe.

Of course my canoe, meant only for one person with his requirements, was now going to be much heavier, and the provisions for my own use would naturally need to be greatly reduced, and I was not able to buy larger quantities. Nevertheless I agreed to accept the young fellow as a companion; he had an open and honest face and seemed in any case to come from a good family. It would make the journey easier for me, as long as he turned out to be of some use, and less dangerous for both of us, as we would be able to take turns keeping watch in dangerous places. Our departure was therefore set for the following day, and I now looked forward to that moment quite impatiently.

That Sunday we wandered in and around Albury, but, dear God, there was nothing comforting in the surrounding landscape, and everywhere I heard the saddest tales of the dreadful shortage of fodder and the ensuing plagues.

The area really did look quite desolate. There was not a single blade of grass to be seen, neither in hill nor dale. Livestock were wandering about as if at any moment their sharp bones would pierce their skin, and beside the lagoons in the interior lay half-submerged and starved cattle. They had got stuck in the mud there and were so weak and exhausted that they had not been able to clamber out again.

Furthermore, among the herds of several sheep breeders the insidious glanders, the so-called catarrh, had broken out, so that one breeder, in order to save the rest of his sheep, had had to cull 900 animals in one go and have them burned. Others had lost two, four thousand or more and did not know how many of those remaining they would be able to save. Further inland there was said to be some grass, and so all the livestock that was slaughtered in Albury came down from Billabong[6] and was very expensive here. It was, of course, no surprise. With no showers to speak of in the last sixteen months, where was the vegetation to come from? The gum trees, which, come think of it, are rather sorry specimens even in the best circumstances, looked miserable in this drought as they rustled their long, dry lanceolate leaves. The leaves themselves do not contain any moisture either and break like glass when you hold them in your hand. On account of their very strong taste of eucalyptus oil, they are not eaten by the livestock either, and the small gum bushes therefore stood untouched in spite of the total lack of any green fodder.

And this was the Australian paradise, about which I had heard and read so much? These were the lush pastures, the park-like lawns? Oh divine fantasy, please come to my aid and cover this dusty, grey area with lush green, and then cover the lush green with well-fed cattle, chewing the cud, and then grant these areas ... But no, these areas are really only to bear the best grass and significant herds of livestock in a more or less favourable season. At this moment these areas were merely desolate, sad and dry, and the cattle were standing in despair among the dry gum trees, thoughtfully ruminating on the long since digested fodder. Poor beasts, as far as the eye could see, not a single blade of grass, and even quenching their thirst could lead to death.

The Murray itself is a fairly significant river, at least the most important or rather the only one in Australia, as it actually remained the only river with running water in this year of drought. The other river-beds were reduced to just a chain of stagnant puddles. The Murray is about 60 to a 100 paces wide and of a very indeterminate depth; here gravel and sandbanks with only 10 to 12 inches of water, there spots where a three-masted ship would remain afloat. The water itself has a lovely, pure taste and is said to be very good for you.

What seemed particularly threatening for my canoe trip was the large number of gum trees that had fallen in to the river and which, of course, could not float down the river because of their enormous weight, but which lay where they had fallen. Only a storm surge and flood might sometimes be able to pull them into the current for a short stretch. But there they soon sank to the bottom because of their weight and now lay for centuries – for I think a gum tree never rots – and stretched their black, slimy, rigid arms in sharp jagged shapes through the clear waters flowing above them. And I was meant to steer my canoe through these trees.

On Monday morning I finally had everything in order. The boat was tarred on the outside and all cracks and wormholes – this best of all possible types of wood is also blessed with cracks and wormholes in addition to other virtues – had been plugged. Our equipment lay on the landing stage, and among a crowd of people that had gathered, quite a crowd for such a small town, we pushed the canoe into the water. Mrs Heaver broke a bottle of brandy on the bow and christened it Bunyip;[7] we climbed in, pushed off and rowed into the quiet forest, amidst the three rousing cheers of those left behind.

My canoe was the first boat to attempt the journey down the Hume River, as the Murray is called as far as its confluence with the Murrumbidgee, about 300 miles away.[8]

3.

A Canoe Excursion on the Hume

The last time I had paddled a canoe was in Arkansas, down the Fourche la Fave, the canoe hewn from a light pine trunk so that it shot like an arrow, more on the water than through it.[1] What a difference here! My canoe was certainly built in the right proportions, about fifteen feet long and something over two wide in the stern, and worked as thin as the brittle wood allowed. Nonetheless it sat deep – very deep – in the water under its own weight, while the weight of two of us, with provisions and other luggage, added not inconsiderably.

The bends in the river at the time were so tight, and the gravel bars formed as a result were so high, and extended so far, that they typically forced the channel right up to the bank. As a result, the channel was filled with fallen and half or entirely submerged trunks and branches, or at least it was in danger of being so, and at such places the journey was not only extremely difficult but also perilous.

Our provisions consisted mainly of hard bread or ship's biscuit, tea, sugar and salt; for fresh meat we relied entirely on my shotgun. Very soon, however, I would find that hunting on the Murray and the Hume was not as easy or as relaxed as I initially thought. Because of its winding course, constantly interrupted by obstacles, it bears almost no similarity with the beautiful American rivers, and one could not possibly imagine gliding noiselessly along its surface to sneak up on wildlife approaching the water. Constantly, and with the full use of all my strength, I had to try to avoid the snags or tree branches in the way, and the noise caused in the process, along with the unavoidable movement of the boat itself, would have scared away any nearby wild animal. It soon became apparent to me that we would possibly be entirely dependent on ducks, of which there are great numbers of the most varied kinds. As I was very aware of the shortage of ammunition, I shot two at a time – for our evening meal and breakfast.

That night we camped on the left bank, carried our things onto land, and slept sweetly and soundly despite a light rain that fell between 12 and 2 o'clock, probably because we were exhausted by our unaccustomed exertions. The river, by the way, had such great bends that we were firmly convinced that we could not have made it very far from Albury.

On the second day we had very shallow water, and because of the eternal bends, in which the channel was so thoroughly full of snags that very often we had to climb out in order to pull the heavy canoe through six or seven inches of water. It was quiet cold, and the reader can well imagine that such a journey, with constantly bare and wet feet, also had its down side; there was more to it than the romance of an expedition through the wilderness.

On this journey I also had, by the way, a somewhat fantastic hope, namely to get to see the bunyip, the Australian monster of the Murray, of which many spoke in these parts. With this extraordinarily low water level I hoped to see at least a trace of him, so as to be able to confirm his existence. Until now he lives only in the somewhat fabulous legends and tales of the blacks, who describe him as a monster of the size of a small ox, with a horse's mane, a frightening jaw and needle-sharp claws. Whites have never seen the creature, which the Indians call 'Devil Devil' in their English–Indian pronunciation.

If it existed at all, then it *had* to at least leave its tracks on the banks of the Murray or in the various lakes, or perhaps at night I would be able to hear its snorting and roaring, with which it is supposed not infrequently to drive fear into the timorous tribes of the Murray.

Perhaps in the end I might even find his bones, and then I would suffer the same fate as Mr Koch, the discoverer of the mammoth.[2] Afterwards a certain man by the name of Galway approached him and told a long and rambling tale of the capture of the Hydrarchos.[3] This, however, could not happen to me just yet, because I did not yet have the Bunyip. I was nonetheless firmly determined, should I find a trace, to devote weeks as necessary to catching such a monster or at least to seeing it.

That afternoon it began to rain in an extremely inconvenient way, and the clouds hung so low and threatening that one had to think that the fear of a horribly wet night ahead was all too well founded. It is true that undertaking the journey at this time of year we had to expect this from the start, and we paddled on but were indeed very happy when, just before nightfall, we discovered a hut on the left bank. Naturally we paddled quietly toward it and found at least shelter against a storm which, as presumed, raged the whole night.

The next day the weather had calmed somewhat, even if showers fell now and again. At about midday the sun drove away the rain clouds and warmed our limbs, half stiffened by wetness and cold.

The river remained the same – its bends driving us to despair. Often we had to paddle for hours and then carry the canoe over gravel and sand and tree trunks blocking the stream. At the end we had returned to the same place, or had advanced not even a quarter of a mile from where we had started out.

The only thing that interested me was observing the riverbed and calculating the risks that would confront a steamer if it were to make a voyage charting a course. For centuries these indestructible gum trees have been thrown in and remained there, and I did not doubt in the least that most of the gravel bars we found in the middle of the current were nothing more than trunks that had fallen there, against which over time sand and gravel had accumulated to such an extent as to form a bar. In most places the riverbed consists solely of this chaos of trunks and accumulated sand, and from it protrude the bare, tough and slimy branches of those great tree skeletons.

Through these trunks which appear, as I have already said, most commonly in the channel itself, that is, at the very edge of the banks, runs the strongest or rather the main current of the river, and this is where the deepest water always is – seldom shallower than two or three feet, even at this extraordinarily low water level. Usually, however, another channel has formed on the opposite side of the bed, but naturally with a much weaker current and shallower water, sometimes not more than four to five inches, and, as a result, in many places a small gravel bar forms as an island in the middle.

These tree trunks which now obstruct the main passage must of course be removed if the river is ever to become navigable for even the smallest steamers, otherwise they would seal the fate of all who tried to force a passage through their rigid, treacherous and often so well – and also so perilously – concealed ranks.

Below its confluence with the Murrumbidgee the Murray has relatively few tree trunks on its bed compared with above it; the bends there are no longer so tight, and the river is somewhat broader and deeper. Below the influence of the Darling it is almost free of trunks; here and there, however, some branches do protrude, and even here it would be necessary to make at least some changes.

Every piece of wood must, however, be removed entirely, especially in the upper part of the river, whether by humans or horsepower, with saws and ropes, because there the bends are much too tight, and the channel is too narrow, to allow for the use of steamers, the so-called eradicators, although these could perhaps be operated further downstream. The removal of those trunks is certainly possible, and in some of their rivers such as the Red River and the Rio Roxo, the Americans have already overcome significantly more difficulties. Will, however, the banks of the Murray ever be in a position not only to repay such considerable expense but also to sustain a steamboat company, in part by delivering supplies but also by transporting produce? That is a question which I, at any rate, could not answer for now, just as for the same reason no settler on the Murray would offer a guarantee. For now it rather appears that the country in its terrible drought would not want to justify such an expense and make the pecuniary sacrifices. Nonetheless, it is capable still of achieving certain things which no one hitherto thought possible because of the high transport costs.

For the moment the settlers or station-owners there concern themselves exclusively with stock-farming, and in future too this will have to remain the primary, if not the sole, source of income. However, a larger and indeed much more significant advantage could be extracted if freight becomes cheaper and large-scale transport possible.

From the sheep presently almost nothing is used but the wool. As for cattle, whose numbers are growing at a great rate, the meat is used almost solely for the needs of the stations. Here and there it is also boiled down to tallow, but this could much better be viewed as a misuse rather than a use, and in any case the meat of these numerous herds could be put to excellent advantage as soon as the Murray is really navigable.

Along the banks of the Murray there are, it is worth noting, masses of small salt lakes containing the most wonderful salt, which is now even being imported into the colony. The Murray could therefore provide a huge mass of the most beautiful salted meat, if only the settlers on its banks were prompted to develop this source of income. The salt itself could be exported, legs of mutton smoked, hides salted, and other items which are currently going to waste could be exploited. From the gum trees, which could serve perfectly for smoking legs of mutton, one could also burn charcoal, and perhaps by salting the Murray's excellent fish caught in the numerous lakes and lagoons one could provide further goods for trade.

I did, however, hear a substantial objection to this – if it were fully thought through and tested – and it came from the perspective of the individual settlers themselves. It was that the salt from those lakes was not suited to the long-term preservation of meat and hides, that is, to transport over great distances, and the tests already carried out had not ended happily, as the salted meat had spoiled. Individual attempts – and I believe there was just one over a really long distance – may well have been done, but the Murray flows through a very wide stretch of land, and those salt lakes are to be found at very many points and therefore probably have different levels of salt. This has not yet been closely examined, because until now there was no prospect of moving the salt in great quantities from where it is found to where it could be used. This branch of production would therefore in any case need to be subjected to close study.

The Murray will hardly allow crop farming, not because the low and flooded river valley is incapable of producing good crops, but the lack of flow through autumn would destroy the crops every time. Moreover the valley is not broad and fertile enough to permit levees or dams of the kind, for example, that hold back the waters on the banks of the Mississippi. In addition, it is quite impossible to determine in advance all that the Murray might be able to achieve, because to make it navigable would certainly also engender a new eagerness among the residents along its banks and many would move there who at the moment would not even contemplate settling in a district which is connected to the civilised world by nothing more than an ox-drawn cart.

But I am chatting here about the possibility of future shipping on the Murray and in the process am completely neglecting my own journey.

I do not wish to bore the reader with the details of the admittedly long – and now all the more monotonous – journey, so I will jump directly to its conclusion, its dismal catastrophe. Just as one gum tree looked like the next, so one bend resembled the other, and constantly we performed this same work of jumping out of the boat and dragging it over the stones. With great effort, and with considerable risk, we avoided the dangerous trunks, which repeatedly threatened to block our progress. Precisely because of these monstrous bends and obstacles, the way became so terribly long and tiresome that I was able to calculate with some certainty that at this rate – if we were not eaten by the savages – we would barely be in a position to reach Adelaide in three to four months. At this point our journey on water reached a long feared and – despite the intervention of fate – still fortunate end, obliging us to continue our path on foot.

We had not yet, it is true, been molested by Indians, indeed had seen only very few, and the black fellows were too timid to show themselves so close to white settlements. At night we did not even keep watch, but soon the river itself would become a much greater enemy than the blacks.

One sunny morning, after we had slept particularly well and had enjoyed a generous repast of ducks, of which we even kept a few for the coming days, we climbed aboard once more and paddled with favourable disposition down a long and unusually open stretch of river. Our joy would, however, not last long. Suddenly it seemed to us as if the entire stream before us was completely blocked, cut off by a solid mass of fallen tree trunks and roots, and, even as we approached, no passage through opened up. As a result I had to land and walk toward the trunks in search of an opening through which we could manoeuvre our slender craft. I managed to find such a spot, but the entrance and passageway were so narrow and dangerous that we needed more than two hours to slip through this fateful place, and on top of that in the process our canoe twice filled with water, whereby the first time I had to bail it out mainly with one hand, while with the other I supported the entire weight of the canoe, as a strong current pressed against it.

Finally, after strenuous efforts, we forced a passage between whirling eddies and great, dark, slimy trunks and stumps which offered grim resistance against the bubbling torrent. It was an eerie experience to stand so close, as it were, to the edge of an abyss, where the slightest movement of the body would determine whether we sank or swam. If our canoe had sunk here – which would occur if no more than a bucket or so of water flowed in – then I can barely believe that one of us would have reached the bank again. The crazy mass of pointy, threatening branches was too much, and the current would have cast us into it, beyond rescue. It would not, however, come to this.

At this fateful place we again reached roughly a mile of quite open water and believed that we had already escaped all danger, when we suddenly reached a bend in the river, where the current shot through a narrow passage on the right side, while several trees hung down over it, and on the left bank a high gravel bar stubbornly blocked any passage.

I ran my canoe first onto a sandbank in the middle of the stream, so as to be able to establish in advance how the channel really looked, and to this end sent my companion over to the bank. He soon returned and assured me that beyond the tree everything looked fine. Placing our canoe at the mercy of the spirits of the Murray, we set out again, and I steered into the middle of the fast flowing channel, which shot just under the tree hanging down above it. Under the tree things went quite well; the passage was free there, even if only three feet wide, but immediately behind it, some six inches under water, there was another trunk, and approximately 30 paces further hung yet another tree, which I could not have seen from upstream, also hanging so low over the channel that it did not allow the canoe to pass beneath it. We managed to get over the trunk just below the surface, but as a result the progress of the canoe was totally impeded in avoiding the second, much more dangerous tree. We ran up against it with a full broadside, and the entire current, at this point forced into a passage a few feet wide, pressed against our canoe and pushed it, despite all our efforts to keep it free, half under the trunk.

For a few minutes we resisted the current in this way and tried to pull the canoe forward to free it and set it again into safe water, but that was not to succeed. Suddenly the pressure of the water forced the side closer to it down slightly, so that a narrow stream of water could shoot in. I tried to restore the balance on the other side by raising it once more, but in vain. The water had gained entry and would not be turned back. Ever more powerfully it rushed in; in a few seconds our little barque was filled, and all that I remember of that moment is that I reached for the gun beside me in order at least to save it.

The boat had sunk in about six feet of water, and everything had washed out of it, but because the gravel bank was right up against it, we were able to grab the rope tied to the front, and with no little effort we at least were able to pull the empty boat onto dry land. In the bottom of it remained only the long-handled frying pan and a harpoon, which had hooked itself into the wood. As it happens, the frying pan was a godsend; with it we were able to bail out the canoe quickly so as to rescue at least some of our things, and, using it as a rudder, were able to refloat the canoe. In the meantime probably more than half an hour had passed, and I was able to fish out only those things which clung to protruding branches in the immediate vicinity. Among them were two of our lightest woollen blankets, my little tin box with my letters and papers, my coat and the tea tin.

By wading, swimming and diving, my companion meanwhile brought up a few more minor articles, among them the bread-sack, by now almost totally dissolved. Some two hours and ten unsuccessful attempts later, and after we had finally made an anchor out of the bread sack filled with gravel, with the harpoon we retrieved my hunting pouch, which contained our entire supplies of powder, tobacco, fish hooks, some medicine and a few other minor objects.

With that we set off once more, travelling perhaps another two miles downstream until we came to a good camp-site, and there as our first priority we lit a good fire so as to dry ourselves, to rest, and to be able to assess the damage incurred. Unfortunately it was significant, and the worst thing was, much could not be undone. Our powder was wet through and unusable, and even our boots were gone. What a predicament we found ourselves in, we poor devils! Moreover we looked like we needed some attention, as we were cold and wet like a couple of half-drowned rats, barely able to carry our possessions onto land and to dry them before the blazing fire.

As a matter of urgency I devoted myself to restoring my shotgun to working order, unscrewed the pistons, poured in fresh powder – at least the powder which I still had in the powder horn had remained dry – and fired it so as to dry it out completely before reloading. That done, we hanged out the blankets to dry and also spread out before the fire the tea we had saved. The powder in the canisters was, however, beyond saving, as were most of the other things, and without shoes we could not even continue our journey. What now?

I did not have enough money with me to replace everything. Without provisions and powder, and without sufficient blankets, we could not even imagine remaining on the water for several months in the worst season. Even our oars had been washed away, and our situation would have been desperate if it had not had contained such a wealth of comedy. My good spirits did not desert me for even a moment – I was now once again in a particularly bad 'scrape', as the Americans call it, and for now I had nothing more to do than to find a way out of it.

If during the day we had been in danger from the water, at night, as if for the sake of a change, it was fire that threatened us. Because we were cold we had lit the biggest pile of wood we had been able to find nearby, and that happened to be at a place where, apart from a hollow tree trunk some sixteen to eighteen feet in height, the dry tops of three or four trees had also broken off. The fire blazed happily away, particularly in the evening, so that we even had to burn off the dry grass around it so as not to cause a forest fire of the kind that had already caused such horrific damage closer to Melbourne. Thus we had wrapped ourselves in our blankets and were sleeping deeply, and I dreamed of climbing a mountain spitting fire and seeing a crater spurting lava and flames. I could even hear clearly the dull roar deep inside. It must have been around midnight that I was awakened by a quite distinctive, uninterrupted sound, and when I opened my eyes I continued to lie for quite a while and would have sworn that I was still dreaming, because right in front of me I saw clearly and distinctly – as well as any human with open eyes and apparently fully conscious can see – flames and sparks climbing up into the dark night sky. It was as if I had stumbled my way to Hawaii.

When I jumped up somewhat perplexed, and by now fully awake, I saw the bright, glowing flames around the old trunk, licking at it like flames from a chimney, and the flashing sparks were flying high above us. Not content with that, they then fell down onto us, carried by a light breeze, and had already burned more holes in our blankets.

The following morning we held a brief war council, but there was not much to discuss. There was only one path to be taken, and that was on the river, until we either reached a house in order to acquire some boots, or shot some kind of animal from whose hide I could then make moccasins.

Thus we took to the water once more at 9 o'clock, and I paddled on all day using the terrible frying pan, without reaching a place as treacherous as on the previous day.

Dear reader, have you ever paddled with a frying pan? Not yet? Well you have missed nothing, because it is the most uncomfortable thing one can imagine, and the heavy chunk of iron, along with the relatively thin handle, numbs the hands and tires the arms. This was, as it happens, one of the worst days of my entire journey, and not only because I had lost almost all my equipment, along with part of my modest cash reserves. No, the thing that weighed on my mind most heavily was that the journey by water had been rendered impossible, and even if I were firmly determined to continue my march under all circumstances by foot, I had to abandon my long-held, cherished plan of travelling further along the quiet waters of the Murray.

'Who knows what all this might lead to', I told myself many a time, but I truly did not know the answer, and I had to trust in time's ability to heal everything to reach a happy end.

During the day I shot a few ducks once more. To sneak up on them I had to climb out of the boat and walk along the bank several times. The grass here was burnt and its short, sharp stumps, not visible to the eye but all too obvious to the feel of the foot, stuck up everywhere and caused the most grievous pain to my soles.

We camped for the night on the left bank, and in the morning the river had climbed more than two feet. Fortunately the previous evening we had secured the canoe well; the branch to which we had tethered it was, however, already under water.

Paddling calmly on with the frying pan, we finally came across a fence, and soon thereafter we saw the bright roof of one of the low-set bush huts looking out from among the drab green of the forest; we greeted it with not a little joy.

But who lived here? Reader, do you believe in miracles? Just between you and me, I would not believe in them either unless I saw one with my own eyes, and in this instance a miracle really did happen. In order to make it all the more obvious to you, let me first recall to you an anecdote known to every German.

When Mozart one day was sitting quietly alone in his tiny study, a stranger came to him and placed a request for a requiem on a certain day. It was Mozart's last work. He completed the requiem, died, and it was performed for the first time at his funeral. The stranger never returned – it had been an angel.

Reader, the man who lived in this place was a cobbler, and not much earlier a stranger had come to him and had ordered two pairs of shoes – he called them boots – which he had just finished, and which fitted us as if they had been made for us. The stranger had not yet returned to collect them. Reader, we negotiated with the man for the shoes. This upright gentleman accepted an agreement that he would give us the boots in exchange for the canoe with rudder (frying pan) and the tea tin, as well as some somewhat sodden tobacco. For the 'stranger' he would make another pair of boots. I did not wish to dissuade him, but the two other pairs were surely never collected, because who ever heard of an angel needing shoes?

We stayed the night there, then put our luggage in order and marched off downstream the next day, with sore and wounded feet. In spite of all the terrifying stories of blacks – come involving murders committed just recently – we headed toward Adelaide, which, we were told, was 700 English miles distant.

The march, it is true, would have been quite pleasant if I had had a different travelling companion. He was a fresh-faced chap who, however, would not accept any advice, and who would not have been able to offer me even the slightest help if we had really been in peril. I could not exchange views with him, could not teach him anything and could learn nothing from him. What benefit was there then for me in sharing with him at this time the rigours and the perils – and later the honour – of such a march through the wilderness? Nonetheless, I did not wish to leave him to his own devices, so that not until we reached the so-called Woolshed – by land about 120, by water perhaps 400 miles from Albury – and with it an entirely safe and populated road leading directly down to Melbourne some 180 miles away, did we come to an agreement, according to which each would go his own way.

We spent the night here together one more time and parted ways the next morning in peace and friendship.

Now with a lighter heart I shouldered my rifle and wandered alone and with firm resolve into the grey-green wilderness of dreary gum trees in order to commence the wildest and most adventurous march of my entire life.

4.

March through the Murray Valley

Generally the Murray follows a course from east to west, perhaps a west-north-west course, until it reaches the so-called 'Northwest Bend', where it suddenly makes a sharp southerly turn. From the 'Woolshed' also it runs a good distance down to the south, until in the vicinity of the Murrumbidgee it resumes its old course, before its final turn south at the Northwest Bend.

This southerly turn traverses a broad swamp-land, which is pocked with thousands of now dry lakes covered with lignum and a great variety of gums and boxwood. Particularly at this time of such drought this forms the most desolate image one can imagine in a forested region.

There now runs in a fairly straight westerly direction a kind of emergency channel, which because of the wide bend in the river breaks its bank at high water and does not join the main stream again until near the confluence with the Murrumbidgee. This channel is called the Edward River, but it does not contain any flowing water, except when the Hume has risen high enough to fill it.[1] In summer, like all other water-courses in Australia, it is distinguished by a chain of ponds, so that the lakes or even the billabongs, as they are often called by the settlers, retain the foul-smelling green waters from the last flood only at their deepest points here and there. It was horrifying to be trapped in there, as I often observed with a shudder. Poor, unfortunate animals, in particular cattle, which found the ground bare of anything from which they might derive the slightest nourishment, and too exhausted even to go down to the Murray where the steep and perilous banks seldom offered a safe drinking place, sought to quench their thirst at the nearest place which seemed to offer them the opportunity – and paid a frightfully high price. The wide, muddy edge gave way under their hooves, and with their mouths reaching out to the water's edge, tongues sticking to the gums, they did not wish to step back until they had had at least one sip, and in the process they sank deeper, ever deeper. In their weakened state after months without a decent mouthful of food, languishing and miserable, they were no longer in a condition to extract themselves from their perilous situation, nor could they even quench their thirst. With strength drawn from desperation they struggle on for a short time, only to sink deeper and deeper into the mud and, with all four legs stuck, tongue hanging out perhaps just a few inches from the edge of the mudhole at which the unfortunates expect to ease their torment, they lie there quietly to die. Quietly? They would have been happy, if they had only died of hunger and thirst, but their weakened state only led them in this instance into a state of unconscious exhaustion, from which animals appear better able to go more easily to their deaths than we would otherwise like to think. But no, crows and magpies which gathered around in great numbers in the trees, their feathers greasy, and glossy, had an abundance of rich and easy spoils on offer this year. Carrion? It did not even occur to them to touch carrion after they had flown many a long mile. They knew a tastier meal, and they swooped down to the dying animals as they bleated or lowed in vain for help. Sharpening their greedy beaks on the horns of the half-sunk animals, they mercilessly pecked out their already glassy eyes.

No more sympathy was shown by the wild dog, to which it did not occur to ruin its teeth by waiting until the flesh turned cold and hard before sinking its fangs into the still living, warm flesh of its easy prey. What did it care for the terrified bleating – it was music by which to eat its meal, and it ripped open the body of the animal as it lay on its side or tore its way into its flanks.

But let us banish those horrific images. It shook me deeply to have to watch this torment, and nonetheless, although I had just a few loads of powder in my horn, a few times I was unable to resist the urge to free these unfortunate creatures from their suffering, and I shot a bullet through the brain. If I had wanted to help all of them, I would have needed to have a cart loaded with ammunition.

Around the Edward the country improved somewhat, because here for the first time grew the real vegetation, the kind that makes this river so well-suited to sheep breeding – the saltbush. Even if the name does not exactly sound inviting, it really has become a blessing in this country, especially for animals.

The Australian sheep farmer and settler, by the way, understand by the name 'saltbush' a variety of plants. The main saltbush has a not very large, heart-shaped, bright green leaf which is rather lush, looks like it is covered with flour and has a more or less salty flavour. Another type of succulent with short, thick, fleshy, juicy leaves, and also with a salty taste, bears the same name. Some of these look really quite pretty and lush, and I do not understand at all how they are able to draw up and hold such an amount of moisture in this terribly dry soil.

The main source of food for the sheep here incidentally is the so-called 'pig's face', certainly a very unpoetic name. It is a kind of cactus which in autumn, after producing a red blossom, is able to produce an extremely tasty berry, also red. The pig's face itself protrudes from the soil in triangular, thick, fleshy leaves or stalks, and the sheep enjoy eating it greatly. There are, as it happens, various sorts of it which resemble each other in appearance, but in which clear differences of taste are evident. One sort tastes very salty, another is simply watery with a slight bitterness, a bit like raw gherkins, and a third one, from which I myself have made many a hearty meal, has an aftertaste almost like ripe cherries.

The blacks consume this pig's face in great quantities, but it is also eaten a lot by the sheep, and I believe that it would make an excellent salad. Many a lost soul has managed to stay alive by eating it.

The vegetation otherwise remained fairly constant: gum trees in the vicinity of the river, and tea and broom bushes with the saltbush on the so-called flats. The saddest of all the plant species however is the lignum, which flourishes on the flood plains. It looks exactly as if all its thin stems had been eaten off by animals, and as if it had been robbed of all its leaves. It grows back, however, immediately after being eaten, and the animals are quite innocent of its desolate appearance – they do not touch the bitter, wooden branches.

The country on both sides of the Edward was flat and laced with numerous lakes. The soil was a grey and, in moist weather, clay-like loam, which, however, cracks when it is half dry. Apart from the vegetation which thrives here, the land would scarcely be able to support other crops.

Through these woods I commenced my lonely journey, albeit in the midst of a good number of stations, one of which – even if one could not always count upon it – could be reached each night. To a certain extent just the knowledge of their existence provided a kind of protection against brazen hold-ups by Indians or blacks.

On the very first night I camped in the open on the Edward River in a small grove of so-called Borewood – gum trees too, but with a somewhat different bark – and my evening meal was a cockatoo. Its meat incidentally is tough, dark-red and dry, and only the severest hunger enabled me to tolerate the smell of parrot which I usually find disgusting. I plucked the feathers off this fellow, which in the evening in the depths of twilight I had pulled out of a gum tree, and fried it on coals. I had made a decent fire, because although I had seen Indians during the day, it was said that they were not dangerous in this district. In any case no instance was known in which they had murdered a white man. The next morning I did not wish to dine on cockatoo again for breakfast, but I needed to march a good 12 miles before I came to a station, where I ate my fill of cold beef, tea and damper, as the English call it.

For the sake of clarification, because the word 'damper' will probably appear many more times, it may be helpful here to say that damper is a quite common form of wheat dough, made simply with water and without yeast. It is just pressed flat and baked in the coals. For a civilised taste it may certainly be difficult to digest, but it totally satisfies the 'bush stomach'.

Until 23 May nothing of note happened to me. The area was quite monotonous, consisting mostly of saltbush plains and borewood woodlands, low-growing trees like apple trees with a dull grey bark and dull grey leaves. The entire natural scenery looked like a worn-out Styrian hunting jacket, and a matching steel-grey sky stretched over it. Rain was always threatening and kept me constantly anxious, because if it had rained in this district, then I would have found myself in a really awful predicament. The soil here consisted entirely of grey, dusty loam, which with even the slightest moisture stuck cruelly to one's soles. Even the use of a long stick could not remove the heavy clumps, so later when I walked such routes in the rain, I carried my knife in my hand so as to keep the heels free, or at least every now and again to clean off the awful appendages.

On the evening of the 23rd I reached a small creek, the Mouleman,[2] which flows into the Edward (that is, when it has water, because now it was only a dry bed bearing the honourable title creek). There was an inn and a police station here, but I learned some disheartening news about the blacks, who reportedly had just recently committed a number of murders of lone travellers journeying from one station to the next. One of these rascals, 'Billy the Bull', was locked up here at the police station. He had committed two murders of whites and named the places where the bodies were buried. In one case he had hidden the body in a truly diabolical way so that the police would not find it. After he had bludgeoned the unfortunate man to death and removed his kidney fat, he carried the body down deep into the bed of the Murray, and here, after he had first cut open the body of the dead man and filled it with stones, he had driven a stake through the man's breast into the bed, a good fourteen feet under water, so that later the body, when it became lighter, would not be brought to the surface by the current. He was accused of many other murders, but it was not easy to gather the evidence, because he had summarily dispatched all of the witnesses with a club – including even one of his wives.

Apart from him the police were also after another two of the devils, namely Bill and Peter, who had also murdered white people and simply thrown their bodies into the bushes. They had not yet succeeded in capturing them, and one of the police said innocently that I would probably encounter them on my travels.

After hearing this frankly quite disturbing news I would gladly have taken a black man with me from here to accompany me, but the same thing was said to me here as it had been in Albury and Sydney, namely that I would first of all not find one who would travel with me, and, secondly, if that did happen I would be exposing myself to an even greater danger than if I were travelling alone and armed, because often it was not just the desire to rob individuals – particularly individuals from another tribe – which drove these tribes to attack. Rather, it was a kind of religious mania or superstition which then came to the fore as soon as someone was cast before them, and this was much more dangerous than simply a wild tribe's instinct for theft and violence.

These savages here do not believe then in a natural death, and everyone in the tribe who dies is – in their opinion – the victim of the magic of another tribe. This magic can be conjured in a variety of ways, but the method is not the issue – what is important for them is the result. The women decorate themselves with white clay and howl and scream, whine and lament, until the men – they themselves driven to despair – set off in order to bring back to camp the fat of some enemy beaten to death as a human sacrifice. Then the wailing turns suddenly to joy, and the faces of those enraptured by magic are now entirely becalmed.

The inevitable result of this is that the neighbouring tribes live in a constant state of hostility and do not dare to cross the boundaries they themselves had determined, except to conduct raids into their neighbours' territory to avenge all manner of deaths. For this reason a black man seldom ventures into foreign territory, even if accompanied by a number of Europeans. Once he has crossed the boundary, and a hostile tribe is between him and his own, it will never occur to him to make his own way back, and he views the white men as his only protectors.

For that reason, then, it can be the case that white men who travel with a black man are almost unavoidably exposed to the danger of being attacked by another tribe, while a white man alone has a much better prospect of getting through unharmed.

Here I saw also for the first time a small detachment of the so-called 'Black Police', who 'in the bush' especially are of inestimable importance for the security of settlers, not only by punishing other tribes for their heinous deeds, but also by preventing robberies that have already been planned. They received a good salary from the government, along with clothing and board, and they are under the authority of a white commander. Their uniform is a blue jacket and trousers, the latter with red stripes down the sides and a round cap. Their weapons are primarily bayonets, but they also carry shotguns, and it is remarkable how soon they become accustomed to the use of them and how wonderfully well they learn to shoot with ease.

For the most part this 'wild police force' is selected from and supported by the neighbouring tribes. In this way the whites, moreover, have the advantage that all the nooks and crannies of the district are known intimately, and even the characters from whom violent acts might be expected are known personally and can be watched carefully. But they have even recruited individuals from hostile tribes who, protected and supported by the whites and their weapons, then feel themselves sufficiently safe to enter territory which they would otherwise never come anywhere near, except in going to war.

One tribe of the Mouleman blacks was camped on the left bank of the small, almost dry stream, and a number of black policemen, who had set up their station there, roamed around among them. Like a flash they appeared before me when they saw me coming through the scrub, armed with a rifle and knife, and while they allowed me to pass by them at a distance of some ten paces, they quickly exchanged some words among each other. Then, however, like dogs when a stranger approaches, tracing a tight circle around him as they bark to impede his progress, they allowed me to proceed perhaps another 50 paces toward the buildings, and then they followed close behind in my tracks, until they reached the place at which my footprints were so well formed that they knew exactly where I was headed.

The station itself consisted of a small number of buildings to meet the needs of the police. In part they were to serve as a prison, and in part as accommodation for the employees, and then were two private residences and a guest-house.

The conversation revolved almost entirely around the subject of some just recently committed murders of travellers, and around the likely verdict that would be reached on the perpetrator who had been caught and handed over. It was assumed that after issuing a harsh warning, the courts would give him a woollen blanket and let him loose, as had happened until now with most of the others.

I am truly not disposed to giving encouragement to acts of cruelty against Indian tribes. It is only right and proper to apply restraint with the Indians, who have quite a different conception of human life than we, and from whom we can hardly expect that they should immediately conform to rules and practices, which, after all, have been imposed on them by the whites. It would not be right to bring the full weight of the law to bear against them from the start. However, this rascal Billy the Bull knew as well as any white man just what he was doing and how he was thereby exposing himself to the whites' thirst for revenge. If the courts set him free again, then that could only be taken to mean 'go forth and murder as you please'.

It was very much like the murderer Merryman in Albury, and there the whites were almost to a man of the opinion that if they came upon him in the forest they would simply put a bullet through his head. I myself would not have troubled my conscience in the least if I had shot him down like a wolf. That aside, in the district there had already been far too many such murders. Where it was not just travellers but also individual shepherds who were abandoned to the insidious lust for murder of particular rascals, then it could do no harm at all if, for once, an example was made, and these fellows were shown how one can deal with them if one wishes, especially if the culprit was one of the well-recognised murderers such as this Billy the Bull.

I must make mention of a remarkable circumstance which delivered this Billy the Bull into the hands of the whites. It might perhaps be a circumstance whose origins lie with the savages themselves. They seem to believe that after the course of a certain, not very long, time – perhaps a matter of six months – a kind of statute of limitations applies, according to which they would no longer be punished and could once more visit their hunting grounds, which they commonly leave after the murder of a white man. Even 'Billy' had removed himself for six months after committing a murder whose consequences, he knew, he could not escape. After his capture he confessed to this murder and happily declared he was responsible for still further murders which had been committed 'long, long ago' (more than six months), and for which, by his calculations, he could no longer be held accountable.

The next night a settler named Mr Smith came down the river from the next station to stay in the guest-house, along with a preacher who had been brought up from Melbourne. The settlers, it appears, have made a subscription so that a preacher might remain in the area, and he was the first one in the district. There was much said in favour of this; it was believed that one was meeting a long felt need, because the average man, no matter how basic and uneducated he might be here in 'the bush' (as the Australian wilderness generally is called), every now and again wishes to hear the word of God, and for that reason would make a small contribution to maintaining a clergyman. Moreover, there were already families living there, and for the sake of weddings, baptisms and funerals it seemed desirable to have religious assistance.

My march and the nature of my travels brought me, much to my benefit, in contact with all classes of society along the Murray, and above all as a traveller on foot, a so-called 'bundleman', with the lower classes. Whenever I reached a station to spend the night I generally slept in the shepherd's hut or in the kitchen, but I was constantly plied with food and drink and warm sheep skins.

In the evening I reached Mr Smith's station some 25 miles distant. He returned there in the afternoon, and I slept in the so-called 'hut' with the shepherd and the stock keeper. Of course the conversation revolved around the topic of the 'natural curiosity', as they called it, of a 'bush preacher', but by no means with the reverence which Mr Smith or the preacher will have expected.

'I bet he came to deprive us of our six pence,' one of them said. 'Damn the penny he takes out of my pocket,' replied the other. Everything spoke against a sermon, as indeed against any kind of spiritual consolation. I also believe, after everything I have heard, that this is pretty much the general mood in the bush, and in the whole wide world there is surely no more thankless place for a clergyman than in the Murray scrub. And surely nowhere in the whole wide world is there a rougher, rawer people than these inhabitants of the bush – with the exception of course of the settlers themselves, or at least the tenants, of the various stations and 'runs', who in a distinctly aristocratic manner fully isolate themselves from the 'people'.

These people do, however, have one virtue, the virtue of hospitality, which would not be observed more conscientiously by an Arab. If a traveller arrives at one of their huts, if one sees just one person coming from a distance, then the 'hut-keeper' sets the quart-pot with tea on the fire and the damper and meat on the table. If he arrives around evening, than as a matter of course he spends the night there, and indeed in many huts I have been requested most warmly to stay the next night as well to rest. The few settlers who provide the exception to this rule are known all along the Murray, and they are spoken of only with contempt.

The population otherwise consists to the tune of at least three-quarters of people who were transported here in their youth and, deprived of any opportunity of education, grew up in a land as wild and raw as they. Almost every word they speak is testament to that, and 'a bloody fine day' and 'a bloody bad road' are the constantly heard expressions, even if they are meant favourably. Nonetheless, these people exist in a kind of legal straitjacket with which the equally wild but not so raw backwoodsman in America is unfamiliar. There reigns a sort of congenital inhibition regarding the law, which in many cases is not in a position to protect them, but which the bushman very seldom or never breaks. By this I mean lynch justice, which perhaps nowhere else in the world would play a greater role than here. And there is nowhere else where, if there were not such a benevolent fear of the law, things would be in worse hands.

It is the case that even here in the bush thefts occur commonly. These, however, are all the more dangerous, because the shepherds and stockmen are unable so much as to lock their huts. Even the hut-keepers, especially in the vicinity of the animal pens, sometimes have to leave their dwellings. All too often it occurs that wandering vagabonds, always alert to the possibility of stealing blankets or supplies – because, apart from those, there is seldom anything else to take from the huts – or even of breaking open a box in which a few painstakingly saved shillings might be found. Alternatively, to continue their journey they catch horses, which they then, when the opportunity presents itself, sell, trade or even let loose.

If such rascals were caught in the act by the rightful owners, then a police officer would have to be fetched from perhaps 60 or 70 miles away in order to arrest them. Chasing after them is similarly difficult. If one wanted to call on the police, then the thieves would gain such a head-start before the police could arrive that one could hardly imagine catching up with them. When, on the other hand, the people themselves take up the chase, then upon catching the thieves they are not permitted by law to do anything more than retrieve the stolen goods from them – and I understand that even that is not entirely lawful. The thieving rabble that hangs around these parts knows that all too well and continues its disgraceful business without fear. If one only applied the old lynch to them a few times, without intervention by the authorities, then the rascals would no longer feel so secure in carrying out their crimes. Say what you will against lynch justice, in certain cases I am in favour of it, and everything I have seen and experienced of it in America has been confirmed here in the Australian bush.

On this day I had come across several empty shepherds' huts. It was supposed to have rained here several times lately, and further up to the north, in the so-called scrub or the mallee bush, the grass was beginning to germinate, so most sheep stations were now being moved further inland. At this time of year the sheep do not need the pig's face with its high moisture content, so it can be sent by cart to the shepherds for their own needs.

Today for the first time also I came across the mallee bush, of which I had heard so much earlier, and which is such an important plant for so many Australian tribes.

The mallee bush, like almost every Australian tree, has long, lancet-shaped gum leaves, identical top and bottom, which are filled with an oil. It grows only as a bush, on which there are six to 12 main branches, and then 20 smaller branches, thin and without leaves, growing upward from a central root, while a dense crown of foliage forms a broad, symmetrical canopy. The green of these leaves is vibrant, and their stem has a reddish hue, with the result that with the thin, distinctive growth they form groups which do not look at all bad. Among them there usually grows the Australian spruce tree, a truly beautiful though not tall tree, which, with its wonderful shady, lush green and its needles, contrasts most pleasingly with the surrounding and often prevalent mallee bushes. The wood of the spruce is thin, white and firm, and is ideally suited to woodwork, with the result that almost all of the huts in the bush are built from the small, thin trunks. The bark is of a very pretty grey and consists of long, deep strips, which stand out wonderfully against the pine-like growth of the tree itself and beneath the deeply shaded foliage.

The ground where these mallee bushes stand consists entirely of red sand, and wild oats thrive here with just one half-decent rainfall. In some places, indeed, as I was assured, they taste quite exquisite. But for now only the first signs of them were visible in the shape of thin, green stalks, and it would take a few more good showers even in this rain-deprived area to bring them to full and lush growth.

On both sides of the Murray the mallee forms an almost impenetrable scrub, often right down to the river itself, but particularly further back. Woven into it is the thick, cactus-like porcupine-grass in various shapes – wreaths, half-moons, snakes – in which only the kangaroo and the emu can find a home alongside the wild dog.

Yet many tribes of blacks gather here, the Mallee blacks or Worrigels,[3] as they are called by the tribes on the Murray, and live on kangaroos and wallabies (a smaller species of kangaroo), kangaroo rats, wombats (a kind of badger) and emus. Not a drop of water flows in their territory, and they gain it in a sensible and unusual way. The roots of these mallee plants are full of moisture, so they dig them out, break them into pieces and put them in a container made of bark built especially for this purpose, whereby from some of these pieces of root a completely clear, from others a somewhat reddish, but constantly clean and sweet tasting water flows. Of course, these people do not wash themselves, and therefore they do not miss having water for this purpose, but for drinking these roots are entirely sufficient.

In this so overwhelmingly dry summer, however, some of them found it necessary to leave behind the mallee scrub, which otherwise meets all their needs, and to go down to the Murray. Here they entered the river territory of hostile tribes, and in cases where they were not strong enough to establish their presence for a short time on the Murray, then at night – although this goes very much against their nature – they secretly go to the river and collect the barest quantities of water they require in bark pans.

I will return later and in more detail to the customs and practices of these tribes, because apart from my own experiences I also found some excellent and even official sources, which I was able to use, and from which I was able to create a good overview.

I was now drawing ever closer to the territory in which the blacks were supposed to be particularly 'jolly', as was the strange term used. The word 'jolly' actually simply means cheerful or merry. The response to my queries suggested, however, that it was not a harmless kind of happiness that was meant. Rather, 'jolly' here signified cheeky or cocky, and the most terrifying stories were told to me by a so-called 'bundleman', a traveller on foot, who had worked in a small district below the stations and had come up here with one companion. On the way they passed a tribe of savages, and two of these had separated themselves from the others, and they approached them with spears and clubs demanding 'smoke', that is, a light for their tobacco. The travellers assured them that they had nothing they could give them, but one of the black scoundrels set eagerly about removing the blankets from their shoulders and then searching through their pockets. He found a few shillings of silver, and each of the travellers also had a pocket knife. While this took place, the other man remained and simply wore a friendly grin on his face. The travellers were robbed of everything and had to be happy that they were able to continue their journey unharmed and with their kidney fat still in place. A short time earlier, members of the same tribe had taken tobacco and a knife from a lone traveller. These two also took the opportunity to enquire after a comrade of theirs who was supposed to have passed this way earlier, but had not been seen here by anyone.

At this point I need to say a few words about the weapons of the blacks, which, when one hears that all are made solely of wood, can be underestimated. The tribes have a very sophisticated knowledge of how to use them, and the accuracy with which they throw the light spears in particular is extraordinary.

The latter consist of two quite different parts: the roughly two-foot long handle is made of a kind of firm tube, usually from the so-called grass tree, a plant bearing a resemblance to one which we call in colloquial German a *Plumpkeule*. Then there is the tip, some three to four feet long. They are usually made from the hard wood of the iron bark tree and are smooth and needle-sharp. The spears are thrown not just with a swing of the arm; much more power is added with the use of a so-called throwing-stick. This is a narrow piece of wood roughly two feet in length and equipped with a kind of hook at the upper end. The back end of the spear is placed in this hook, and the spear is thus hurled to a certain extent with the aid of this leverage. They normally carry four of five such spears on them. Apart from the spears, they also have a club – a short, heavy piece of wood with a thick pommel in various forms – and a long, narrow shield with which to deflect spears and clubs. Then there is the throwing club, a narrow, bent, very thin and sharp instrument made of hard wood, with a broad head like an erasing knife. The most distinctive thing of all is the woomera, as I understand they call these objects in Van Diemen's Land, or the boomerang, as they are called on the Murray.[4] This boomerang has often been described by Englishmen, but I have never been able to gain a really clear understanding of it just by reading about it, so I want to attempt here to see if I am able to explain it more comprehensibly.

The design of the boomerang, as simple as can be, is based on a pure mathematical principle which has been discovered by these blacks, and certainly not by calculation or thought but rather by coincidence. The boomerang is a roughly two to three-and-a-half inches wide and perhaps 18 to 20 inches long – but not more than half an inch thick – piece of hard wood. Both ends of it are not sharp but are rounded off to a half-moon shape, like a sickle; on the inner side they are not so gently curved but are quite sharp. There are two kinds of these boomerangs: one is a normal throwing weapon which, as a result of the curve, makes a much deeper impression on impact; the two sides of the sickle are completely identical. The other one, however, on which one side is a little shorter and the instrument itself has a somewhat greater curve, is not simply hurled forward in the same manner but also, if it does not encounter some resistance, that is, if it has missed the object at which it was thrown, then as a result of its own rotation it returns to its thrower, and even with increased power. This kind of boomerang is not thrown directly at the object which it is meant to strike, but rather it first touches the ground some 29 paces distant, and then bounces off it with increased energy, flying toward the envisaged target. If it strikes man or animal – and the thrower knows exactly how to determine the required height above the ground to achieve this – then the sharp, hard wood inflicts a nasty wound with its powerful rotation. This wooden sickle can slice through even the thickest cloth, and even in its irregular flight is almost impossible to deflect. If, however, it misses its target, then it flies on another 100 to 120 paces and climbs to a height of up to 20 feet above the earth, describing a short turn to the left, whereby for a few seconds it almost looks like it comes to a complete standstill, and then suddenly hissing and buzzing it whizzes through the air and, almost in a straight line, flies directly over the spot from which it was thrown, back perhaps a good 10 or 12 paces.

This boomerang is not so well known further down the Murray in South Australia and not used at all, while however according to Dr Leichhardt's report it is found in the very far north of Australia.[5] I did not see it among the tribes in the Torres Strait, however it may be the case that they did know how to use it so well, because on the islands there is no game on which to use this weapon, and one can imagine that they left behind on the mainland everything that they did not require for their stay there.

Once again on 25 May I approached the Murray, which I had left in following the Edward, and now wandered along the Logan, which bears this name for just a short distance, and is formed by the Edward and the Wakool, both of which are overflow tributaries of the Murray. Here I shot my first black swan, although I had previously seen several without being able to fire a shot. I plucked it and took the pelt with me.

These black swans have an excellent plumage. The back is rather black, and the stomach turns into more of a dark silver-grey. The valuable thing about it however is the snow-white, almost one-and-a-half inch thick down, which appears when the black feathers are plucked, and which provides the softest and most beautiful fur for a lady's coat. The largest of the wing feathers are white, and a red ring appears around the eyes.

Frankly there is not much in the way of game to be hunted in these parts, and the kangaroos are perhaps the only thing which could stake a claim in this regard, because one does not only chase them but can also stalk them as one does deer. However, I got to see only very few kangaroos; during the terrible drought they remained deep in the mallee bushes, where just about all decent food is supposed to grow, and where they survived on the young grass as it appeared. Kangaroo hunts have been described much too often and in much the same way, so that it is not worth wasting more words on it. Much more interesting in contrast, it is said, are the Aborigines' emu hunts, which typically target this Australian version of the ostrich. When it is discovered on the plains an entire tribe will stage a genuine mass hunt for it.

This emu bears a close similarity with the South American cassowary, yet it appears to constitute a quite different species and is also somewhat larger than the American bird. The one, at least, with which I almost collided on this day was definitely over seven feet tall and was a colossal fellow. I was walking through a small brushwood grove, my steps on the soft, dusty ground barely audible, and was just arriving at one of the thousands of small dry creeks or gullies which cross the flat countryside in all directions, when I heard a sound in the gully. Because of the Indians I was carrying my rifle at the ready; in a moment I had it cocked and stopped to listen in silence so as to establish the direction and nature of a second sound. I did not, however, remain in doubt for long. In the very next moment something came at me from a tea-bush, like a storm unleashed, and naturally I at first thought it to be a murderous Indian. I raised my rifle to my cheeks in a flash, following an instinct to defend myself.

Before I even had a target in my sights, and before I could recognise what it was emerging suddenly from the bush, a dark shape passed by so closely that it almost brushed my rifle, and I now recognised an enormous emu making good use of its long legs. With fabulous speed it really flew over the soft ground, throwing up a cloud of smoke behind it. All of that happened so quickly, that I genuinely forgot to shoot, and two seconds later it would have been too late, because the whole episode was over in a flash.

This, by the way, also had its positive side, insofar as it made me more circumspect thereafter. Just as in the gully I had not seen that tall emu, which was making no effort to hide itself, there could have been a half dozen blacks comfortably lying in ambush, and they could have plunged their lethal spears into my body. Now I began to be more alert, and the consequence of that was that as early as the following day I secretly observed a kangaroo which had come down to the water in the Logan.[6]

The emus are eaten by the blacks; the young ones are said to taste quite good. The pelt with the plumage is of no use except for protecting the feet. The blacks might at best use it to lie on.

Apart from the emu and the kangaroo, there is almost no game at all, just a few kinds of kangaroo: the wallaby, which is somewhat smaller than the kangaroo, and the kangaroo rat, which when stirred shoot through the bushes, half jumping and half running. At first glance, as they disappear at great speed, they bear a similarity with the rabbit. The funny thing about them is that in flight they always hold one of their front paws in the air, first the right, then the left, so that at first one thinks they are limping. That, however, is by no means the case; they are simply sparing their feet for as long as they can disappear from the spot as quickly as they need to. The blacks catch them in traps, which is all the easier because they live in burrows and consequently have regular exits and entrances.

The only four-footed predator in Australia (at least in these parts of Australia, because the north is still largely unknown, and, in contrast to the fauna of these areas, crocodiles have been found there), is the wild dog, a kind of jackal, somewhere between a wolf, a fox and a dog. Its colour is not constant, unlike the consistently grey coyote of California and the pale colour of the prairie wolf of the western steppes of North America. Most of these 'dingos' are, it is true, yellow or bright yellow, but there are also brown, tan, and quite black ones. The last, however, in most cases then have a tan shadowing reaching back from the stomach and onto the legs. The wild dog lives an entirely natural existence and wants nothing to do with civilisation, although it has been tamed by the blacks and, in rare cases, also by whites. These dingos raised by whites are renegades, deeply loathed and pursued by their free-running brothers. Their approach to civilisation is much like that of Mephisto: 'You can do nothing to change the world at large, but you can start with the small details.' They can do nothing about the entire civilisation with its stations and its flocks of sheep, and they would be foolish to try, because it is precisely this civilisation which keeps them well fed. Thus they stick closely to the individual sheep, which they molest in a truly despicable way. The situation, by the way, is extremely dangerous for them, especially where kangaroo dogs are kept, because if one of the kangaroo dogs catches them at their handiwork, then their fate is sealed. Even with a head-start of half a mile they cannot escape a kangaroo dog, which is able even to catch up with an emu running at breakneck speed. If they are careless they often even fall victim to slower dogs, because these clever animals, particularly if they feel that in terms of pace they are no match for the dingo, lie in wait at the corner of a fence not far from the stockyards. Goodness help the sly thief venturing too brazenly into their vicinity. Nonetheless, he attempts to get at the closely watched flocks, which are safe from them neither during the day, when they are in the scrub, nor at night when they are in the yards. The bloodthirsty beast creates the most horrendous devastation among the animals, and not just because he tears apart everything he wishes to eat – that could be excused – but because he murders everything left alive around him.

Some of the English settlers even keep foxhounds and hunt the dingo in the style of the English fox hunt, whereby they sometimes have quite lovely hunts. On the Murray I found such a 'kennel' on the property of Mr Jeffries, and in other parts of the country they are said to exist here and there. The animal's penis is valued highly as a trophy and is taken home, just as is that of the fox in England, and there is never any worry that they might ride out for the day without coming across a fresh scent to follow. Seldom, if ever, do they return home without their catch.

There are said to be large numbers of snakes here in Australia, but now, in winter, all of them are hidden underground or in hollow trees, and even if every now and again I came across a fresh track of one on a fine warm day, I did not ever get to see one. Incidentally, one can count among these creatures a large species of lizard several feet long. The blacks regard it as a delicacy, and many whites like to eat it too.

As far as poultry is concerned, one finds the black swan, the pelican, the wild goose, a great range of many different kinds of ducks – one in particular has the very pungent smell of musk – and a wonderful kind of crane among a large number of so-called 'native companions'. The last grows to four or five feet tall, and in its movement and appearance, but not in its colour, which is a very beautiful steel-grey – it bears a striking resemblance to our German stork, to which species it unquestionably belongs, except that its beak is shorter.

The solemnity with which these native companions strut along is really amusing to observe, and quite often in their gait and movements – as strange as this might sound – they resemble humans. Sometimes they appear deep in thought, sometimes they wander idly, and sometimes they stride purposefully. Thus I once saw two of these creatures making their way from one lagoon to the next. Previously they had stood at the water's edge and observed with unusual attentiveness the mud and the dull water; I could not hear their remarks, as I was too far away, but after they had turned to each other a few times, and then one after the other turned their gaze to the terrain, they simultaneously made their way up the flat riverbank and stepped slowly, side-by-side, through the open forest toward another lagoon, or even the same one, which at that place formed a large bend. For all money they looked like a couple of elderly gentlemen dressed resplendently in steel grey, chatting with their hands on their backs, and promenading contentedly in the forest after their repast. Slowly they ambled along side-by-side in this manner, and soon thereafter they disappeared behind the grove of trees bordering the other arm of the lagoon.

I have seen the platypus, famous because it is hitherto the only animal known with a bird's beak, on a number of occasions on the Murray, where it often jumps into the air, so that one thinks at first that it is a fish breaking the surface. Twice I met it also on firm land, but always close to the bank, and before I could get a close look at it, it always dived under.

As poor in four-legged creatures as the animal world in Australia may seem, so infinitely rich is it by contrast in birdlife, and in no other part of the world have I hitherto seen such a variety of plumage and such a blaze of colour as among the parrots and cockatoos, waterbirds and pigeons here.

The white cockatoo occurs in huge flocks, and processions of them often sweep through the woodlands, stretch across the banks of the lagoons or, screeching and squawking, flutter up to the broad branches of the gum trees on the riverbanks in flocks of three or four hundred. The black cockatoo is less common, but it, too, appears in great numbers, sometimes together with the white ones, but more commonly alone. Among these I have seen two easily distinguished kinds, one with a deep red, the other with an orange-yellow comb and a horizontal stripe above the tail.

Among the birds that can be hunted is another kind of yellow and brown forest hen, about the same size as a common hen.

That is enough now for the animal world. Let me return now to my lonely march.

The night of the 20th I stayed at a station I had reached just before nightfall, and the next morning I left quite early. Strangely, however, I felt somewhat dizzy in my head, as if I were drunk, and on level ground I tumbled over a few times. The strongest thing I had drunk that morning was tea, and during the day water from the Murray, so that could not have been the cause. Apart from that I felt entirely fine, just in my head something was strange, and sometimes it seemed as if the whole bush was dancing around me. I did not want to fall sick here, right in the vicinity of the worst of the Indian tribes – the very thought sent a cold shiver down my spine – and so I wandered on, not exactly in the best of spirits. The dizziness grew stronger and stronger toward evening, and finally I could go no further. I did not wish to camp by the river itself because of the blacks prowling back and forth there. So I staggered – one could no longer call it walking – some quarter of a mile into the mallee bushes, with huge effort lit myself a fire, wrapped myself in my blanket with my rifle on my right, open side, and soon fell into a kind of half-sleep, in which state I spent the entire, rather miserable night. The next morning the dizziness had somewhat subsided, but my head was burning as if on fire, and my stomach similarly was making it rather apparent that it wanted something more from me than just pig's face and Murray water. Luckily, when I had packed up my blanket and went back to the Murray I shot a wallaby, a piece of which I was able to cook on the fire, and yet I was still unable to continue my march that day. God knows what was in my limbs, but it was as if my bones were crushed, and I feared I was becoming seriously ill.

So as not to lose the day entirely, I decided to wash once more the only shirt I had rescued from the wreck of the canoe – simply because I had it on. The weather at the time was favourable, and on a sandbank in the river, the cocked rifle lying across a few pieces of wood put in place especially so that it would be in easy reach in case of an emergency, I completed my entire washing within something like half hour, using sand instead of soap, and then consumed the rest of my wallaby. My stomach was still in perfect shape and not at all affected by the dizzy spell. The next morning, thanks to my strong constitution, I was completely recovered – the dizziness, it is true, had not yet entirely left me, but I noticed it only when I stood still and focussed my eyes on a particular point. During the day this feeling, too, left me, and I followed my course once more, happy and fresh, through the eternal gum forests.

On leaving my campsite I had, however, lost the only tracks which led to a station, probably lying some distance back. Following a straight course, which would bring me back to the river, I reached the Murray at about 2 o'clock in the afternoon, at a place where, on the opposite bank, there stood a little hut on a sandhill surrounded by spruce wood and banksia. On the other bank I saw a few blacks with one of their bark canoes and waved to them, and soon they were next to me. From the blacks who live on the stations there is nothing to fear, at least as long as they remain in the vicinity of the whites' accommodation, and for a piece of tobacco these fellows would be willing to take me across the stream.

These bark canoes of the Australian savages are, by the way, curious things, and very different from those of all other tribes I had hitherto come across. The North American savage, for example, on the big fresh-water lakes of the inland fashioned for himself out of the tough, elastic bark of the birch a canoe with which he can even shoot boldly and at great speed over the wild turbulence of those mighty waters. But it does not even occur to the Australian savage to go to any effort to achieve what can be achieved much more comfortably and effortlessly. Therefore he simply strips off a piece of bark from a gum tree and lays it on the water – he always chooses curved trees from which he takes the outer layer, so that almost no effort is involved beyond the stripping. If the water runs over the side every now and again, then with a few handfuls of clay he builds himself fore and aft a barrier. Carrying just his spear he paddles back and forth across the river and sometimes a short distance up or down it. He must, however, constantly keep his balance, because not uncommonly – for example in the canoe in which I was carried – the edge is barely an inch above the water, so that even the slightest false move can fill the canoe beyond saving, so that it sinks. Fully aware of such a possibility I sat there with my rifle hung around me, while my powder horn, which I had been able to have freshly filled at the last public house where they had some things for sale, was tied to my head.

We managed to cross without incident, however, and I spent the whole night in the hut with the people there, who took me in most hospitably. Through the night the rain poured down from the heavens, and I was very happy not to be in the open.

Here I also heard that the two blacks who were being pursued because of two murders lived quite nearby. The constables sent out to bring them in had, however, returned with their job not done, because they did not know these men personally and were unable to find out from any of the others who they were. But they were expected back any day, and the shepherd hoped very firmly that these two dangerous rascals, of whom one moreover was armed with a gun, were rendered harmless.

On 29 May, a quite beautiful day, I walked along a rather well-trodden path. I was not expecting to see a house for the next 20 miles or so, and was therefore very watchful in this somewhat desolate area. I was below the mouth of the Murrumbidgee, and this was where some of the nastiest tribes were said to gather. It was already the afternoon, and I had not yet seen a single one of the blacks, and had not even found a fresh track left by them, when suddenly on the path ahead of me I saw something move, and a dark body slid across the way ahead of me into the thick tea-trees and lignum bushes. I proceeded forward another 30 or 40 paces and then stopped and looked for my gun, because with good reason I suspected that I was being observed from one side. I tapped the trigger a few times, and to be safe I inserted new percussion caps and then left the path, which just at this point passed through rather thick bushes, and turned right toward a small and more open sandhill. In case one of the scoundrels really had evil intentions, I would now have a better view over the terrain and would not have bushes all around me through which the blacks would easily be able to creep up on me.

It was a case of out of the frying pan and into the fire, however, because on arriving at the top of the hill I suddenly found before me an entire tribe of blacks who were on the move, and just at that moment, for reasons I cannot guess, they had had to stop. Not a single fire was burning, and even the few women whom they had with them were carrying their packs on their backs.

In any case, I had already been noticed by them, because some of them looked toward me when I appeared so close by – I would not have been more than 100 paces from them – and four or five old men were engaged in a lively discussion. I myself at first did not know what I should do – foolishly I had brought with me from Sydney just my gun and my knife, and I had left my royal Saxon passport in my suitcase, so there was no way now to prove my identity. Thus I was dependent on my own devices, and this time I did not believe that there was any way to avoid an assault. I was, however, completely prepared for it, because when I had been unwell I had made a round of shot for my gun, which was a source of some comfort now, and in the large pocket of my belt I had quick-loading pellets ready to insert in the barrel at a moment's notice.

The appearance of this dark gathering was by no means inviting, and one could not fail to recognise their real intent. They were prepared for battle, having painted themselves extensively with white and red clay in the most fantastic manner, and they were travelling, I would say, armed to the teeth. Almost everyone carried two boomerangs, three or four spears, and in their hands the small war club with the long, narrow shield. One can imagine that these fellows, who even in times of peace were hungry for murder and booty, would not be more placidly inclined now that they had their weapons and had adopted the firm resolve not to return home without the kidney fat of one of their vanquished enemies.

The target of this procession was, incidentally, not the whites, otherwise they would have attacked me long ago, but probably one or other of the neighbouring tribes (and that was definitely the case, because later I heard that they had set out against the Swan Hill blacks). In any case, I arrived in their midst quite alone, and with weapons which they knew well to fear, and I do not believe that I was mistaken when I understood the fierce debate among the elders to be about me.

I now regret that I did not observe more closely my advocates back then, that is, those who were perhaps voicing their opposition to attacking everyone they came across. At that moment, however, I really did not have enough time to do so, because after casting a quick glance around me, I once more saw a figure behind me. On this occasion, like the earlier one, it did not step openly before me but rather, when I turned around, sought the cover of the bushes. As the English say, the episode was 'too exciting to be pleasant'.

By the same token, I also did not wish to assault them head-on but at least allow them to be the aggressors, a role which they normally eschew, and so I turned once more toward the path I was following and decided to stick to it and to wait to see what the black rascals might do.

I did not remain in doubt for long. I had barely gone 200 paces, when to my right through the low tea-trees I saw two powerful young men cutting over to the path, as if they wanted to cross there; I was perhaps another 60 paces distant from them when they stopped and waited for me, though not with a hostile posture. By turning away from the hill I was no longer within sight of the rest of the group, but I now saw how they, too, gathered on the hill, obviously so as to observe the negotiations. It had already been said to me by many with whom I had spoken, and who had considerable experience of their own, that under no circumstances, if I were ever to come into such contact with Aborigines, should I show fear. I myself had already had this confirmed in a great variety of situations, and even if now my heart was beating loudly, I determined that the black fellows would not notice it in the least. I therefore removed the rifle slowly from my shoulder without cocking it, placed it under my arm and calmly continued walking forward toward the two who were awaiting me.

'You smoke?' said the first one, when I was right before them, thinking now of course that I would stop next to them. The question was not really to find out if I myself smoked, which was of too little interest to them, but rather whether I had tobacco on me.

'No', was my short answer, and with that I veered to the right and, keeping free my right arm with the gun (because of its sheath I carried my hunting knife on the right side also), I passed them quickly by and continued on my way. For a few seconds they stood still as if undecided, but then after exchanging a few quick words they followed quickly behind me, and I now had to turn around to await them, because I did not want to be within range of their spears with my back turned.

'You smoke?' repeated the one who had spoken earlier, now impatiently, not merely as a question but demandingly, and I told them just as curtly and clearly that I had no tobacco on me. To be honest that was not the case, and I would gladly have offered them a cigarette, but if I did that, then ultimately they would think that they had intimidated me and then, their greed awakened, they would be emboldened to do much more.

'That damn gammon,' the speaker continued, now enraged. 'You smoke.' 'Gammon' is their English expression for lie or deceit, and now I was thinking that I had let them go so far as to think that I was just a peaceful bundleman with whom they could do what they wanted. In order to prove to them as a matter of priority that I was not in the least afraid of them, and to show that I had the upper hand, I reached into my pocket, pulled out a stick of chewing tobacco, showed it to one of them and said to him that he could have the tobacco if he gave me one of the boomerangs he was carrying in his hand.

The effect that this suggestion had on him was truly comical. At first he looked at me for a few seconds, then at his comrade, and suddenly jumped high in the air, as if in a burst of joy. Now, however, he gripped one of the boomerangs in his right hand, ran back a few steps and called, 'I give you boomerang,' and then swung the weapon as if he were going to hurl it at me.

Perhaps the whole thing was just a joke; in any case it showed me very clearly how very differently these fellows setting off for battle behaved, when they found among them a single man with whom they could do what they wished. But as he now stepped back and swung the boomerang in the air, I had already put my tobacco back away again and cocked both barrels. Both blacks reached for their spears when they heard the sound they knew all too well. They have a very healthy fear of firearms, especially double ones, among which they know how to distinguish, and they looked indecisively at one another, no doubt convinced that what happened next depended entirely on them. Then one of the Indians standing on the hill, whose movements I had quite lost from my sight until that point, emitted a curious cry. In a flash my two friends turned toward it, and when I too turned in that direction, I just managed to see another three of the blacks run in a mad hurry down the hill, spears at the ready, and jump into the bushes out of which I had come.

At first I could only believe that the cry and the attack were directed at me, and that the whole band would set upon me, so there was nothing more for me to do than shoot a few of them and then allow my skin to be transformed into a sieve by their spears. A second later, however, I was set at ease and convinced that no one was thinking of me as the cause of the commotion, and even the two who had been dispatched down to meet me now ran back as fast as their legs would carry them. Of course, I myself did not stand around awaiting their return. Neither, however, did I quicken my pace to reveal my fear – though I must confess that I found that very difficult – but calmly continued on my way, following the path. When, however, after some time I turned around, I saw all too well that no one was paying me any further attention, because the women, who were now the only ones standing on the hill, had all turned their backs to me and were looking in the other direction.

At the next station, which I managed to reach that same evening just before nightfall, I received a partial explanation of this mysterious behaviour.

These Indians belonged to the Murrumbidgee blacks. A short time earlier one of the Swan Hill blacks had come over to a small Murrumbidgee tribe. He is alone, and he comes across two Murrumbidgee blacks, of whom one is carrying a red shotgun. These two ask him where he is from and what his name is, and when he answers the questions, one of them says to him that everything is fine and he should go with them. He even gives him the loaded gun to carry and lets him lead the way. When, however, they walk a short distance in this direction and reach a suitable place, the one who previously had had the shotgun takes out of the hand of his comrade the waddie or small war club, knocks the outsider to the ground, and smashes in his head, cuts him open, removes the kidney fat and covers up the body with branches and bushes.

The tribe of the murdered man, however, learns of this and declares a desire for revenge; the other Murrumbidgee blacks, in contrast, wanted to protect the black man from their tribe against this threat, and therefore came together from all directions, with the result that the settlers in the entire district presumed that there would inevitably be a battle between the tribes. As far as I was concerned, the strange behaviour of the blacks, from which I emerged unscathed, could only be explained if that black man who had twice crept across my path was perhaps a member of the hostile tribe sent to spy and was discovered by his enemies. If that were the case, then it was naturally of utmost importance to get hold of this spy, and for that reason they let me pass untouched. But it is also possible that this was only a pretext to find a convenient way of getting rid of me, because the blacks are as cowardly as they are treacherous, and for as long as they can avoid it, they are reluctant to make an open attack on whites, since such an action might later be betrayed by one of their own. If it could happen secretly, in cases where there are at most two of them together, they are less concerned. Almost all of the murders of whites were committed by one black or perhaps two.

I had now been on the left bank of the Murray for some time, but now I was advised by the people at two stations through which I passed on the way to the next police station that I should cross over to the right bank, at least for a while, because in that way I could cut across a significant bend in the river at that point.

Following this advice, on the 30th I reached the so-called police station. Here, however, it is somewhat isolated in the desert, and is maintained more for the sake of its name than for any other purpose. The only thing that the commissioner there, a certain Mr Macdonald – a much respected and generally well loved man – has to do is settle boundary and other disputes between neighbours. At the same time the commissioner is also the Protector of blacks and has already done many good things for them; on this occasion though he was not present. If I am not mistaken, he had made a journey to Melbourne for health reasons, but he was already on the way back and was expected any day.

Next to the police station was a guesthouse in which I spent the night. Upon my arrival the proprietor asked me immediately if I were a German who had set out on the Murray from Albury in a canoe. With good reason I was astounded that this man here, in the middle of the wilderness, could already have known about this, because no traveller had come down the river, or at least I had seen no sign of one, and who else could have told him? When I answered in the affirmative and asked him how he knew, he showed me with a sly look a Sydney newspaper, which one of the members of the mounted police had brought with him from Melbourne, and in which my plan of leaving Sydney to make a journey by canoe along the Murray was mentioned. The man made much of his own shrewdness in identifying me and was extraordinarily friendly.

Some 20 blacks were camped here, and when I arrived I gave one of them the swan skin which I was still carrying in my blanket, with the request that he scrape the fat from it with a shell, which they are said to do with great skill. When half an hour later I went out to see how far advanced they were, all of the blacks looked so shiny and covered with fat from top to bottom – because despite the rather cold weather only two or three of them were wearing blankets – as if all of them had just been cooked in oil. Their hair, faces, arms, legs, in short everything, glistened, and I could see how they viewed each other with mutual admiration. They had, however, in their eagerness removed so much of the very popular fat from my swan skin, scraped it so thoroughly, that in a few spots the skin itself had been removed, and it seemed high time for me to take it back, or there would be nothing left but the feathers.

This custom of the Australian tribes of rubbing fat into their bodies appears to derive as much from the nature of the climate there as from fashion or from superstition. The air dries out the skin to such an extent that even Europeans, in particular on a lengthy stay in the interior, have sought refuge with the same means – Leichhardt also mentions it in his travels. The savages use the fat also in roughly the same way and to the same purpose as we do, washing frequently, even in summer, when the skin is so clean, and it is said that blacks in the vicinity of settlements often plead with whites to give them even a small piece of fat, if they are unable to provide it themselves, just so as to be able to soothe their skin.

Two Englishmen were spending the night in the guesthouse. They had come from the Darling, and some 16 miles from there had also been stopped by blacks, but due to the arrival of a traveller on horseback had been able to get away. The tribe was allegedly camping very close to the route, and one of the Englishmen tried to dissuade me from going down there alone, suggesting I wait here until I found a travelling companion. I could not even consider that, however I did decide that when I reached the vicinity of the location, which they described for me quite precisely, then I would turn off to the right into the forest in order to avoid any kind of contact with them.

On this day my march proceeded largely through the endless mallee bushes, where at least I could walk with ease (because the ground was firm and hard), but I could not see very far around me. At 3 o'clock in the afternoon I reached roughly the area which the Englishmen had described to me, and where the blacks were said to be camping by a creek. Soon thereafter I did see the creek and, as I proceeded with caution, the smoke of their fires. I turned left into the bushes, circumventing the camp-site by a distance of about a mile. Around evening I reached the road once more, and now I could follow my path unhindered.

When I turned off the road to march through the mallee bushes, I saw several kangaroos and an emu, but in this instance I did not wish to make use of my gun, much though it pained me to knock back such a convenient opportunity of a good roast. At night I reached a station, and the next day I continued over the river to the left bank, because it had been said to me at the previous house that I would be able to reach a house on that side before evening. The coach tracks, however, were very unclear, because in some instances they led off to the right, then into the bush on the left. Until evening I was able to stick quite well to the most-travelled path. At nightfall, however, by which time I had not yet reached the house, I lost my way and now believed that if I maintained a course toward the setting sun, that is almost north-west, then I would have to reach the station or a least the river, and would find a path there. Alas, it grew darker and darker, the stars were already twinkling high in the sky, and the Southern Cross was climbing higher and higher, yet there was still no sign of proximity to the river or a station. Deeper and deeper I entered into the mallee wilderness, kangaroos and wallabies appeared out of bushes before me, every now and again I heard a wild dog creeping through the scrub, and finally I had little choice but to believe that although I had faithfully maintained the course I had set, I must have completely lost my way. At the time I had no explanation of how that had come about, but I knew that I was on the southern side of the stream. If I were to strike out directly to the north, then I would surely reach a path, or at least the river. Turning my back on the Southern Cross, I marched, that is I laboured and dragged myself in the direction of due north.

If I had not been so certain of my bearings, I would surely have gone crazy, because now I passed through a terrain – steep, sandhills covered with thick bushes, and then a wide saltbush plain – with which I was not familiar, and which was nothing like the path along which I had come. Yet the stars in this case were surely not lying, because even if I did not wish to place my fate entirely in their hands, I am very inclined to trust their guidance in gaining my bearings. I had to walk for a full two hours, and in these six miles passed through some of the very wildest, roughest terrain, whereby the 'porcupine grass' almost drove me to despair. Porcupine grass? Why should one flatter it in this way? One could just as easily have said 'Porcupine bristles', because the tips penetrated my skin like sharpened tips, and now I understand completely why the Indians do not like to travel at night – one does not need to be superstitious to keep a prudent distance from such a perverse plant in the dark. Lack of water and broken mallee branches added to my woes. It was only the thirst that tortured me, because that whole day not a single drop of water had passed my lips, that persuaded me not to lie down right where I stood but to continue my attempt to reach the river that same evening.

When, however, I occasionally took time to stop for a moment and cast a glance at the wild chaos surrounding me, the scenery was glorious. The coarse sandhills covered with mallee, the wonderful bushes and beautifully formed little spruces growing out of them, surrounded me like a surging tide. The stars, sparkling brightly in the sky, gave off just enough light so as to recognise the peculiar and often wildly fantastic shapes of individual bushes and tree trunks. At the same time there was a rustling and whispering through the bushes of a mad and eerie kind, because the strips of bark which hung down from all the trees were beating against each other. The mallee leaves produced their own drily whispering rustle, and the breeze which wafted through the swinging bark sometimes sounded like the genuine singing and whistling of human creatures.

I am not a timorous person, and as I knew myself to be fairly safe from Indians, who would not have been on the move here so far from the water and in the porcupine grass, I was able to abandon myself to these strange impressions with utter calm. It is not easy, however, to indulge in such natural beauty when one's shins have been jabbed to bits, and I gradually turned my thoughts from the surrounding trees and bushes, which had already troubled me enough with their unavoidable obstacles, back to my travels.

The chains of hills in Australia are quite distinctive in their formation, unlike anything I have seen in any other country, and unlike anything existing in any other part of the world. The entire landscape here shows no trace of water, not even a dry riverbed or the sign of a dried out creek. The wave-shaped hills – or at least rises, since none of them is more than 60 to 70 feet high – extend, at least in this chain, from east to west. Like the sea, if its waves suddenly froze as they reached beyond the horizon, so these mallee hills stretch into salty deserts hitherto unvisited by humans, rigid and terrible. This uniformity is all too often the reason why shepherds and hunters get lost there, and the unfortunate person who loses his way, and with it usually his mind and his wits, has nothing to orientate him but the skies. If they are covered, or if he does not comprehend the language of the stars, then he might as well lie down and die.

I was told of many such cases by the station owners, and when I had first truly entered the wilderness, I could easily understand why. Moreover, nothing in the world can have such a paralysing effect on human nerves as the thought of being lost. Even the strongest man, if he is unable to preserve his powers of reason and keep his head with the greatest of effort, turns into a child and runs away in a blind, crazed hurry. It is as if his life depended on the part of the track that he might yet come across, until he falls to the ground, almost dead from exhaustion, and then takes a fresh breath, only so as to begin anew his mad run. In every other country one at least has the aid of a formation of hills or mountains, with gullies to collect water in the rainy season, so that it flows down into a valley. Even on the prairies and steppes, where there are no rivers, there are narrow ravines channelling the rainwaters, which then become like rivers. If he follows these, then the lost traveller must eventually reach a larger body of water, and then come to some kind of settlement, providing he has not already expended all his energies or, as is mostly the case, follows such a course for days and then, close to his destination, sets off in another direction to begin his wretched journey all over. All such signs are missing here. The falling rain is eagerly soaked up by the sandy soil, and wherever a genuine gully has formed, and which appears to have been shaped by water, one only has to follow it a distance to find out that it was coincidence or some other such circumstance that must have hollowed out the flat and narrow valley. After a few hundred paces it disappears again, and it is sand, eternal, horrible sand, that confronts the dying traveller.

I myself was not too bothered with gullies or hills. Certain of the right direction, and maintaining the course set from the beginning, turning off the left or right very rarely in the hope of circumventing a steep or heavily overgrown hill-tip, I eventually reached a wide saltbush plain, and beyond it saw finally a dark, wooded strip, which signalled to me the proximity of the river, and almost simultaneously met a narrow and quite well-trodden path, next to which I could feel a cart-track, because there was not much to see. This path in any case led to the station, which I must have by-passed, because in the strip of forest in front of me I saw that the stream just at this point unexpectedly made a huge sweep to the north, which was the reason why I had had to march for so long before I came to it. As, however, I knew that toward the west there was no other shelter for the next 25 to 30 miles, and as I was carrying no other supplies on me, I decided to go back the short distance – as I presumed – to the house.

Thus following the path, which at last led me beneath tall gum trees once more, and in any case was in the vicinity of the river, I wandered once more mile after mile without coming upon even a sign of human habitation, until finally in the distance I saw a light glowing, and now thought that at last my march had finally on this evening reached a happy end.

5.

March through the Murray Valley
(Continued)

I walked toward it quickly and had closed in on it to maybe a hundred paces, with the thick undergrowth preventing me from seeing exactly where the fire actually originated. At that time I was so utterly convinced that I would find a hut here that I did not even entertain any other thought and emitted the usual Australian call, the commonly known *cooey*, so that the inhabitants would be aware that a stranger was outside and would have a chance to restrain their usually ferocious dogs. Some poor lost soul who once – in the Sydney district – forgot to do so was attacked by the vicious kangaroo dogs just as he was climbing over a fence and was literally torn to shreds before the home owner had a chance to come to his aid.

Here, too, the dogs gave a bark as soon as I called out, but there was no reply, and the next moment the fire had been extinguished or at least covered over. As I had by now come even closer to the fire since first calling out, I could hear some whispering in hushed voices, accompanied by rustling in the bushes to my right.

I had, without giving it any thought, headed toward a fire of the blacks, and by covering up their coals they gave me a clear enough indication that they did not want to have all that much to do with me. I for my part felt no great longing for them either, and so, once I realised how close I had come to playing a very thoughtless trick on myself, I moved off quietly to the left and stayed behind a tree for about a quarter of an hour to await whatever was to come. However, there was nothing to be seen and not a single sound to be heard. At one point

I felt I could hear a dog approaching quietly, but that might well have been an illusion, and there was silence again within seconds. Neither did the fire ever spring up again, and so I finally started making a slow retreat down the same path whence I had come.

After I had put approximately half a mile between myself and the blacks, I decided to make camp. By now I was dead tired and hardly able any longer to put one foot in front of the other. It must have been near midnight, and I had been tramping since very early in the morning – it was no surprise then that my feet were aching. However, I still did not dare light a fire, even though the night was rather unpleasantly cold. I simply did not want run the risk of falling asleep near a fire, with those Indians, whose intentions towards me I could not fathom, so close by. So I rolled out my blanket, placed my bag, with the swan pelt on top, under my head, wrapped myself up tightly, and in no time was fast and sweetly asleep.

But this was not to last for long. Very soon a bitter cold wakened me again, in addition to which a rather dire and plentiful morning dew was settling down, thwarting all my attempts to warm myself. I jumped up a number of times to walk back and forth but was just too tired and, in the end, had to lie down once again in the grey dust of that bare earth, by now saturated with morning dew.

One thing, though, that particularly annoyed and angered me was a small little field mouse or some similar critter that, every time I thought I might finally fall asleep, started to nibble at my backpack or the fur. But as soon as I made the slightest movement, it was gone without a trace. The first time I even got quite a fright and jumped up in a flash with my gun at the ready, thinking the savages from the now deserted camp had felt an urge to creep up on me. However, even after discovering the source of this annoyance, I was still not able to remedy it until I had shifted my campsite and moved on some 20 paces to another bush.

It was a sad old night I spent there, and God only knows the longing with which I was looking up time and again at the Southern Cross, which, in my opinion, had never moved so slowly and simply did not want to bring on the new morning. Finally, it came nonetheless with a piercing wind blowing down from the sun, as dawn broke in the bleak stand of gum trees.

I now also realised that I was not at all on a path trodden by people, but had probably missed the correct one in the dark and had followed a cattle track that was leading God knows where. I therefore resumed my direction toward the river and, within a short time, came indeed across the right path, which I then followed until I finally reached – exhausted, hungry and thirsty – the station. Here I was received in the most hospitable and friendly manner and was able to strengthen my tired limbs by way of a nourishing meal and a short rest.

Near the station I walked once again into a small Indian camp, because the savages like to move closer to the whites from time to time in order to obtain various useful items from them, and especially, for some small services, an occasional piece of bread, which they eat with gusto. When they arrive, their lodgings are set up in a flash, since there is indeed nothing simpler than these huts which, in all honesty, do not really deserve the name hut. These are just pieces of tree bark placed together at an angle towards a centre point, crookedly supported by a stick rammed into the earth, and with a fire on their open, leeward side.

I doubt that the Indians do not feel any chill simply because they walk around naked, since I have actually seen them lying by the fire, shivering with cold. Nonetheless, they never, not even in the most severe of winters, erect a more suitable home, and they do not even bother at least to place pieces of bark on the ground to protect their bodies from the continuously rising damp. That might also be the reason why one finds so many cripples and emaciated individuals among them. I have never seen as many blind people, for example, in any savage tribe, as I have among the Australian blacks. Another disease – if that is what I may call it – occurring among them is the wasting away of the flesh from individual limbs. I saw a number of otherwise well-built men and women who had one perfectly shaped arm or leg, while the other was completely without flesh, effectively just a bone covered in skin. In women, this seemed to affect mainly the arms, while in men occasionally one of their legs had withered. And I saw two cases where both men's upper body was perfectly well developed, but the lower part literally resembled a black skeleton, so that they had not even retained the strength to walk on fleshless legs and had to slide along on their hands. However slow and awkwardly each of these unfortunate beings moved of course on terra firma, the more agile they were in the water. It was most eerie to see how, after finally arriving at their canoe, they shot off at great speed and even jumped overboard, disappearing under the water and resurfacing amid loud cheers a hundred paces from the spot where they had dived under.

What is very strange is the difference between the two neighbouring countries of the South Pacific and Australia with regards to their main diseases. The South Pacific islander with his elephantiasis gathers so much flesh under the skin of his legs that it threatens to burst them, while in the Australian savages it disappears completely from under the skin. If they only knew what voluminous legs their neighbours often have, I am firmly convinced they would say they had been robbed of it in a treacherous manner by some shameful magic potion.

The most terrible looking of all among the blacks are their old women, who truly resemble black living skeletons. And there is no more dirty people than the Australian savages, their most awful features being their noses, which they clean only occasionally of the coarsest substances by using a hard gum leaf. They are supposed to look even worse in summer when there are flies sitting all over their mouths, without being barred or driven away. That is why the intrusiveness of the small Australian flies is put down to them having been 'spoilt' by the blacks.

On 4 June I crossed over once again to the right bank of the Murray. Here I was told by the blacks I met near a station that a *devil devil* or bunyip was living where the river made a bend and had washed a kind of sinkhole into the steep embankment.[1] Up to now, whenever I came upon the river, I had thoroughly searched the bank for any signs of strange tracks, but to no avail. I did not find a thing. So I now resolved not to leave this area until, at the very least, I was convinced that this fabulous beast had not set foot on this piece of land. To that end, I crawled and walked around that whole bend, and even hiked a certain distance back upstream in order to check the bank up there as well, but found not the slightest track, neither up nor down. My only hope of finding any trace of the monster had to be reserved for a couple of lakes further downstream where, especially in the largest of them, also known as Lake Victoria, there had been alleged sightings of the bunyip at the time.

On that same evening I managed to reach the Darling, where a few houses had been built, and where I stayed overnight on the other side. At least as far as distance was concerned, I had by now completed the longest part of my arduous journey, and even though the Indians in these parts once again had a particularly bad reputation, I was beginning to feel impervious to such claims. During the day I hiked along as if stalking an animal, with my fully loaded shotgun at the ready and carefully scanning every bit of shrubbery in front of me, listening out for the slightest of sounds. And on those nights when I did not make it to a station, it was an unpleasant sensation to have to abandon the nice fire and, instead, to stretch out behind some damp old bush and try and steal a few hours of sleep from the darkness. I had a fair few misadventures during these quiet, lonely nights, when I woke unnecessarily, startled by some false alarm, and then stayed awake for hours. Many strange noises pierced my sleep, and soft footfalls passed by my camp, most likely those of the red dingo or of wild dogs. However, it would be an impossibility to go into all those details here. I would have trouble fitting even half of it into one volume, and, after all, I want to concentrate on only the most important points of my march. And if, after that, the reader still has any interest in Australia, there is a lot left I can tell him about it, and we could spend many a jolly evening, maybe in one of the shepherds' peaceful bark huts, or even in one of the wild forests of that curious country.

Here, or at least 20 miles further downstream, the bank of the Murray changes entirely. It no longer flattens out gradually toward the interior of the country but rather becomes an often 100 feet deep riverbed, formed by steep, wildly fractured and perforated layers of limestone. It is in this sometimes narrow and sometimes wider bed that the river now meanders, without taking any of those terrible bends it did further upstream. Moving from bank to bank, and depending on which side it flows, it now leaves behind either on the left or the right a so-called flat, on which the gum trees grow to their usual height. While these flats, which one would call bottoms in America, are never very wide anywhere, they nonetheless make for splendid pastures, since they are so easily fenced in, specifically because of their narrow width. Besides, with their steep cliffs toward the land side, and the Murray itself on the other, they already keep the cattle in place purely by natural means. The soil of these flats, however, is not at all as excellent as one would expect from their location. And I saw especially here on the Murray proof of the lies that are often being told in all those country portraits usually distributed by so-called shipping agents, whose only objective it is to fill the ships, in which they have an interest, with any number of heads or souls. So they mess with the hopes of some poor devils by promising them heaven on earth, and any number of them fall into despair, because they have come to this foreign land with unreasonable expectations and simply cannot bring themselves to give up on their dreams, however drily and rigidly reality stares them in the face at every step. But these shipping agents do not care one bit. They, after all, have already been paid their pound of flesh for that 'poor soul' who now must come to terms with his own misfortune all alone.

In this spirit accounts and maps often portray the Murray valley as so very fertile and marvellous, but how little arable land did I actually come across! In fact, it was found only further upstream on its banks, while down here not a single bushel of wheat can be grown, and all the flour must be brought in by oxcart from the next settlements, which more often than not may be 400 to 500 miles away. Only in a handful of places do the stations have small gardens for a few vegetables. But even these are located in the sand of the hills, since the ground down at the Murray, which at best might bear some wheat or corn, gets flooded every year, always exactly at harvest time, by so much water that it washes any crops away each time. The valley floor is made up of a grey, light clay, which at the very least should be ploughed when it is in a dusty, powdery state. Once it receives any moisture at all, it develops such a terribly sticky character that it can drive anyone walking on it to the utmost despair. But then this grey loam dries out again very quickly and does not seem to hold even the slightest bit of moisture. Indeed, just hours after rain, the ground which has only just dried will crack open again at the surface. Nevertheless, all this could be improved if it was not for those constant floods which make any cultivation of these broad stretches of land simply an impossibility. Of course, the terrain could be kept free of water by levees, as is done for example on the Mississippi, but firstly the Murray is not a patch on the Mississippi, and, secondly, there is simply not enough land in these valleys to make it worth the effort of all that cost and labour. The Murray valley will never be able to provide even the grain that the cattle breeders need just for their own consumption, however little that would be.

That day I spotted a very beautiful lagoon from one of those limestone cliffs. Surrounded by a belt of rather impressive gum trees, it was the shape of a crescent, with its ends littered by a large number of spindly trees with jagged branches. These trees were arranged there in such a way that the rays of the sparkling, glistening sun were refracted among them in a most peculiar way. Hundreds of cockatoos, their white gleaming plumage contrasting starkly with the dark-grey background of the earth, filled the scene with life, while the occasional long-legged bird stood in the sun-drenched waters, earnestly examining its territory to fish for its 'daily bread'. Among them I recognised one of the *native companions*, which now seemed to have completed its day's work and was just wandering up and down the bank. Every so often it would angrily shake its head, obviously annoyed by the awful cackling and racket produced by the endless cockatoos. At some point it halted its stroll and looked over to the gum trees, but at that same moment it rose with flapping wings and then fell to the ground. I myself reared in astonishment, since I could not understand its behaviour and had neither seen nor heard anything that would make sense of it. Nevertheless, I was to discover the reason soon enough, because while the bird was still fluttering about on the ground, a dark figure slid out of the surrounding undergrowth, grabbed the *native companion* and, surrounded by the cockatoos who had all flown up by now and were screaming blue murder, carried it back into the bush. Almost by instinct I turned around to see whether I, too, had an old gum tree at my back from which a boomerang could have done its dirty deed. But there was nothing to be seen along the whole length of the 'bluff', which extended into fairly open saltbush flats, and I continued on my route unhindered and without being harassed.

On 6 June I had a long, lonely march through sand dunes and plains, with barely a few trees along some creek beds. The only living things were the madly screeching cockatoos and the sporadic herd of semi-wild cattle which roam the mallee and are often not seen at all by their distant owners for years on end. I also came across a few emus, which ran off at explosive speed among the saltbushes, and the odd, venerable kangaroo sunning itself under a tea-tree, but hopping off in mighty leaps across the low shrubbery when I approached, disappearing very quickly into the far, far distance. In the evening I reached the so-called Lake Victoria, which had often been mentioned to me for its natural beauty. All I found, however, was a large puddle from which I could not even collect water for the night, since its edges were formed by nasty, cruel mud.[2] I arrived there just at dusk and saw all around several fires belonging to the Indians, but I did not let that stop me from lighting a decent fire myself, just as they had done on the shores of the lake. The blacks do not much fancy walking around at night, and even if they noticed the new fire, they took it to be, especially right in their midst, one of theirs. So nobody bothered me in any way, and I was already up again at the crack of dawn, fried myself another duck (I had shot two of them the day before when I passed a creek) and rolled up my swag. I was still in the process of doing so when I spotted three spear-carrying blacks approaching me, and they seemed not a little surprised to come across an unknown white-fella here, who, moreover, was all by himself. During the day, though, there was not much to fear from them, even when armed. And anyway, these blacks even if from the Darling, who are part of the Victorian lot and have one of the worst reputations for deceit and cunning, are nowhere near as dangerous as the Murrumbidgee ones, who are far superior to them in the use of their weapons and in the weapons themselves. For example, this is where the six foot spears start, of which each Indian carries just a single one, at most with a fish spear, and it can be thrown only by hand, and that means not anywhere near as far and forcefully as the small reed spears of the tribes further to the east.

That aside, these three boys came across as friendly enough. They fetched me a cup of water, and one of them offered, in exchange for a piece of tobacco of course, to show me the way to the next white settlers' station on the Murray. But first I wanted to search the shore of Lake Victoria for bunyip tracks, and I took the young black – the other two had gone fishing by a different route – along with me. He was well enough acquainted with the bunyip or *devil-devil*, and also maintained in his broken English that it could be found here in the lake and in the surrounding gullies, but he himself had not yet seen it. Nevertheless, he assured me that it had once killed one of his fellow tribesmen. My question whether it had then also eaten him, he answered in the negative. I would now have liked to find out what its natural habitat was and what it actually lived off, but he did not seem all that clear about it himself and thought it advisable to answer by shaking his head in a somewhat secretive manner.

As we continued along the soft, muddy shore of the lake, of which we skirted the best part, I kept a close lookout for any imprints in the soft dirt, but could find no tracks other than those of the usual animals of this country. When I finally asked the black whether he could not show me any trail of the bunyip, he shook his head and replied gravely: *'devil-devil no trak – butchery jabon devil-devil, but no trak'*, which was meant to say that the devil-devil, even though very large, thought it far beneath its dignity to leave any tracks.

In the meantime, by always following the edge of the lake, we had been heading towards an Indian camp, in which I saw roughly 16 to 20 figures moving about. While I was not particularly happy to step right into the middle of a whole band of blacks, even if it was bright sunshine and the terrain entirely open, I also did not want to show any fear, and, besides, we would have had to make a huge detour in order to evade the 'mob' directly in my path. I therefore calmly followed the savage who – as he had obviously noticed that I was quite interested in the topic – kept telling me the most curious stories about the bunyip: how it had not that long ago attacked a woman and removed her 'butter' (their expression for kidney fat), and that the woman, even though there were no visible injuries on her, had nevertheless died after two sleeps (two nights), and how it crept up at night on sleeping people and breathed its noxious breath upon them, which caused them to go blind, or how it robbed them of the flesh from under their skin and caused their arms and legs to wither.

All that, and much more, was related to me by the black as he walked beside me with an easy spring in his step, carrying the long spear in his hand, with his dark expressive eyes all the while restlessly scanning from side to side. Their eyes are without doubt the most beautiful feature of this race, and one would long and happily look into them – if they did not sit so very near their terribly neglected noses.

Meanwhile we had got close to the camp, and even though I automatically and by force of habit checked the bolt action of my rifle, I realised very soon that there was absolutely nothing to be afraid of here.

With the exception of two or three adult men the camp was made up solely of the old, the infirm and of women and children. These two latter groups were diligently at work, using little sharp, flattened pieces of wood to dig through the light, damp beach sand from which they then proceeded to collect the cockles contained in what could nearly be described as layers. In places there were already whole nets full of these, and the people were roasting that simple meal over a number of fires. Most of the tribe had gone fishing, as I was now told by my companion, and the women and girls crowded around me as soon as I was close enough and wanted hooks for fishing.

There were a lot of young girls among them of every age, and just a very few were actually dressed in at least a small possum coat. However, there was not a single one of noble or beautiful form, and I did not make out any friendly features in any of them. And the dirt that accompanied them was just terrible. I gave them a few fish hooks and then called over to me half a dozen boys who, above all, had to wash their faces before I took out a few of the sheets of vermilion I was carrying and painted these boys' noses right in the middle of their black faces in a brilliant red. The impression this made was enormous – the noses were glowing like carbuncles, and not just the boys themselves, but indeed the whole tribe seemed to be dancing with joy about it. But I also had to leave them some of the vermilion because, as the men assured me, they needed it urgently for a corroboree, or ceremonial dance, which they were going to hold these days. I would say they needed it just as urgently for that purpose as most of our European Indians would need a tailcoat.

In the meantime, however, the sun had risen ever higher, and the black urged me that we had to leave because he wanted to get back to his tribe that same evening and was not allowed to march at night because of the *devil-devil*. I therefore set off with him and walked down some distance along Rufus Creek,[3] as the English now call it, and at about 3 o'clock in the afternoon came upon the Murray once again, and on it a small sheep station whose residents welcomed me most cordially.

I stayed there the night to have a proper rest, because the next day, as the people here told me, I had a long march ahead of me before I would get back to the river again. This was due to the Murray having a very considerable bend here, but I would be able to cut my route by a fair bit if I maintained a straight direction. While there was no dedicated path leading away from here, a few drays had come across some weeks ago, and if I managed to follow the tracks, they would surely lead me in a direct line back to the banks of the Murray.

This may have been a rather uncertain guide, because since then it had once rained for a full day, and even here the tracks I was shown seemed somewhat indistinct in the sand. But since the route was described to me in quite a bit of detail, and I would keep elevated sandy land, the typical mallee scrub, on my right-hand side, allowing me to gain an overview over the low river valley at any time, I set off confidently.

My route on that day passed very close to the foot of the sand dunes, but it was mostly along the riverbank flats, where the vegetation was once again developing very particular characteristics. Not that the previous dreariness had given way to a more welcoming scenery, oh no, it was still just another page in the thick and monotonous book of Australian landscapes. However, even as far as that was concerned, it had gained a certain attractiveness.

The path I took that day led mainly through saltbush flats, but the saltbush itself now displayed two different species that I had never seen before. Until then, it had been mostly shrubs two to five feet in height, which, with their pale brown stems and light green, seemingly frosted leaves, might have looked very attractive to sheep, but rather sad to human beings. These saltbushes were now changing less in colour than in shape and, really, they were actually more like some other type of plant and belonged more to what we would call ice-plants. Their leaves were thick and fleshy and, in shape and colour, the spitting image of sugar-coated aniseed – but with a different flavour. Scattered fairly evenly among them stood another type of saltbush which, with its succulent, deep dark-green, nearly velvety, fleshy leaves, was offset in a peculiar manner against the surrounding grey of the rest of the landscape. In fact, that whole area before me resembled one giant, grey embroidery into which small bouquets of juicy green chenille had been worked.

Far away in the background a band of pale-green gum trees ran through the scene, and when I finally arrived there, I found that the trees marked the banks of a small creek or waterway. In the Australian usage, however, creek always means 'stagnant water', and since this one was also rather salty, I could not even get a fresh drink from it. Nevertheless, it was highly welcome to me, since there were masses of wild ducks between its steep, narrow banks, and I hit two of them with one shot, one for supper and one for breakfast.

Incidentally, by now I had long lost my cart tracks. After wandering around in the scrub and following fresh kangaroo tracks a few times, I had not the slightest idea any more whether they might have veered off to the left or the right, but that bothered me little, and, maintaining my direction to the best of my ability, I calmly continued on my way, until near evening I saw the blue smoke of a campfire rising just ahead of me. While I was acutely aware that there would be water around here, I did not feel the slightest inclination to spend the night in the proximity of a number of those black rascals and therefore wanted at least to try to avoid them. It was already too late, however, because straight after I found myself to be excitedly surrounded and yapped at by half a dozen mangy and skeletally thin dogs that seemed unlikely to wait for an invitation before attacking me and eating me alive.

As fast as I possibly could I found myself some open space, where I awaited the approaching blacks. While there were only three of them, they were bizarrely decorated in their war paint, white and red, and they were exceptionally well-armed, with each of them carrying even two boomerangs, something I had very rarely seen among these tribes. But they seemed friendly enough – the devil may trust them, though – and asked me for some tobacco.

As we were still standing next to each other, the dogs suddenly roused a wallaby that had, God knows how, remained hidden all that time in the bushes right next to us. The smallest of the blacks, a shrivelled-up, old and exceedingly ugly little man with the most spiteful face I had ever seen amongst the blacks, jumped forward as quick as lightning, dropped his spears, picked up one of the boomerangs and threw it, practically without aiming, at the fleeing animal just as it crossed a slightly elevated, open position. The boomerang touched the ground after approximately 20 paces and then went in a dead straight line towards the wallaby. I was absolutely convinced that it would have to be hit, but the ground was in its favour at that particular spot, in that there was a slight dip, and just as the nimble animal touched the ground once again and bent down for the next leap, the otherwise deadly weapon whirred right over its head. Shortly after, the boomerang rose higher and higher, before seemingly standing still for a second, and then, with a slight arc to the left, returning whistling and whirring to the ground. In the process it came so directly toward me that, to this day, I do not know whether that scamp had actually aimed at the wallaby or myself. I got out of the way of that whizzing weapon by quickly jumping aside, but even then one of its tips still brushed my arm and, with that barely noticeable touch, left a deep, blue bruise. The blacks nearly died with laughter.

Of course, I showed not the slightest concern, but as a souvenir got the little bloke to barter away his boomerang for some tobacco and two fish hooks. After having them describe to me the way to the river, I set off once again with evening fast approaching. I walked probably a further eight miles, according to my calculation, in order to put as much distance as possible between myself and those fellas, whom I did not trust in the least. It was a moonlit night, and

I reached the river about one hour after dark and, first of all, quenched my thirst. I then walked a good distance into the bush, where I lit a fire, grilled my duck and had an excellent night's sleep.

I was by now between the two inland lakes Victoria and Bonin[4] – the main abode of the mysterious bunyip – and even though several whites had predicted that I would find the blacks here rather numerous and deceitful and wicked, I had so far come across only a relatively low number, and those few had, maybe with the exception of that somewhat ambiguous throwing of the boomerang, been friendly enough toward me. Mind you, I had kept them at arm's length as much as possible and was under the impression, probably justifiably so, that the most dangerous stretch in that regard was now behind me. But I was not yet completely out of harm's way, as I was to find out soon enough.

I had covered around five English miles that morning, when I suddenly spotted several Indians on a small hill to my left. Since they had yet seen me, however, I would not allow myself to be panicked and just kept walking straight on until I saw, also to my left, the whole camp, which consisted of some 30 gunyos or bark roofs.[5] A bunch of white-haired old fellows sat around the fire, but they must have been informed of my approach, because before long – after they had called out to each other from one fire to the next – three young lads, armed with spears, headed toward me and, as in the past, tried to block my path. This time, however, I was not at all in the mood to be drawn into any form of conversation with them or have them move in on me again. I therefore halted my step, slipped the gun off my shoulder, cocked both barrels and motioned them in a completely unequivocal way not to come near.

They immediately stood still like a brick wall, and just one of them called out to me that all they were after was a little bit of 'smoke'. However, I declined any deal by shaking my head and, deviating a little from my previous course, made my way into the scrub to my right. The blacks, possibly somewhat baffled by such an unsympathetic refusal from a single traveller, stayed where they were. I was not at all sure that they were not going to follow me after all and took cover several times after walking a certain distance, but I could detect no sign of life and, finally, continued on my way, feeling completely safe.

Around evening, with still no road to walk on and just maintaining roughly the same course, by the banks of a small, dry creek I came upon three Indian graves which lay silently and eerily in the wilderness, shaded by a few strong gum trees.

The graves consisted of three simply piled-up mounds. Each had a small hut of saplings and brushwood erected above it, so densely covered with foliage that there seemed to be total darkness inside. The space in front of the hut showed everywhere fresh footprints, and when I passed in close proximity and glanced inside, I was greeted from the gloomy death mound of one of the huts by three gleaming white hemispheres, much like skulls, but far larger. They attracted my interest to such a degree that I paused, first looked inside and then all around, and felt very eager to inspect these strange items from close up.

I would have really loved to crawl in, but the entrance was extraordinarily narrow and low, because the grave, raised and covered by leaves and small twigs, occupied nearly all of the interior space. And besides – may the devil trust those black wretches – just one of them might still have followed me despite all my vigilance, and would I then, by desecrating their burial places, not have given them proper cause to attack me?

I was already turning away again, but then, aware that such an opportunity might never present itself again, I made an instant decision at least to have a look what these white items in there might mean. I quickly threw down my blanket and hunting pouch, checked the gun, felt for the knife at my side, and then, after taking a careful look around, crawled into the grave hut.

Once inside I was enveloped by a fatal odour of decay. The blacks bury their dead not very deep, and I nearly had the impression that the thick layer of leaves and brushwood lying on the mound merely covered the top of the corpse. I climbed over it without wasting any time and reached for one of those white heads, which by now appeared to be giving me a particularly gruesome smile. These were not skulls, however, but rather some form of bowl modelled from white clay and rushes; which lay upside down on the graves, their meaning not easily explained. I wished I could have taken one with me, but they were too large and too heavy to carry. And breaking off a bit of them would not have been easy either, since the rushes that had been kneaded in with the clay had turned the whole thing into one solid and tightly-bound block. Besides, I did not feel like staying in there any longer. The hut had been too tightly woven or covered in shrubs to scan even the immediate surroundings from inside. All of a sudden I had a sensation of not being able to breathe in there anymore. It was the same feeling that had once grabbed me under a huge fir tree under which I was working in California, and which, after I had barely got out, without making any further sound or breaking any of the roots we had not yet cut, suddenly crashed to the ground with terrible and irresistible force. I quickly crawled forward, and when I stuck my head out, I could have sworn I saw a black shadow just behind the nearest saltbushes. I did not even take the time to pick up the bag and blanket but instead ran straight toward that spot, where I actually did find some tracks, but no further signs of any human being. The footprints might well have been older, since the whole ground around there had been stamped on by bare feet of all sizes.

The faster I got out of there, however, the better it would seem to me to be, especially since the terrain was covered in a mass of rather dense tea scrub and so-called lignum, and the blacks, if they were indeed plotting something against me, could not have chosen a better place for it. I therefore quickly threw the blanket and the bag back over my shoulder, and, still somewhat on guard, took the gun under my arm and marched off.

During the morning I had been marching along the sandy slope of the mallee, but since then had now veered off too far to the south. As I had come across a dray track running roughly in my direction through the bush, I was now following it through wild and dense scrub. I had run out of water as well and intended to walk on until it got dark, then to light a fire and lie down beside it. Before that, however, I wanted to satisfy myself once more that I really was not being followed, and that the black shadow I had positively glimpsed was not that of a black, but a wallaby, or, if it was a black, then one who had just coincidentally been strolling in the area. I therefore left my trail, lay down behind a dense saltbush and decided to stay put there for a full hour, and if I did not notice anything suspicious, I would set off again. However, I had hardly been lying for five minutes when, without a care in the world, one of those black scoundrels approached in my tracks, closely followed by a second one. And I was not a little surprised when one of those two turned out to be that little old shrivelled-up fellow, whose boomerang I was still carrying in my pouch, and who I had presumed to be at least 20 miles away from here. What had motivated that black Satan to follow me all this way, and why was he now creeping around here in such sneaky, stealthy fashion?

I had come into this wilderness with a truly peaceful disposition toward the blacks and had intended from the very outset to spill blood only if the worst came to the worst, and only in self-defence or in order to protect another white. Now, however, the gun was raised nearly in spite of myself, and its sight focussed, as of its own accord, on the body of the black rascal, but eventually I put it down again and decided to see how they would react once they spotted me.

They were still about a hundred paces away and approaching quickly, when, suddenly, a small flock of black cockatoos swooped screeching and whistling over the bushes and attempted to settle just where I was lying. I turned my head to look at them, and the moment they spotted me, they scattered amid ear-piercing shrieks. This had, above all, a wonderful effect on those Indians snooping around out there. I was very confident that they could not see me since I was lying behind dense, low scrub, but when I turned my head back toward them, I just caught a glimpse of them disappearing into the undergrowth to their left and right, and even though I stayed put in my position for nearly a full hour or so, I neither heard nor saw anything of them again.

There is nothing more awkward on earth than the uncertainty of finding oneself in a dangerous situation, but not being able to identify its type and cause. I would have preferred it twentyfold for these chaps to confront me head-on rather than creeping around in the bushes in that treacherous manner and spoiling that last bit of fresh air one was still breathing out here.

My initial inclination was to end the matter quickly and turn the trick they had played on me back on them. I therefore picked up their tracks in order to follow one of them, but to my surprise, instead of two, I found three tracks, of which two went off to the right and one to the left, even though I had only seen two blacks. That led me quickly to the realisation that, by following these tracks, I was exposing myself to far greater danger than if I continued on my own route. I could not hope to compete against these clever blacks where this kind of warfare was concerned.

But why were they pursuing me so doggedly? The shadow at the grave mounds had probably not been a delusion after all and, who knows, maybe they were seeking revenge for that desecration. If that were the case, then that would be far more dangerous than a mere lust for loot, because religious fanaticism has provoked people into crazy shenanigans forever and made them impervious to reason. Evening was approaching, however, and since I felt a rather urgent thirst, I resolved firstly to beat my way to the river, and then come to a decision on how I would spend the night without exposing my kidney fat to any unnecessary risk. It is a pretty damned feeling if one cannot even be sure of preserving that little bit of fat one had a hard time acquiring in the first place.

Just as it was dark, perhaps three quarters of an hour after sunset, I reached the river, chose a decent spot for camping, cooked myself a few pigeons I had shot during the day, had an excellent meal, and then turned my thoughts to what best to do now. If there had been two of us, one would have had to keep guard, while the other could have had a restful sleep and gathered strength for the coming day. That, however, was impossible here at the fire, and yet I was so fatigued that I could hardly keep my eyes open. There was absolutely no doubt that I could not lie down right here, and even though the night was very cold and inclement, I decided that I would nevertheless rather abandon the fire and squeeze in behind some bushes. Before that, however, I collected a lot of wood and stacked it in a long pile against the wind, so that the embers would keep some heat for most of the night. I then gathered my belongings and made my way down to the banks of the river, and followed it for about a quarter of a mile downstream. I was pretty certain that *here* the blacks would not be following my tracks during the night, since this close to the water they would be too afraid of the devil-devil. Without a fire, however, I myself did not want to camp near the water either, because it was terribly cold. Therefore, once I felt that I had left my fire far enough behind, I climbed back up the bank and lay down between two saltbushes standing close together and covered with dense foliage. There it took me just a few seconds after the anxiety and exertions of that day to fall into such a deep sleep that I am convinced that, if the blacks had found me there, I would have been totally at their mercy.

When I finally awoke I jumped up with a start, because I had dreamt around morning that I could see the blacks creeping up on me again, and the sun was already high in the sky. With daylight, however, all danger had disappeared, or at least I did not fear it anymore, and my main concern now was to go back to the fire to have a look in the soft sand whether those black scoundrels had not paid me a visit at night. I was able to congratulate myself that I had not slept at the fire – their footprints were everywhere, leading all the way up to it, and I even missed a piece of cloth which, in damp weather, I usually wrapped around the lock of my gun, and which I had taken off last night and forgotten by the fire.

As I was by now completely convinced that my pursuers did indeed have evil intentions, I slogged on again in a straight line through the lower country saltbushes and tea-trees toward the sandhills, at the foot of which I had at least open terrain and could not that easily be surprised. Besides, I had to be near some station, and if I could make it there, I was more likely to be safe from my former shadows.

During that day I had a most unnerving march, where one had to be constantly alert, with the gun always at the ready, being hungry and tired on top of it – such marching is no damn good to anybody. My neck nearly twisted off from all the looking left and right and, most likely as a result of the constant stressful use of all my senses, as well as having nothing but a bit of pig's face to eat for lunch, I developed such a stinging headache in the afternoon that each step felt like a knife being driven into my brain.

It might have been around 3 o'clock in the afternoon when I first spotted once more the dark shadow of a black slipping across my path, and this time it was in front of me. At least, the wretches were shy of creeping up on me in my tracks, and, in making a detour, they had arrived a bit too far ahead of me. But by now I was utterly sick of being stalked and surrounded by such a mob. Raising my gun in one swift action, I fired a round of lead shot in the direction where I could assume that character to be hiding amid the swaying bushes, and the shot rattled into the branches. Practically at that very moment and so fast that, after turning around by sheer chance, I had just enough time to jump aside, a spear flew past me before getting stuck in the sand only a few paces from me. It must have been thrown from a fair distance because it had already no power left. But even though the scrub in the direction where it had come from was sparse and low, I was not able to spot the enemy who had thrown that weapon.

Naturally, I did not waste any time, but reloaded quickly and then held my position, from which I had a decent view to all sides, for quite a while. At this point I was determined to singe any black hide that might show itself, but nothing came into view anymore. So I finally continued on my way, very cautiously at first, but without being molested at all from that time onward. And I took the spear with me.

In the evening I found sheep tracks and, by following them, reached a sheep station where I was at least able to have a secure night's sleep, and where I gorged myself on a quart of tea, a piece of damper and some mutton chops.

The shepherds, when I told them of my adventure, thought that it was definitely my crawling into the grave hut which had caused the blacks, and probably the relatives of the deceased, to chase me, since they might have been of the belief that I had performed some magic in there. Otherwise these tribes had been reasonably friendly toward whites in recent times.[6] Having said that, the stories they told me straight after about all these 'friendly tribes' were not exactly in the latter's favour. It seemed that just in the last three months they had not perpetrated 'anything new', at least nothing that had become common knowledge.

For readers not familiar with the circumstances it may seem somewhat strange that the shepherds who, during the day, travel among them with their flocks, are hardly ever attacked, even if that does occasionally occur here and there. And in the past, the blacks have indeed done so, but had to find to their own cost that such people were always missed after a very short time, and that the neighbours, together with the police, were then mobilised to conduct search and revenge parties. While they always came off second best in those encounters, they got away with murdering single travellers at will without any enquiries being made. These people would usually walk from one station to another, looking for work. Nobody was expecting them where they were heading, nobody missed them where they had come from. Nobody knew on which side of the river they were walking and cared even less. Such people mostly remained missing unless individual murders came to light by chance, often as a result of a voluntary confession by the savages themselves, who, as has been mentioned, believe in a certain kind of statute of limitation.

Incidentally, as the shepherds assured me, from here on in I had nothing to fear from my previous pursuers, because I was now entering the territory of another tribe, onto which they were not allowed to follow me. While I still found plenty of other Indians, I must not tire my readers any further, nor do I have the space to tell them how I came across a tribe doing their corroboree or dance the very next evening, and how I circumvented it in one of their own bark canoes, because the possum-hunting dogs blocked my path through the bush. Or how, later and further downstream, I met a jolly company of white labourers who, in the caves in the limestone banks on which they were meant to build a house, had literally made themselves nests to sleep in. I have already filled too many pages with blacks, and shepherds, and 'hut keepers' and must now continue on my path a little more rapidly.

Here, as a result of the banks of the Murray itself, the scenery assumed a somewhat different character. Just below Lake Victoria there had already been the first limestone embankments here and there, often rising quickly from the water in hundred-feet-high jagged cliffs. But up there they had lasted only for short stretches. Here they started to form a continuous riverbed often several English miles in width, where the watercourse would flow sometimes on the right side and sometimes on the left, shooting at speed under a series of rocks while, at the same time, leaving a wide low 'flat' or 'bottomland' on the other.[7]

The flats are made up purely of alluvial soil, that grey tough clay which stays completely uniform all the way up to the Edward River, where the saltbush begins. It would most likely be able to bear a good crop at a favourable time of the year, if it were not for the river bursting its banks always exactly at harvest time and thereby making any cultivation of these stretches completely impossible. Thus all they are good for now is pastures, which nature has already provided with enclosures in the form of steep riverbank cliffs and the river itself, with only a little bit of work to be done at the top and the bottom. By the way, nothing at all was growing in that grey 'loam' at the time, and the spots which still had some water remaining from the recent flood period were lying there, picturesquely surrounded by the ever indestructible gum trees, all denuded and cracked. It was a landscape where a man could have put a bullet in his head with total peace of mind; the beautiful scenery would certainly have provided no reason not to do so.

While the stations were a fair distance apart, I was from then on able – except on a single occasion – to reach one of them every evening as long as I kept following the Murray, which made it a far more relaxed and also safer walk.

I now approached the big 'Northwest Bend', as it is called. This is the large curve in the Murray which, to this point and all the way from its source, flows largely due west, but here it takes a very sudden turn to the south in a real elbow, less than an English mile across, before it empties into Encounter Bay via a large lagoon which is called Lake Alexandrina or Lake Victoria (because the English name practically any puddle in Australia after their queen).[8] That said, Lake Alexandrina is no real lake anyway, since even the small craft which have hitherto travelled across it must, once they come out of the Murray, or more precisely, once they reach open water, stick to the Murray's bed or channel *through* the lake, if they do not want to get stuck in the mud on the left or the right. Either way, the Murray will remain cut-off from the sea forever, because its mouth into the actual ocean, through Lake Alexandrina, is blocked by such a mighty surf that entering or exiting it would be, if not completely impossible, probably too dangerous for any ship.

The character of the landscape here is the same as further upstream: mallee scrub on the sand dunes and gum trees in the valleys, with sand on top and grey loam below. And this clay is so tough and sticky after even the slightest bit of precipitation that I am totally convinced that if a regiment of soldiers were to march from the river up to the cliffs after a light rain, they would carry the whole valley with them onto the hill.

Twice I had to cross the river in order to avoid bends, once in a bark canoe, and once by wading, but even here the water was at least three feet deep, and that was in the shallowest places. Once I had passed the large bend, I hardly saw any blacks at all anymore. Most of the tribes living around here are completely peaceful, and, as various station owners told me, usually move down to Adelaide in winter where the government supplies them with clothes and provisions, which, of course, I was not that unhappy about.[9]

So at long last I had reached the eagerly anticipated 'Northwest Bend' where, as I had been promised for a long time already, all danger from the Indians would be behind me, and from where it was now no longer very far to the populated, *settled* districts. Here, the river took a wide majestic sweep to the south, and my eyes were able to follow its course far downstream, without having to contend with those terrible turns further up. And there, in the far blue yonder – oh, what comfort it was to my tired eyes – one could see the undulating outlines of the Adelaide Hills. The end of the flatlands was nigh, and I would soon reach the destination of my long and arduous march. It was as if a wave of new-found strength pulsed through me, and that morning I walked off with double my usual vigour. That said, the countryside remained very much the same, and the cliffs, to which I kept myself now, still bore nothing but low saltbush of the sugar-coated aniseed type, as well as small gum trees and mallee scrub.

It was a wonderful morning. The sun shone down so warmly and refreshingly onto the steaming country and was reflected in every single dewdrop hanging from the rare blade of grass or branch of a bush. The magpies which, due to a shortage of leading voices, are all committed here to performing brilliant arias, came up with such a range of new melodies that even my heart began to thaw. Breathing the fresh morning air deep into my lungs, I walked along the cliff edge and rejoiced in that double spectacle of the distant hills in the background and, in places, the truly picturesque valley below me.

As I was walking along, from time to time standing still or even lying down in order to be able to view a particularly pleasant spot with the appropriate leisure, I suddenly spotted a wild dog that, just like myself, seemed to be enjoying that magnificent morning and was simply out for a stroll without any clear destination. Here the high country was made up of an undulating plain, only rutted by low indentations furrowing towards the edge of the cliffs, and it was in one of those that Master Dingo contentedly wandered up and down and, unless I am very mistaken, for mere sport caught the odd fly from protruding branches. In doing so, however, it exposed itself unwittingly to highly dangerous company, because I, now less than 40 paces distant from it, sat right behind a low saltbush with my gun cocked, and in my mind contemplated those atrocities which, as the shepherds had told me in recent times, had been committed by our very Master Dingo here. How it broke into flocks of sheep and went about suffocating the lambs without mercy, how it cut off single ewes from the flock and tore their throats without further ado, how it ... but no more of that. One way or the other, I was fully intent on murdering it.

Meanwhile Master Dingo was coming straight at me, and even though it occasionally stood still and listened, that was done rather from some kind of instinct, and not because it feared any particular danger in this wilderness. Whenever it did so, it sniffed the air in the ravine up to the left or down to the right, while assuming that everything ahead of it was sure to be safe. Occasionally, though, it paused, extended first its right and then the left hind leg, arched its back, had a good yawn, stretch and shake and appeared to be in as fine a form on that fair and sunny morning as any of its race had ever felt on such a day. And yet, that dog now stood less than 25 paces from the barrel of a gun aimed directly at it. A pointed bullet with five grains of powder behind it, and the percussion cap under mortal threat from the set trigger, all aimed at it, and it does its stretching and yawning! It came closer and closer. By now it was less than fifteen paces from me, and then it lay down on the ground, scratched its back on a protruding root, stretched once again, threw its head to the left and the right, and then jumped up, shaking off the dust, before suddenly sitting down again, practically right in front of me, as if to say, 'Well, I have plenty of time, there is no need to rush.'

Did this dog look like a cold-blooded lamb killer? Was this dingo tormented by pangs of conscience for terrible deeds perpetrated in the dark of night? Or was it, perhaps, still a young, innocent dog that, in quiet solitariness had hitherto lived off locusts, bugs and manna? Was it not wandering around out here all alone, caught in deep contemplation? Our scholars, when they ponder something, scratch their heads, and the dingo was just at that moment doing the same. With its hind leg in a somewhat awkward position, it tried to reach behind the last rib. With that movement, however, it had turned its head towards me when, by chance, our glances met. In that instant it certainly forgot the source of its itch, whether idea or flea, and it quickly and alertly turned fully toward me with ears pricked. My finger was on the trigger, the finely focussed sight of my gun was set right on its eye. There was an itch in my finger, and yet this was no evil dog, just a careless one, and I simply did not have the heart, on this beautiful morning, with those long-awaited blue hills in the background, to spill any blood. Nevertheless I wanted to give that fellow a warning to be more on its guard from now on. With a calm, swift movement I raised the barrel of my gun a few degrees, and just when my sight fell on the dingo's right ear, my finger pulled the trigger.

Naturally, the whole thing took less than a twentieth of the time I have needed to relate it. But with the flash and boom of the gun, Master Dingo did indeed have a rude kind of awakening from its Sunday tranquillity. With the first shock it made a giant leap off the ground and then, without ever looking back even once, made good its escape, forever shaking its head. Perhaps it felt a semiconscious sensation that somebody had it by the ear. As fast as its legs would carry it, it raced up the shallow ravine and, very soon, had disappeared into the low scrub. As I discovered, I had actually hit its ear, since some of the sugar-coated aniseed bushes had, in places, small drops of blood scattered on them, which had been shaken off in the speedy getaway.

On Tuesday, June the 17th, I finally left the Murray, which was flowing south here, and turned west towards the hills, which were approximately 30 miles from the river. From there, I had 34 miles to the first settlement, since not a single drop of water is to be had on that whole stretch, and even sunken wells supposedly provide only saltwater. That meant another night in the open, before I would re-enter a civilised and partially cultivated district. Furthermore, by now I was longing more than ever for Adelaide, and if it was only to get out of my scruffy clothes and into fresh new garments. It is a most uncomfortable feeling if one has only *one* shirt and then has to have a 'big laundry' day. As regards my trousers, even calling them by that name would be crude flattery, since I truly believe that by now they contained more grey thread than original wool, and the various patches were reminiscent of a romantic age. The only socks left were in my memory and on my left ankle, and if I had sought to change a Prussian Thaler in that outfit in Germany, people would certainly have asked me where I got it from.

That day I marched some 20 miles and then made camp under a dense tent of branches which I had cut with my knife from thickly foliaged mallee bushes. In addition there was more than enough firewood, and I spent a rather pleasant night, even if it started raining lightly towards morning. Actually, right from nightfall heavy thunderclouds had gathered above the still rather distant hills, and there was thunder and lightning toward the west all night long. I had quite firmly resigned myself to setting off again the next morning without breakfast. However, after shouldering my blanket and other effects at break of dawn, and having walked a mere quarter of a mile, I spotted several kangaroos grazing just where the mallee scrub ended and the land opened up into an open plain covered by the occasional low shrub. I decided to prey upon them quickly, and so I threw down everything I carried, checked my gun, and then went kangaroo stalking.

With the first two on which I tried to sneak up, the terrain was not quite in my favour, and they fled in giant bounds. Not much later, though, I spotted the white belly of a third and managed, by creeping for roughly 20 paces along the ground, to place a small, dense bush directly between myself and the game. I quickly made use of this opportunity, which enabled me to approach to within approximately 50 paces. When I raised the gun, the kangaroo had just bent down again to graze. The moment it took the bullet, it jolted up into the air, before falling on its back without taking a further leap.

Since I did not want any fuss and had no intention of lugging around any provisions, I just cut the skin along its back, took off the two strips of meat from in there, went back to my fire where I had some fantastic embers going and cooked myself a roast, the tender meat of which would always have been a delight, but tasted even better to one as hungry as I was.

6.

The Adelaide District

At about two in the afternoon I set foot on the first hills of the Adelaide district. Phew, how the wind whistled over the naked hills with their sparse growth of everlasting, indestructible gum trees. How coldly and frostily the rain drove into my face, so that I had to lean forward with my whole body to resist the sharp wind that more than once stopped me in my tracks and almost pushed me backwards. Oh, how lovely the dull grey and green landscape looked under the lowering grey clouds, whipped by a sharp south-westerly, in the early falling twilight – it was a wonderful stage setting. But I must not be unfair: there was grass growing here, the hills were green. For so many long, long months my weary eyes had been deprived of the consolation of a verdant hillside! The soil looked arid enough to be sure, but the frequent rains had given it sufficient moisture and the grass grew rather lush – at least it looked lush to me, unaccustomed as I was to seeing two blades of grass standing side by side.

At about 4 o'clock, as the rain poured down whatever was inclined to descend from the heavens, I reached the first houses – Norton's public house – and found myself now about nine miles from the first German colony – the Murray lay behind me, and I had at least successfully left behind me the most laborious and dangerous part of my whole journey.[1]

So it is only right and proper to begin a new chapter with this district, since already on this first night lodging in the hills I was plucked out of my life in the bush; my new surroundings betrayed an encounter of interests different from those of the sheep-breeders and stockkeepers. As tedious as I may sometimes have found the talk of cattle and horses and the meticulous description of certain oxen once owned but now lost – conversations treating with the utmost seriousness the question whether the right or the left horn was crumpled or the right or the left hind hoof was white or the letter 'R' marked on the '*off*'-hip of the one that had a little hook near the bottom and so forth – but I had always felt that this talk was better than the talk of gold in California, where everyone chewed over again and again how they had – one day here, another day there – picked up a rock or broken open a crevice and found a little piece of gold, a quarter or half an ounce, or two, three or six ounces. I was really pleased that now, still half in the wilderness, at least I would be spared such conversations.

In the one room a fire was lit in the fireplace and a crowd of labourers and small traders from the neighbouring houses were gathered around it, for it was in a way a little township that I had come upon this evening. While a fire was likewise being kindled in the parlour I joined the crowd to warm myself up a bit and to hear what they might have to talk about.

'They've found a nugget of seven ounces in the Ophir diggings,' reported an old man holding a newspaper in his hand and wiping his spectacles in order to tell the curious bystanders of even greater wonders.

'California again, as I live and breathe!' I thought with a low-murmured malediction, 'What the devil is plaguing these people here in the middle of Australia that they have nothing else to talk about but that damned Californian gold?' The reader must excuse me for thinking such coarse thoughts, but it can surely be forgiven a man for being a little surly after being plunged from conversations about nothing but gold into conversations about nothing but unfortunate cattle and sheep, only to find himself once more dragged feet first back into the gold gossip.

'Ophir Diggings – Ophir Diggings', was all I heard, and at first I assumed it must be a newly discovered creek in California.[2] But in that I was soon to be disappointed, and it was with a certain melancholy resignation that I heard the news that had set all ablaze, that gold had now been discovered and was being panned in Australia too. 'For this a robber and a murderer!' I could have shouted with Karl Moor[3] – for this I had come through endless forests of gum trees and barren plains, only to hear that in Australia too gold had been found. I had been anxious on that account once before, while I was being broken on the wheel by the Royal Mail crossing the Goulbourn district and the Yass Mountains, the local ranges showed unmistakable traces of gold, or at least – apart from the vegetation of course – the whole region bore an uncanny resemblance to the quartz-sprinkled tracks I had, alas, hiked through all too often in California. There were no reports yet from the Goulbourn district, and the first gold had been discovered in the Bathurst district north of Sydney. It was soon made very palpably clear to the good people here that they were now resident in a land of gold as the price of a barrel of wheat suddenly shot up from 15 to 30 pounds sterling for 2000 pounds, and naturally all now fear the worst.

I was glad when I was finally able to escape the noisy room and retire to the more peaceful parlour. I think it necessary to remark that it was not my dress that procured me the honour of sharing the best room in the house with one other guest, a Mr Scott, station owner on the Murray – I looked far worse than any of the teamsters and shepherds milling in the tap-room. But the landlord had found out that I was the man whose canoe voyage he had already read about in the papers, as he told me, and so he treated me with the utmost friendliness. He had previously been a police sergeant and treated us that evening to several most interesting accounts of the early days of the colony, when the police were constantly engaged in battles with the bushrangers, and it had taken some dangerous expeditions and many a skirmish to entrap and disarm them.

That night it poured with rain, and I congratulated myself on having found such a refuge. Next morning as we were sitting at breakfast a young lad burst in with the news that a black swan had just alighted outside, a most unusual event here in the hills. I already had one skin, and as I would have liked to take two with me I grabbed my rifle and went out. The swan was indeed sitting scarcely a hundred paces away from the house, and I fired the musket at it, but it failed because of the damp weather, and then as the swan rose up I shot it down with the shot muzzle. I rolled up the skin together with the other one in my blanket-roll, paid my bill and strode off directly into the teeth of the south-west wind blowing over the hills with all its might.

The area was absolutely Australian. The vegetation of course nothing but gum trees – everlasting, indestructible gum trees, the land itself undulating and covered with quite a good growth of grass. But still not a trace of cultivation, since the neighbourhood around Norton's gained and keeps its population only through a copper mine located close by.[4] At last at about 11 o'clock I saw the first fences surrounding cultivated land, saw once more straight brown furrows, and over there on the slope of the hill, where the little low cottage peered amiably out of dark, green scrubby gum trees, a man was walking. I was still at least a thousand paces away from him, but I could have sworn that he was a German, strolling calmly behind his six oxen and a plough, with a woman marching along in front leading all seven.

I had reached the outskirts of so-called Angas Park, a rather extensive district that an Englishman, Mr Angas, has leased exclusively to Germans.[5] Each one has built his little house on his own section, and without having the appearance of a village, one suddenly finds oneself in the midst of a perfectly cultivated district criss-crossed by fences, which even at first glance betrays German diligence and German orderliness in thousands upon thousands of trivial details.

The first house, or rather the first hut that blocked my path, stood right by a fence corner from which the fence ran diagonally across the path, reminding me most vividly of my earthen tent – or rather the charcoal-burner's dwelling as it should rightly be called – that I had built myself together with young Hühne back there on the Sacramento, half dug into the earth, half roofed with branches.

The wife was at home, that is, she had just come in to fetch seed-beans for the field, and she seemed rather astonished at seeing a German in such dress, with gun and knife. They were from the Magdeburg district and had only arrived here a short time ago without a penny, and of course they struggled to barely scrape a living. On top of that, because of the huge rise in grain prices, seed was hardly affordable for the poor beginner this year. So it was hardly to be wondered at – with this unusual way of living, half buried in the earth, in dirt and disorder – that the woman, who seemed to have seen far better days, said with a scarcely suppressed sigh: 'I wish we were back in Germany. Last night we were almost washed away here.' She said then, and pointed to a corner of the house where I could make out the traces of fresh repairs, 'The rain undermined the walls and suddenly the water surged in. You can imagine our fright; this morning my husband dug a ditch around the house outside and patched up the wall, but how long will that hold? Oh, if people knew about all this already in Germany before they left, they would think twice about it.'

I tried to encourage her: the first emigrant always has to struggle with a thousand difficulties which he could not have foreseen, and which he would not even have believed if someone had really predicted them. But she shook her head and said that it really was better in Germany. And surely it is better in Germany if – if only we could find a doctor who would cure the root of all our ills.

Although she seemed to be in a hurry, the woman kindly offered me something to eat, but I thanked her and marched on, as I wanted to visit several places in Angas Park and was keen to reach Tanunda that evening.[6] About an hour later, in the midst of friendly little dwellings dotted about to my right and to my left, I came to a farm that I really had to look inside. From the outside it looked just like one of our little German farmsteads with barns, stables and sheds, and I was stopped in my tracks for a minute or two in astonishment. It was almost as though I was not really in Australia, as though a friendly spirit had transported me back home at the speed of thought, but – those damned gum trees! – of course I was in Australia.

In the yard one of the workmen was harnessing the horses. That was a German harness and a German wagon, I could have sworn it, and the maid came out of the stable with an honest German dung-fork in her hand: so I had to get into that house at all costs. I jumped over the fence, walked across the yard, opened the front door – there was no way that door handle had been made in Australia – and it would not surprise me in the least if my beloved compatriots, truly remarkable in this regard, had brought the whole door with them from Germany. I knocked.

'Come in.' I stood in the middle of the room, and here, dear reader, if you really want to get a clear impression of what I saw, you must leave me standing here a minute and walk into the very first farmhouse that you happen upon beside your path in Germany: so absolutely accurate in both appearance and even smell was the quiet little chamber I had entered. But not really quite so quiet, since the white-haired, red-cheeked and extremely dirty little brat that the old grandmother sitting by the stove was holding on her lap and trying to feed a spoonful of mush, was screaming for all he was worth and had successfully managed to kick every stitch of his clothing off up to his chin. The old grandmother was such a faithful and consummate exemplar of an old German farmer's wife as you yourselves could possibly find in the heart of Germany, and I am firmly convinced that everything about her was authentic, right down to the pins and shoelaces, and not one English or Australian article, whether it be of dress, under-clothing or footwear, had ever touched her body. But that was not all: the stove, chairs, tables, cupboards, footstool, spittoon, earthen dishes, iron pans cooking pots, the plates engraved with texts, the bowls with verses from the hymn book, the great trunks with green roses and yellow forget-me-nots – in short, everything was German, and if you picked up by the roots an authentic room from a farmhouse in Saxony or Prussia, packed it carefully in cotton-wool and planted it again here, you could not have preserved its character better. The housewife was in the bedroom making the beds, but came out when she heard that a stranger was there. The husband was out ploughing the fields. She straightaway set tea, bread and dripping before me on the table. I had to eat first of all, and then she wanted to know if I had just come straight from Germany and how things looked there. Strangely, of all the Germans I have met abroad – and under 'abroad' I do not mean Schleiz or Lobenstein or the like as it is always understood in Germany – I have always found that the men are not in the slightest interested in their former fatherland, it is always only the women who ask after it. But dear God, I was not able to tell these good people anything of home, for more than a year I had not had a letter, and the latest reports that I had seen simply said that Germany – I mean Prussia, Austria, Bavaria, Württemberg, Reuss-Greitz, Hanover, Sigmaringen, Saxony etc. were perfectly peaceful. And as it happened they seemed to be quite satisfied with that, enquired which region of Germany I came from and asked if I knew the Schulzes in Radegast. Unfortunately I had to say no, but we soon got to talking about economic matters. These people had been in the country six or seven years, had leased their land, if I am not mistaken, for 14 years with the option to purchase at £4 sterling per acre, and were quite well-situated. The land was not particularly good however, and they could have got better soil for that price at many other places in a more favourable location. But when they came here years ago, they had nothing, and were happy when Angas set the conditions they had entered into. I heard the same in many different places.

Mr Angas has in fact favoured and given clear preference to the Germans in letting his land, and many have therefore called him a 'benefactor' of the Germans. But he knew very well why he did so and still does. The Germans are his best workers – they are at least the most hard-working and persevering, and apart from the excellent rents he receives, he knows he can count on them most reliably to get the remainder of his land made productive. He adds 15 % interest to the money owing to him, and he holds the land as a permanent mortgage; and he has already shown through more than one confiscation that he knows how to pull in the interest money. But in spite of that, he is a true friend of the Germans, self-interest makes him so, and self-interest rules the world, no matter what one may like to say about it. If the Irish were more convenient for his land, the Germans could do nothing more than see to it themselves where they might be accommodated. And of course the best and firmest contracts are those where the interests of both parties are represented most equally – then capital and labour do not confront one another but shake hands instead.

I entered many more houses and farms that day, and although here and there a few individuals complained of the highly variable weather and the dangers that the crops were exposed to by the hot winds and excessive drought or damp, on the average I saw that the people here were at least able to make a living, and some had already established property that they would never have been able to establish in Germany in that time and with those means. The German is surely never totally satisfied on principle, and disputes with the neighbours, the impounding of stock and the like can occur at any moment. But the reality was constantly the same – hard work at first, endless difficulties to overcome, old habits to change, new customs to adapt to, but then the reward for hard work, and old age secured against need and care. Now the question still remains of course, how much the heart is still attached not only to old habits but also to old friends and loved ones and perhaps even the old homeland itself, and whether it really was so impossible to secure a living back there that one really had to tear oneself away from everything one held dear and transplant oneself in cold foreign soil. Sometimes – and how often! – a slightly better living is too dearly bought through emigration, and many an individual would, oh so gladly! return even to the old oppressive circumstances, where he at least had someone with whom he could share his joys and sorrows. But those are matters that each one has to work out for himself, though they should be considered before it is too late.

I visited various little farms that day and found many quite comfortably furnished. In every instance their German origin was unmistakable. But it did me a great deal of good to hear my mother tongue again after such a long time, not just at one place but wherever I turned; it called to mind so many a fond image. I was to feel this even more strongly when I arrived in the little thoroughly German town of Tanunda in the evening. The stretch from Norton's place to Tanunda was only 15 English miles, a march that I could have put behind me in three-and-a-half to four hours, but I had spent so much time on the various farms in Angas Park that night had already fallen when I was still at least five miles from Tanunda. But even that was not a great distance, and I strode on energetically.

On the road I met a cart with two people. I asked the first in English how far I still had to go to the town. The answer said in good honest German: 'It will be about six.' When I responded to the German with German the man became talkative, was pleased to have found a countryman on the road, although he could barely see my shadow, and assured me it was just 'three quarters of the way' to Tanunda. To this day I have no idea how far that was supposed to be.

At about seven in the evening I reached Tanunda, although in the pitch dark night I could see little enough of the place. But I soon found the public house – naturally it was German – for wherever our dear God stretches out His arm, as one says in our country, the publican kindly hangs a lantern on it.

The publican in Tanunda was indeed a friendly man who kept quite a good public house, the Tanunda Hotel, and it was a very strange feeling for me to leap in one bound as it seemed from the bush and the blacks and to land in the midst of an entirely German way of life.

After my evening meal the room filled up around the fire crackling in the hearth; a young German doctor and several shopkeepers and traders came in, the pharmacist and a few others, not forgetting a little tailor who was staying here too, all of them Germans, and a lively conversation ensued on a thousand things, but above all about the newly discovered gold. I sat there quietly; I was rather too bedraggled to take part in the conversation and was not in the least in the mood to tell these people my whole story.

Dr Behr in San Francisco,[7] and later Fritz Meyer in the mines, had already told me so much of the strange life and doings in Tanunda that I would gladly have spent more time among these people here, but above all I had to go down to Adelaide, where I expected to find letters and knew my trunk was waiting. I could always come back to Tanunda afterwards. In fact I intended to make several little side trips into the German district.

I had a short march of 16 English miles in front of me the next day to Gawlertown, and there are likewise many Germans living on the way there. From Gawler I went to Adelaide next day by mail coach. The distance is about another 26 miles, and the mail covers them in five hours. In the evening, before Gawler, I joyfully tossed my staff away and spent the night in a German public house, and next morning I rattled on break-neck roads into the capital of the Adelaide district – the long-sought city of Adelaide.

Leaving Tanunda I found the country was quite good, and Lyndock Valley[8] is indeed one of the most fertile parts of the whole of South Australia, and – not counting the everlasting gum trees as the only vegetation – even has quite a romantic location. I saw a few very pretty farms on the way. Toward Gawler however the soil gets worse and worse, although the valley of the Gawler River itself offers a lot of good land. Beyond Gawler the so-called Gawler Plains began, meagre pasture land without trees. From 18 miles away we could see the masts of the ships lying in the harbour five miles beyond Adelaide. The roads got a little better approaching Adelaide, that is, harder. The unevenness of the road had earned it the name 'nutcracker road' from the humorous coachmen; the clusters of houses became closer together, on the left and on the right the presence of larger buildings announced the proximity of a significant city, and at the stroke of 10 in the morning we drove into Adelaide to the cheerful tones of the post-horn of our postillion, who played the *Fahnenwacht*[9] with real skill, and stopped in front of the post office.

On the way I had found among my travelling companions a German who was going to Adelaide on a rather delicate mission to recover his runaway wife, as he said. It seems to me, by-the-by, that runaway wives here in Australia are more like an infectious disease than anything else, as the rage for running away from their husbands is spreading like an epidemic throughout the land. Between the three stations I encountered on the Murray I heard of a runaway wife on at least one of them. On the evening I was in Tanunda three cases were mentioned, including the one I have just named; in Gawler there were two more, and in Adelaide I was about to hear of the strangest one. It is truly a risky business to take a wife here in Australia. But what will happen when they eventually have railways in this country? If I were a married man here, I would use all my influence to prevent the establishment of railroads.

The German acquainted me with local circumstances in the city, and I made my way first of all to the firm of Meyer and Noltenius to take delivery of my mail and my trunk.[10] I felt a little bashful at appearing in respectable business premises in such dress, or rather undress, as I had upon me, but it couldn't be helped – in a few hours I would be in a position to change all that. And I found the firm, Mr Meyer as well as Mr Noltenius, but neither mail nor trunk had arrived for me! So now for the third time since I had left Germany I found myself without any belongings. That had happened to me once in Valparaiso, when the *Talisman* had taken the whole catastrophe to San Francisco, and once in San Francisco itself when I came back from the mines and found that all my things had been plundered.

And now here. I really had to laugh when I considered what an accursed situation I had landed in. But it really was no joke, though it was indeed tragicomic. But I was nevertheless very warmly received by the two gentlemen, and they offered in the friendliest possible way to do all within their power to assist me. Above all, I had to procure new clothes, and that is what happened. They could be replaced, but I found no letters from Germany, and they could not be replaced. It was so long since I had received any news!

Combing the city in search of a new wardrobe above all, I naturally got to know it straightaway from the dark side; the dirt in the streets made me shudder in fact, and only lengthy habituation could render the inhabitants of Adelaide indifferent to such mud baths in the guise of footpaths. Adelaide is still a young city, and one should not make extravagant demands of it.

For all that, Adelaide is extensive and laid out on a rather grand scale, with the public buildings scattered wildly in all directions, so that one must often traverse virtually trackless stretches, still totally undeveloped, in order to reach them, but in spite of that until now the city has only one main street, bearing the name Hindley Street in one half and Rundle Street in the other. Even this street has no footpaths, and all the streets would be wrapped in total darkness were it not for a very beneficial law commanding all public houses to have a light burning before the door, and there are many public houses or dram shops in Adelaide, for Adelaide possesses no public lighting either by gas or whale oil. This is a very wise calculation on the part of the government, for not only do they avoid spending a penny for illumination, but they even get paid by the numerous alcohol licences – granted perhaps precisely for this purpose – for permission to provide their own. Certainly a unique way of effecting the enlightenment of its citizens through the spirit!

In this little Adelaide, which can hardly be called a maritime city because of its distance from the coast, a fairly lively commerce nevertheless prevails, at this time particularly in grain and flour. Of course the world of commerce – and especially the German one – seemed to be experiencing a sort of crisis, since several firms had recently gone bankrupt, and more were prophesied for the coming months. The latter does not seem to have been fulfilled however, and I sincerely hope that the Germans there will soon recover from the indeed quite significant losses that many of them have suffered. But it is foolish to claim, as many have done, that the good name of the Germans will be undermined by these bankruptcies: in the first place they have occurred in such isolated cases, and then the English businessman is far too sensible to extrapolate as applying to all that which concerns only a few individuals.

Just at that time great excitement prevailed on account of the rise and fall of grain prices, which were wholly dominated by the Sydney market, and news from there was always awaited with great expectancy. After the first news of gold the price of wheat had risen to such fabulous heights that it was impossible for it not to spur the speculative spirit of the merchants to the utmost.

One thing that I was very sorry to find here in Australia, and even more so here in Adelaide than in Sydney itself – because there was even more fuel here to feed it – was the disunity of my compatriots. Of course that could no longer surprise me; it was unfortunately not a rare occurrence, and it would really have amazed me if it had been otherwise. But it hurts one all the same, and a proper, oh so evil curse seems to rest upon our poor nation, to nourish and nurture its fragmentation not only at home in its own nest but also to transport it with fearful care to foreign continents, and see how the weed flourishes in fertile foreign soil. In North America the devil is on the loose among them, in Chile they hack at one another just as in California. Here I was to find exactly the same thing confirmed, and the only place so far where I have found my German compatriots really united was in Tahiti, but there was only one German living there, and I would not guarantee anything if a second one should join him.

Some time ago the Germans in Adelaide felt the need to establish a German reading club too, but right from the start they did the one thing that is most effective in destroying such a club before it even begins: a large committee was elected and the most restrictive statutes were drawn up with a rigid voting system for membership. Instead of granting such a club the most necessary principle for its survival, fresh air, so that every respectable German could have access to the club as long as he conducted himself properly in it, the whole enterprise became a matter of party politics from the outset, and on top of that, a matter of the weaker party. The end result was unavoidable: the first newspapers were cancelled even before they had arrived, and the German Reading Club died at birth.

As far as German literature in general is concerned in Adelaide, there were still two German newspapers in existence. Dr Otto Schomburg[11] holds the honour of establishing the first German paper in the Pacific Ocean – the *Südaustralische Zeitung*, with Dr Mücke from Berlin and a Mr Dröge in Adelaide as his co-editors – but Dr Mücke went to Tanunda and Otto Schomburg a little later to his own property near Gawlertown, and Mr Dröge carried on the paper alone.[12] Then Mr Reimer founded another paper, the *Adelaider Deutsche Zeitung*, but both of them soon realised that it was impossible for two German papers to exist side by side when the existence of even a single one was so uncertain, and the two parties concluded a treaty by which Mr Reimer purchased the *Südaustralische Zeitung* and only the *Adelaider Deutsche Zeitung* continued to exist.[13] The former had until then been printed in German type and the latter in Latin type, and the former was then also transferred to the latter. In spite of his specific contract with Mr Dröge, this gentleman had intended (as I heard later) to make use of a subsidy which had previously been provided by the government for printing public notices in his paper – which obviously by rights should have been retained by the newspaper he had sold – to establish a new paper once more. I have not been able to ascertain since whether he had actually carried out this intention, but so much is certain: Mr Reimer had disposed of this paper once more, for the last issue of the *Adelaider Deutsche Zeitung* I saw was signed by a Mr Eggers as responsible editor.[14]

Apart from that there was no trace of German literature in existence in Adelaide – apart from the *Spenersche Zeitung*[15] which Pastor Kavel subscribes to, and I believe one copy of the *Weser und Kölnische Zeitung*. There was no lending library or even a bookshop where German books could be obtained. Sydney has to admit the same reproach: not a single German paper is subscribed to there, in fact not even the *Spenersche* penetrates that far. The Germans there believe in God alone, and the *Sydney Morning Herald*.

The only social association in existence among the Germans in Adelaide is the *Liedertafel*. Singing is the one positive element holding them together. There are some really competent singers among them, and I can only hope that this enterprise may continue to exist and to flourish. I was unfortunately only on one occasion in a position to attend an open *Liedertafel*, but that evening is among the most pleasant that I experienced in Adelaide, and that is saying a lot, as I found many dear friends there.

In regard to the location of Adelaide, which so many emigration guides have confabulated enormously, it can only be excused by the lack of harbours in South Australia. Adelaide lies on a plain between the coast and the so-called Lofty Ranges – a chain of hills stretching far inland roughly north-south – several English miles from each. The little river or large stream which flows past it, and which someone has committed the terrible injustice of calling navigable (I believe that some lithographs have even appeared showing steamships on it), is called the Torrens. Five miles away from Adelaide lies Port Adelaide, a dirty little mud-hole on the North Arm, that is, one arm of the sea that stretches up this far, and into which or out of which ships can exit with *one* wind only. The largest ships can indeed enter here, but the transport of goods from here up to Adelaide, by cart and in winter on bottomless tracks, is the saddest thing imaginable, and many goods which have survived a sea voyage of four or five months unharmed, have suffered more damage on that short stretch than previously in the whole process of embarkation, transportation and unloading. Only in most recent times has a railroad to the port been commenced.[16]

The streets of Adelaide scorn all paving, and as terrible as the dust is said to be in summer, particularly during the hot winds, the mud in the wet season is just as fearful. Of course the city is still young, and so far both the funds and the work-force have been lacking. But so much is certain: the current gold mania in Sydney can only serve to its advantage in future, and the solid foundation on which its economy is based – agriculture – will allow the still insignificant city to make rapid progress.

Just at the time I was in Adelaide a crisis had befallen the working classes, with a by no means favourable impact on them. The Burra Burra Mine,[17] which otherwise employed thousands of workers, had at that moment thrown a mass of workers into the city, while the unexpectedly rapid rise of grain prices surely did nothing to render such a misfortune less palpable. The terrible drought this summer had so weakened the stock unable to find more pasture that all the work of transporting timber or sand for the mine works, as well as freighting the ore itself, had to cease, naturally putting an enormous number of labourers out of work. The significant rains that fell while I was still there promoted the vigorous growth of grass; new stock was brought down from the Murray; and while work recommences up at the mines, Sydney attracts a mass of workers to its mountains to look for gold. Flour has likewise fallen back down to a price which is still unusually high but nevertheless affordable, and the labouring classes in Adelaide surely have much better prospects for the moment. On the whole, any tradesman who is not ashamed to do ordinary manual labour, if the worst comes to the worst, can constantly count on employment, and even if he may not find all his dreams realised, he does not need to fear poverty or hardship.

Regarding the South Australian mines, especially the world-famous Burra Burra Mine, so much has already been written about them by people who understand the subject that I can happily remain silent on that score. Because of the bottomless roads and the terrible weather I did not even visit Burra. There is nothing up there that suits my purposes. Mining I do not understand, the region is barren and desolate, and I would just have been wasting money and time on a visit to the mines about 180 miles away – not to mention that one is always putting one's neck at incalculable risk on any Australian mail coach.

Copper is, by the way, not the only metal that South Australia produces.

Mr Osmond Gilles, a native Englishman but also a citizen of Hamburg who has been residing in Australian for many years, owns an uncommonly rich silver-bearing lead mine in Glen Osmond which yields 75% lead and 25 ounces of silver per ton of ore.[18] And right on his land on the Onkaparinga near Mt Barker, gold has also been found and panned but the business is not yet profitable, and I am not sure whether the extensive panning works and the significant side-costs are responsible, or the meagre gold yield. It is possibly the latter, as the Adelaide Hills are not high and I can hardly credit that they will contain significant gold deposits. Nevertheless, gold will in any case be found sooner or later in the Adelaide district, since the Gawler River, the Onkaparinga, the Torrens and several small streams above Tanunda are surely gold-bearing; but whether it will repay the labour expended on it remains to be tested.

Since I am particularly interested in the school system of the countries I have visited, I asked Mr von Schleinitz, who is to be credited with founding a respectable German school in Adelaide, for some notes which I could work on later.[19] Mr v. S. however gave me such a complete overview that I cannot possibly improve on his own words, and therefore append them here:

State support of school and church in South Australia

The boundless religious freedom, or one could say anarchy, that prevails here also determines the educational freedom of the schools in every respect. No supervision at all takes place on the part of the state. The populace is free to believe whatever it will, and to educate and instruct its children however it will, the government does not concern itself with this matter.

The school is completely independent of the church, educational freedom is granted by the state to the utmost extreme, and it is only to the extent that religious congregations superintend church and school within their self-enclosed disciplines that the school finds itself in any greater or smaller dependence on the clergy within these circles. Schools that appear independently outside of such religious societies draw their support exclusively from the trust of the public. Financial support from the state is granted upon application to all schools, communities and religious societies – even the non-Christian – for the construction of houses of God and salaries of priests, in the following manner:

School

Support of schools consists in the payment of 5 shillings per quarter to the entrepreneur for each child over six whose regular attendance can be demonstrated, without consideration of what is taught in the school, i.e. whether it is purely an elementary school or whether the higher or even the most advanced sciences are taught. It should also be noted here that the support comes into force only if 20 children attend the school regularly, and it is withdrawn as soon as pupil numbers fall below 20.

No sort of examination is demanded of the entrepreneur or teacher on the part of the state; the criterion for his competency is based on public trust.

If someone wishes to establish a school, he does not even have to apply to the government in the first instance but can begin when and where he will – only when he comes in for state aid, he sends in a declaration signed by the parents or guardians of the children in which they state that they entrust the education of their children to Mr So-and-so. A Justice of the Peace must also sign that he knows the names and addresses of the undersigned persons, and that the necessary arrangements have been made for a school room.

From that time on, however, the teacher must keep a roll book in a precisely prescribed manner, in which he first lists the names of the children and then separately enters how many children over and under six attend his school, and marks each day exactly which child was present for instruction and which was absent. Twenty days are set as the accepted number of school days for monthly school attendance. He must send in a signed extract from this book each month.

Every now and again a person specifically delegated by a magistrate has to visit the schools, but this is done only to check that the number of students provided by the teacher is accurate – nothing else is of relevance.

Aid is withdrawn only from absolutely incompetent teachers, if that fact is demonstrated, but even they are not forbidden to conduct a school. As long as there are still people who entrust their children to such a character, the school may continue, since running a school is considered a business like any other.

Currently (1851) state aid is received by 28 English and two German schools, one in Adelaide and one in Tanunda. Of the latter the government demands only that the children learn to read and write English. The English church receives no specific aid for schools; the English Methodists and the Free Scottish church and the German Old Lutheran congregations refuse to accept any state aid for church and school on principle, in order to pre-empt any pretext for intervention in their religious affairs.

The present system is, however, too illogical to survive for long after the first session of the new parliament. As stated, only schools with more than 20 children receive state aid, although that makes the opening of schools almost impossible, especially in the country, for it is precisely the schools with a small number of pupils that need aid most, and they receive nothing.

Since, on the other hand, in granting aid no consideration is given to whether the school is just an elementary school or whether more advanced subjects are taught, the teacher who restricts himself to the simplest primary instruction receives a double advantage: that he is able to run the school without outside assistance, so without cost, and secondly, because he is in a position to charge lower school fees, he attracts a greater number of pupils and thus gains higher support.

Schooling is not in the slightest compulsory. Every father can send his children to school or not; the state does not care. The greatest regularity of school attendance therefore always occurs within the various congregations where the clergy exercise a decisive influence on the members.

Higher schools are represented in South Australia as follows:

1. St Peters College, funded by the English High Church. Based exactly on the same principles as the English colleges in Oxford etc. – 45 pupils.

2. Two private English educational institutions for boys, with about 80 pupils at £40 sterling a year.
3. The German School in Adelaide, established on the plan of the higher citizens schools in Germany, for both boys and girls in two separate classes with 33 boys and 22 girls.
4. A boarding school for young girls with 11 boarders, daughters of wealthy families.

In all schools the children barely learn to read and write, with a little arithmetic.

State aid to churches

This is divided into two elements:

Subsidies for the erection of houses of God. Every religious society receives, up to £300 Sterling, as much money from public funds as it can collect from its own means and deposit in a bank. So if such a society deposits £200, the support or subsidy from the state amounts to the same, but if it deposits £300 and more the subsidy does not exceed £300.

For the salaries of priests. This aid is calculated according to the number of pews actually rented in the church to members of the society, and amounts to 15 shillings per pew per annum.

This last point, the so-called church grant, has at the moment become a political issue, in that it is considered a criterion of a liberal, i.e. an opposition, member of parliament for South Australia, to vote against the grant, but to advocate greater and better organised support for schools.

Soon afterwards, the entire time and attention of the city and surroundings were monopolised by the election of 'members of parliament'.[20] Atop all public houses and even some private homes fluttered flags and banners, and indeed the church grant did seem to be the only axis around which the pros and cons of the candidates revolved. Often one could hear the words, 'Yes, I know that the man is suited to be anything but a member of parliament, but he will vote against the church grant'. 'Mr Peacock Esq.', as he is supposed to have called himself, and several others got elected in this way, and the Methodists were particularly diligent in sifting through the members of their congregation, and they did indeed become popular since – according to their religious principles – they had no intention of tolerating any state interference in the church, even if it was to their benefit, so that they would not have to put up with it later if it were to turn into the opposite.

The people wanted to have nothing more to do with a poll-tax – if that term can in fact be applied to a *seat* in the church – and the excitement surrounding the election was as great as can otherwise exist only in England. In an absolutely American fashion, no effort was made to praise or extol the virtues of one's own candidate – and for that in many instances the material was perhaps lacking. No, all contented themselves with the much simpler method of tearing down and vilifying the candidate of the opposing party, and for that purpose both parties seemed to find a superfluity of material. As a result of this anti-church-grant mania, a number of representatives of the people were elected of whom one was ashamed afterwards, and even during my stay several were called on to relinquish their seats voluntarily – they will of course do nothing of the kind.

I will give as *one* sample of the verbal battles fought out in the paper, word for word, the thanks expressed by one of the failed candidates to those who had been active on his behalf:

> MY FELLOW-COLONISTS – I thank you for the very hearty support you rendered me in the recent contest, and though your efforts were not crowned with success, the defeat was, under the circumstances, rather a credit than a disgrace. I did wish to be returned on the shoulders of the 'working men' exercising the franchise soberly and discreetly, but I had no ambition to owe my election to the worthless votes of a drunken mob. Captain Hall calls his return the triumph 'of principle over prejudice'. I call it the triumph of beer over brains.
>
> Yours faithfully,
>
> WILLIAM GILES
>
> [*South Australian Register* Tuesday 8 July 1851][21]

The headline above this read: 'TO THE LIBERAL INDEPENDENT ELECTORS OF THE PORT ADELAIDE DISTRICT', and Mr Giles was meant in that case to vote against the *Church grant*. By the way, he of course belonged to one of the congregations, and, if I am not mistaken, is a clergyman himself.[22]

As far as the entertainments of South Australia are concerned, or rather of Adelaide – for in this regard the precious little that is to be found is entirely concentrated in Adelaide – they are indeed limited enough. The theatre is all that could make any claim to be reckoned among entertainments, if one did not have to in each instance lament the wasted money. They have only two good actors there, the Messrs Koppin and Lazar, the two entrepreneurs. Mr Koppin is really excellent, but he cannot do everything all by himself.[23] They present comedies, but all too often they make tragedies of them.

There are three German public houses in Adelaide – Brinkert, Pohlmann and Grootegut: I resided in the first and felt as comfortable there as one can in any Australian public house. Another German, Schmidt, has established a fourth entirely in the English manner which is frequented almost solely by Englishmen. English public houses in Adelaide are like sand at the sea, and as I have already said, they serve as the illumination of the city.

A short time ago an elegant French cafe was also established, the Restaurant Parisien, but John Bull would have nothing of it, and the French restaurant soon had to shut up shop. The only sensible and peaceable house where one can go in the afternoon or evening without being afraid of being accosted by drunks is the Cafe National, kept by two Germans, and it does enjoy a very substantial clientele.

In the meantime the elections continued in Adelaide; one heard not a word about anything else, and even the gold was relegated to the background for the moment but still managed to shimmer through. The ships to Sydney were full of passengers.

Even in the short time I was in Adelaide I did, by the way, make several very interesting acquaintances. His Excellency the Governor of South Australia had heard of my safe arrival, presumably through the newspaper articles, and since he was particularly interested in the eventual navigability of the River Murray he summoned me to an audience.[24]

There I also became acquainted with the Colonial Secretary Mr Sturt, who had been the first to travel down the Murrumbidgee and the Murray with an expedition especially equipped by the government, and penetrated far into the Australian desert until the blacks refused to accompany him any further.[25] At that time he lost several members of his party and was himself exposed to endless difficulties and dangers, and is said to have conducted himself in an excellent and exemplary manner. I was very pleased to make his acquaintance personally, and the opportunity to occasionally meet such a man and shake his hand is one of the highlights of such long wanderings as mine.

Accompanied by the Mr Scott from the Murray I have previously mentioned, I was very cordially received by the governor, and at his instigation later wrote a brief article on the potential navigation of the Murray for the *South Australian Register.*[26]

Similarly of great interest was the acquaintance of a Mr Moorhouse, the Protector of the Adelaide blacks,[27] to whom I had been recommended by Pastor Meier in Tanunda,[28] and who most kindly not only supplied me with all desired information but also conducted me to the school of the blacks to witness the lessons there.[29]

The Australian black, who by the way has the skin of the negro but not the woolly hair, but rather long hair sometimes curly and sometimes smooth, has – according to outward appearance at least – originated from a mixing of the Malayan with the Ethiopian race. Now in his original state he is the wildest, dirtiest and most treacherous being that I have found among the Indian tribes at least. At first glance he also seems to possess the least intellectual faculties, since his dwellings are the most primitive possible, his weapons simple and crudely worked, his entire clothing only – in cold weather – a rectangular blanket stitched together out of opossum skins. He does not even use a bow and arrow like almost every other tribe, and knows of no higher being to whom he could pray – he fears only the devil. In spite of all that, however, I believe that there is scarcely a tribe in God's wide world who possesses a better gift of comprehension than this apparently so dull-witted savage, or one who knows better how to handle the imperfect weapons that he bears, and at the same time holds so fast with such steadfastness of character to his manners and customs, not yielding to the civilisation of the whites but only to their violence, resisting them every inch of the way.

Already at the Murray I was astonished at the enormous skill with which they cast their light, crudely worked spears, and with what assurance they found their target; then I was surprised at the ease with which they without exception grasped the English language, while the English themselves, who had already lived among them for years, had retained barely a word of their language.

Here in this school I was to find confirmed that this nation is not by any means as antipathetic to culture as one would believe at first sight and as many insist.

Their teacher was kind enough to put several of his best pupils – they were four boys and one girl – through their paces in various branches of education, and he asked me to have them read something aloud. In the New Testament that he handed me I opened by chance at the first chapter of John's Gospel and said that to the first boy. Each of them had the book in front of them and quickly found the text I had named.

'In the beginning was the word and the word was with God and the word was God', the one boy read with really great skill; the second took the second verse and so forth through the chapter. The pronunciation of all the children was excellent, and although their language lacks some of the letters of our alphabet, they had acquired the English accent perfectly, and even read with far more expression than we find in our village schools.

I asked the teacher if the children also understood what they were reading, and instead of replying he began to ask them the meaning of the chapter. I must confess I was greedy to hear from the lips of Australian blacks an explanation of the meaning of the sentence that Faust had brooded over for so long, until in the end even the poodle became impatient. The explanation did not go smoothly, however, and I hardly think that Faust would have been satisfied with it. The children had nonetheless remembered quite well what they had been told about it some time before. 'The word' here meant Christ and was, according to the explanation, not for example a quality of the Saviour, an intellectual term, but yet another name. Just as He was called Saviour, Redeemer and Son of God, here He was called *the Word*. The Indians are children and must be led by a friendly hand over such difficult places.

In the meantime, while some were explaining the Bible texts, another one of them had picked up a slate lying in front of him and was copying a picture of a white swan hanging on the wall in front of them. Naturally he did not yet have the firmness of hand to copy the outlines sharply and accurately, but his eyes grasped every deviation of the lines faithfully, and though it was crude, anyone who saw the black's drawing could see at first glance that the picture was supposed to represent a swan – and that is more than can sometimes be said for pictures by civilised people.

The talent for mimicry on the whole seems to predominate among them, and that may be a great advantage to them in writing. I saw the copy books of several boys who had been going to school for only a few years, and in those years only for a few months, and there were a couple among them who can truthfully write better than I can myself, even if I took great pains over it. If one could only fetter both boys and girls to the school for a longer period and to a peaceful bourgeois life forever, I have not the slightest doubt that anything would be possible, but the innate wild spirit has too much supremacy over them and culture cannot prevail against it. The black Australian on the whole depends too much on sudden impressions, neither past nor future bother him much. Apart perhaps from the threats of the medicine man, he grasps only what the moment brings and devotes himself to it with heart and soul, and it seems to be of no account whether it turns out for good or ill. No matter how long they have been in the school or how much they have learnt, or how much progress they have made, once the thought of their old freedom, the old, wild, cheerful life in the bush, enters the mind, in a flash it is all over with civilisation. They all at once throw away European ideas and clothing, and leap with a jubilant shout back into their old, wild life, and the teachers are left behind sadly shaking their heads in despair.

The teacher also got the children to count and do sums, and in a very practical, lively and easily-grasped way, with beads strung on a series of wires in groups of ten that could be pushed back and forth.

A number of picture tables hanging on the walls and intended for school use seemed to be of the greatest interest to the little black community in general. They consisted of little pictures of people and animals with captions, individual tables showing the whole process of cultivation from clearing the land through to harvest, others dealing with animal husbandry, hunting etc. And the children were not only able to say exactly what the picture meant but also what the caption said and what the colours were, and while some of them were explaining this, others stood around of their own accord and copied the things that interested them most.

The conclusion of this little examination was an attempt at geography, which could however only turn out most imperfectly. The map showed only the outlines of the various continents; they could of course name them all, and also show where they themselves were located in Australia, and where east and west, north and south were. Locating Sydney was much more difficult, and they had to be guided there step by step, but that too is hardly to be wondered at, since until now their only concept of the whole world had been the little stretch of land that they inhabited and the narrow strip of land surrounding it. How could they be expected to grasp and understand the enormous size and extent of the globe? But all the same, a beginning has been made there too, and they will in time gradually be led further and further towards it.

But just what has been the result until now of all this expenditure and the attempts to civilise the black tribes? Sadly, it is only meagre; they simply do not want to allow themselves to be civilised, and all attempts with the adults ended in hopelessness. The missionaries abandoned their station in despair and realised belatedly that they had sacrificed an enormous number of souls to the evil one. According to the doctrine of various individual Christian sects, savages are still capable of attaining a certain level of bliss after death, as long as they do not know any better; but once the doctrine of Christianity and the one and only God have been proclaimed to them according to God's command, if they reject it they incur the *just* punishment of subjection to the evil one and are irredeemably lost, according to the testimony of Methodists, Baptists and other –ists. It is a strange story with such doctrines: if one wanted to believe them (and anyone who does not is damned as an unbeliever), the Devil would have no better agents in the whole world than the missionaries themselves. How many thousands of souls have they already delivered into his hands in Australia in this way?

Since they could make no headway at all with the adults, they experimented with the children, who did in fact attend school punctually enough in the winter, when they received warm clothing, blankets and good food, but in summer they just as punctually flew off in all directions, returning under the influence of the old men of the tribe, hearkening to their words with innate respect.

In the case of the boys there were always a few who could be persuaded to persist for a shorter or longer time, but the girls fled for good as soon as they had reached a certain age and could never be retrieved. Their own customs, their own superstitions which take root too deeply in young hearts to be easily uprooted again, bear the major if not the sole blame for this. A girl is betrothed to some man when she is still quite young – often soon after birth – and until she reaches marriageable age the tribe is quite indifferent to what she does, but as soon as she reaches that age the groom demands his bride, and the tribe calls her back, while the medicine men threaten her with instant death or an insidious illness if she does not obey the command.

Such an admonition they cannot resist, and no matter how much her heart may at that moment be attached to the culture which has step by step become a habit, they throw it all away and obey the command.

The teacher told me a striking example of this. They had taken a girl into the school when she was small, and she attended regularly for four years, making significant progress. Then she went into service in the home of the missionary for two years, followed by two years in Government House. She was well kept and treated kindly everywhere and seemed to have totally forgotten the old ways and become accustomed to her new life; she liked wearing European clothes and did not have much contact with her tribe when it was located in the vicinity. But after eight years this girl – who spoke English perfectly, had adopted the Christian religion and learned everything necessary for housekeeping – threw away at the same time both her clothes and her new way of life and ran back into the bush just as God had created her, and just as she had been taken from the bush eight years earlier.

This particular case is said to have been uncommonly discouraging for all those employed in the education and civilisation of the blacks. A real obstacle which has an especially detrimental effect on their real and lasting civilisation is the fact that all savage Australian tribes are not inclined to become accustomed to permanent dwellings. Even where they have been built for them, they make no use of them, and often on the Murray I have even in bad weather seen them around a fresh Indian campfire, while only a few hundred steps away there are huts abandoned by whites who had lived there previously. Whether it may be superstition or God knows what that prevented them, they preferred to sleep out in the open rather than under a sheltering roof.

The protector has however come up with a novel way to guard against such relapses, which may perhaps be appropriate for a few of them at least, but whether it can in the first place pass the test of common humanity and not end up instead in some kind of European imposition of universal happiness remains to be seen.

As soon as girls or boys reach marriageable age, they are paired up and married off and then transported to Lincoln Point (as I believe the place is called),[30] where the government gives them a certain portion of land and agricultural tools and puts up a little cottage where they are to live and cultivate their own land. But the area they are sent to is located on a peninsula, and the land route is cut off by hostile Indian tribes inhabiting the intervening land. So they simply cannot return to their old life and are compelled to play the role of Europeans whether they want to or not. This is, by the way, a totally new experiment, and only the results will show how it ends up. I for my part believe it cannot end well, for such compulsion cannot exercise a good influence in the long run, and if a man wants to throw off the shackles that have been imposed on him in this way, he will find an opportunity to do so. If he does not, and if the chains hold, he will be unhappy, and then the question is, are the whites allowed to exercise such compulsion, and are they not making the Indians much more miserable than they were with their old manners and customs in the wilderness?

The children going to school here were all respectably dressed – the boys in shirts and trousers and the girls in long blue dresses – and of course they had to keep themselves clean, that is, cleaner than they were accustomed to in their original state. But the noses, the fearful noses!

Mr Moorhouse was, however, also obliging enough to entrust his journal to me for a time to look through and to make extracts – a journal on the Indians and their circumstances, kept since 1839, in which he has recorded a mass of notes on their manners and customs. Of course I did not neglect to take advantage of his kindness, and I found many highly interesting things therein.

I passed several very pleasant days with Messrs Noltenius and Charnock,[31] who invited me to their hospitable country house in Kensington, very close to Adelaide, where I spent a couple of days and most evenings. But the time for departure was approaching, and in the last days I made a brief side trip to Macclesfield, between 25 and 30 miles from Adelaide, partly to see the land there, which I had often heard praised, partly to make the acquaintance of a Mr Sutter[32] – a cousin of California's Captain Sutter[33] – and I did not regret making the ride.

Macclesfield lies in the row of hills stretching from south to north between Adelaide and the Murray. These hills had uncommonly fertile land, with the region around Barkershill[34] and the German village of Hahndorf being among the best. The country consists of hills and valleys and is fairly densely forested – but ever and always only with gum trees. At least the undergrowth here gave the so-called 'bush' some variety. The bushy little cherry trees with foliage similar to that of conifers and the cactus-like grass trees grew thickly in some spots, and at least varied the otherwise fearfully monotonous green of the gums. There were even a few flowers dotted about, but still it did not manage to constitute a 'region'; only Mount Lofty offered the eye a charming view out over the plain in which Adelaide lies with the sea as its backdrop – really a magnificent sight.

Here there are still significant stretches of uncultivated land, but the price has been driven up so high that nothing is to be had under £4 or £5 sterling an acre.

Macclesfield is a little country town that has just been established, but because of the good soil surrounding it, it will soon grow. Houses are springing up one after another, more and more people are settling there, and the mountains have barely been investigated yet, and they could well contain mineral treasures.

Mr Sutter, too, has had some excavation done, mainly in search of coal, which would be an invaluable boon for Adelaide, but has so far found nothing other than some excellent white clay from which he is burning excellent and high-priced bricks.

These hills also offer greater advantages for agriculture than the plains, since they are almost completely protected from the hot winds; nor do they ever suffer from excessive damp. The drinking water is also better here than in most places in the Adelaide district, where near Tanunda it was salty even now in the rainy season, and is said to be scarcely potable sometimes in the hot summers.

7.

Tanunda

From Adelaide I made one more side trip, back to Tanunda, where I had found the life and doings too interesting to be satisfied with the few hours of my previous stay, when I had only passed through fleetingly.

So one day – in spite of the previous warnings of my friends not to put my life thoughtlessly at risk yet again on an Australian mail coach, since it had already so often been saved miraculously – I headed to the post office, where human freight is loaded and dispatched. I made my booking, paid my passage money in advance – an essential provision for the maintenance of these torture-carts, since they deliver their passengers to their destination only nine times out of ten, and this way they have insured themselves – and climbed aboard.

Four emaciated horses – there were nine persons on the open cart – swung into motion, and we set off at a gallop along the 'nutcracker road' toward Gawlertown,[1] the goal of our provisional destination. The coachman had previously been the captain of a schooner, as he said himself, and now attempted to persuade his horses – which bore fantastic names like Morningstar, Flying Fish, Beauty and Bullet – with an unending range of maritime expressions to keep up a little of the gallop which, as if by chance, they had fallen into at the start and now sincerely regretted. He had no idea whatever how to wield the whip, grasped sometimes by one end of the handle and sometimes by the other, which dealt out lacerations to Morningstar and Beauty impartially. After seven miles the horses were changed, and Jenny

Lind, Robert Peel, Kangaroo and Red Rover were harnessed up. Already in the first quarter of a mile he broke the whip handle upon Robert Peel, and if it were not for Jenny Lind and Red Rover, we would never in our lives have reached the next station. Kangaroo lived up to his name, but his jumping was all to his disadvantage, as he constantly broke down in the hind legs.

From this station we already had to walk a couple miles on foot, although the ground was dry and level. The beasts could not manage it, as our coachman told us, and he wanted to see if he could get a fifth horse to take the lead at the next station. But that was all just a trick to keep us in a good mood. The third stop was brief; the horses seemed to be a little better, and we only had to walk about one mile. But at the fourth station we were to be shown just what the Australian 'Mail' was capable of, and the coachman too seemed to have some foreboding of what was to come. When the four most emaciated knackers I have ever laid eyes on were harnessed up, and the groom, as if in derision, held them fast at the front so they could not run off, I heard him say as he scratched behind his ear: 'Now my troubles begin – stand by the halyards.'

He was right – like a yo-yo we climbed up and down from the cart over the first four miles, and whenever we had travelled a hundred paces we could count on it for sure that we would have to walk half a mile again. In the end I got tired of it: that scoundrel of an owner had taken our money and promised to deliver us to our destination by the 'Mail', and now we had to trudge along a dead-level road just so he could get his cart there on time to load up the next sacrificial victims. I not only refused to climb down once more but also easily persuaded the others to follow my example, and we declared to the coachman – who was of course not in agreement – that 'we had no intention of going on land again'.

For a mile the matter proceeded well; downhill and on solid ground it was possible for the four horse skeletons to make headway at a 'gentle little trot', but as soon as the ground levelled out once more and became a little softer on account of the absorbed rain, we had to 'moor' again, and the coachman declared that if we would not get down and walk we could stay there the whole night. We for our part assured him that we would not be missing anything, and would with the greatest pleasure hold out till midday the next day rather than stumble along in the dark and fog alongside a cart we had paid for. When he saw that we would not relent, he started whipping the poor creatures again, and I must say that I would rather have travelled the road on foot ten times over than see the beasts mistreated so badly, but we had to uphold the principle – and we sat unmoved. We had previously told the coachman that we would get out and walk all the rest of the way, if he only acknowledged that he could take us no further, so we could apply to the proprietor for the return of our fare; but he did not want that, and we had no choice but to keep our word.

The horses, however, knew of no other principles than their bellies, and they were empty, and finally the shaft-horse broke down on a perfectly level path. The shaft of the two-wheeled cart crashed down, and most of the passengers shot forward. I had seen it coming for half an hour already and had braced my foot against the front seat. The most beautiful leap was made by a small Chinaman we had on board. As though shot from a pistol he flew over the coachman and headfirst into the poor horse, and it was lucky that he hit the horse, since he would otherwise surely have smashed his skull.

We helped the poor devil of a coachman free the horse from the harness and onto its feet again, and then left him to see how he would get on with his cart and the other animals. We passengers however walked on to the little town about six miles distant and reached it in good shape about 9 or 10 o'clock.

The proprietor of this royal postal service is called Chambers,[2] and it has long been known for a fact that he does not feed his animals when feed is dear, but simply drives them – as soon as they are released from their harness, half-dead with tiredness – onto pasture where the grass has barely put in an appearance. He had himself once claimed in Adelaide that it was cheaper to have one of his horses break down now and then than to feed them all, and he would rather risk the former than pay the certain expense of the latter. The government does not give a damn about it; as long as the man delivers the mailbags to their destination on time, then he can openly rob his passengers in this way and mistreat his animals to death. Chambers naturally amasses a pile of money in this way, and is therefore 'one of the most respected citizens of Adelaide'. The Devil take such scoundrels!

I stayed the night in Gawlertown and only had 16 miles from there on to Tanunda, and of course I went on foot right from start to finish, saving myself the fare; the roads here were even worse than from Adelaide, and steep hills – I would have had to walk anyway, and that would have angered me more than the couple shillings were worth.

Next day I reached Tanunda at midday, took a little room in the Tanunda Hotel and settled in as comfortably as possible.

Tanunda – named after the Indian locality – is a little town of several hundred inhabitants, its buildings perhaps slightly English in taste, but its population entirely German aside from a couple of possible exceptions.[3] It was a very strange feeling for me to find myself suddenly – in a foreign land and continent and even in an English colony – surrounded by nothing but Germans, and in fact a purely German way of life and doings. On occasion, especially when I saw little groups of people standing here and there in the street and heard *everyone* speaking German, I had to stop and think whether I really was in Australia. But that is exactly how it was, and in the end I even got used to it – I think I would even have got used to it if they had spoken Chinese, since being thrown so quickly from one language into another as I have been incessantly over the last few years makes one rather indifferent to such things.

Tanunda is remarkable not only for its Germanness but also for its religious factions, and I was particularly intent on finding out more about them.[4] The most important congregation among them is that of the Kavelites or Old Lutherans, who have however recently suffered a quite significant dent in their unity because of a few simple arithmetical errors. Previously the congregations of Tanunda, Hahndorf, Langmeil and Lightspass – all German localities – belonged together to one church.[5] Then – and I do not know even myself whether it was in spring this year (1851) or autumn last year – Pastor Kavel had the fateful idea of prophesying in advance the end of the world, precisely to the day and hour,[6] and he was thoughtless enough not to postpone the date for something like a thousand years, but to cut very close to the bone. The result was the same as befell the famous Preacher Miller in the Yankee states:[7] the good Lord did not deign to do him the favour of lifting the world off its hinges at the prescribed hour; everything continued in its pre-ordained path, except for the Kavelite church.

It is said that at the prophesied hour the whole congregation headed out to a small creek about two miles from Tanunda and half a mile from Langmeil to await the Messiah.[8] But what happened instead was a violent storm that drenched them thoroughly, and that night they slept in their beds again instead of in Paradise.

That made a bad impression on the congregation. The people had absolutely counted on their own destruction, and now they found themselves all hale and hearty – apart from an occasional cold perhaps – and as remote as ever from eternal bliss. The unfulfilled prophecy shattered their faith in the prophet himself, and a portion of the Kavelite congregation seceded from Kavel. So Langmeil chose Pastor Meier,[9] a former missionary to the Australian Indians, as their pastor, and only Hahndorf and Tanunda, and perhaps Lightspass too, maintained the true faith, since the Meierite congregation was strongly sceptical of the imminent end of the world.[10] Pastor Kavel, however, undeterred, postponed it to the transition from 1899–1900.

What people in Tanunda – that is in the unbelieving part of Tanunda's population, since Tanunda is divided into the Saints and the Children of the World – have to say about the congregation and its beliefs borders on the fabulous, and one must indeed exercise caution in believing their reports, for I almost fear that the Children of the World have exaggerated a thing or two.[11] But of course nothing is impossible in religious mania. In any case, I wished to gather as much information as possible in that short time, and so I visited Pastor Kavel, and was very amiably received by him. I had arrived in Tanunda at a very interesting time, since Pastor Kavel had just been married to his housekeeper several days previously, and the rather unique situation had arisen that although Pastor Meier in Langmeil[12] and another pastor, Mr Mücke, who had established a liberal congregation in Tanunda (to which I shall return later), were both ordained by the government,[13] Pastor Kavel did not consider either of these gentlemen worthy of performing his marriage ceremony and therefore travelled to Adelaide with his bride in order to be married by the civil registrar. The congregation in its turn was not satisfied with this, neither with the civil marriage – although he subsequently on his return to Tanunda had the marriage blessed by one of the elders – nor with the marriage itself, whereby the people felt that he should have avoided 'appearances' in such a matter. But in the case of marriage, if one wished first of all to ask permission of the entire congregation, nothing much at all would come about in the end – at least, not in such a way that both parties would be comfortable, and this is something that each man can best judge for himself.

The next day was a Sunday, and of course it was taken for granted that I would attend the Kavelite congregation, after which I was invited to dine with the Pastor. The service was of course the Old Lutheran one, but with an enormous number of hymnbook verses and Bible texts. The singing was never-ending, and although I do not wish to present my opinion as infallible, I really do not believe that our Lord God can be so intent on having half the hymnbook sung to Him every Sunday. That day I had to sing 32 hymnbook verses. And the texts? I am firmly convinced that the people who wrote those hymns – for they can hardly be called poetry – surely had the best of intentions and expressed their most intimate feelings therein, but it nevertheless remains difficult to sing or say, for example, 'all-beneficent' in two syllables.

Pastor Kavel preached well and fluently. By 'well' I of course do not mean to say that I was in agreement with the intention of the sermon, but he spoke as though with innermost conviction, and I would like to believe that to his credit. Moreover he spoke in such a way that I can well understand that he could thereby win over the class of people with whom he was dealing. Otherwise his sermon was an extract of the greatest intolerance that any faith is capable of producing. It was only for his chosen few that the kingdom of heaven will be open, and one sentence in his sermon I will never forget: 'Those who really act according to God's word but do not have the true faith will, regardless of their good and otherwise God-pleasing deeds, be irredeemably damned and go to the Devil. In fact, God will *hate* such people all the more, precisely because of their good deeds, as He sees such deeds as a kind of hypocrisy, since they do not hold the true faith.' And that is supposed to be a God of love.

This sermon was cleanly packed in between an indefinite number of chapters from the Bible and the afore-mentioned number of hymnbook verses, but I found it very disquieting. I am not normally an anxious type, but it almost made my heart bleed when it occurred to me that God might perhaps count me as one of this little handful that wished above all to be saved, while remorselessly dispatching down to Hell the remaining millions on planet earth. At that moment I desired nothing more than to plunge headlong down with the others. I am, by the way, firmly convinced that Pastor Kavel had a fair idea of my spiritual parentage, and it is quite possible that at least a part of the sermon was delivered for my own benefit, so that I might have preliminary warning of my ultimate destination in a very warm climate. At the very least he knew that I was not an Old Lutheran, otherwise I would have introduced myself to him as such on my first visit, and the natural consequence of that was my eventual damnation, with which he was kind enough to make me acquainted.

However that may be, when I came to dine with him afterwards, he received me – one of the damned – as heartily and hospitably as could not be bettered for an orthodox believer, and his little young wife was just the same. I can in no way think ill of him for leaving his bachelorhood behind him and assuring himself of a friendly and humane existence for his old age. In his own home he was not in the least inclined to enter into religious conversations and was always able to divert them in a skilful manner, and I cannot think ill of that either. I would have done exactly the same; such things belong in the pulpit, not in the home. However I did think ill of the mass of prayers and Bible chapters before and after dinner – such things also belong in the pulpit, and if one takes them with one into the home, that is a matter of taste.

I cannot and will not say anything about the religion of the Kavelite congregation, their belief in an imminent thousand-year reign, or of their own unique chosen status. That is simply a belief, a religion like any other, and as long as these people are dedicated heart and soul to that for which they pray, and devoted to it with fervent conviction, I do not see why their faith should not be as good a one as any. They will understand their error soon enough when we all eventually meet up above.

The congregation by the way sets itself strictly apart – Article 1 of their constitution says:

> The congregation stands on the principle that only those can be regarded as true members of the Church, who do not think that they can believe in Jesus Christ by their own reason and strength, but who have been called by the Holy Ghost through the Gospel, have been enlightened by His gifts and sanctified in the true faith and seek to be kept in the same. We protest against all Donatist and Novatian errors[14] and for that reason would expressly refer to Article VIII of the Augsburg Confession as well as to all passages in the other Symbolical Books of our Evangelical Lutheran Church, which say the same thing. Into the Church and Congregation only those are received after careful examination, who acknowledge Holy Writ as God's Word and the doctrine of the Evangelical Lutheran Church, as it is presented in the Small Catechism of Luther and in the Unaltered Augsburg Confession, as being scriptural and also the doctrine of the Church, who will accept as valid confessions of faith of the Church and Congregation also the remaining five Symbolical Books of the Lutheran Church, because they are in agreement with the two named above, who promise to read them as much as possible, and who are in agreement with the Church Constitution.[15]

In their congregations they do indeed deal with apostate or disorderly members harshly enough, at least according to the letter of their laws, and I do not believe that they can be reproached in this regard. Article 10 states: 'Church discipline, practised self-evidently according to Scripture, shall apply to all members of the congregation, without respect of person, rank, age or sex.'

In cases of church discipline there are three grades of punishment. The first is simply exclusion from the Lord's Supper for a brief period:

in order to give the opportunity for earnest self-examination and for deeper penitence over a transgression that has occurred, 2) public appearance before the congregation and confrontation with the sin that has been committed, and 3) excommunication from the congregation and committal to Satan, publicly before the congregation, in the case of a sinner who, though fully convicted of his transgression, obstinately denies and impenitently continues his offence, Matth. 18; 17, 1 Cor. 5:1–5, 13; 1 Tim. 1:20. See also the old Lutheran Schleswig-Holstein Agenda.

The Old Lutherans practise a formal dualism in this regard and believe firmly and persistently in the 'gentleman in black'.

The rights of the congregation according to Article 11 include the following:

Pastors and elders are to carry out their offices only under continuous prayer for the assistance of the Holy Spirit, and every church member has the unchallengeable right to draw their attention to this obligation. Heb. 10, 14–15.

Article 11 could, with benefit, be adopted in our new constitutions.

The Langmeil congregation has, I believe, retained virtually the same articles.[16] Their Pastor Meier is, however, a man who has already had to contend vigorously with the world, for a time conducting the most desolate of all business undertakings, converting the Australian Indians to the Christian religion and civilising them at the same time.[17] He gave this up in the end when he saw that all efforts were wasted on these desperate tribes, and took up the position of preacher in this congregation. He has in addition rendered great service through the publication of several little texts, one dealing with the language of the tribes with which he was in contact, and the other with their manners and customs.[18]

So these are the 'Saints' of Tanunda, but on the other hand there are also the so-called 'Children of the World', and according to Article 1 of the Kavelite church constitution one can assume that they cannot hope for much from the other congregations – whose intolerance has become proverbial among them. The Children of the World are of course not all of one mind; there are Catholics and Protestants among them, and then the liberals – that is, those who allow the good Lord to be a good man and purely and simply go their own way, or Deists, who simply believe in a God and contemplate the Holy Spirit with truly awesome indifference etc. But then the Children of the World also include not a small proportion of those who do not wish to follow the path of the Kavelites, brushing all others aside as they go, but are nevertheless still attached to their old customs, and although they are in this context called Children of the World, in many parts of Germany they would have been reckoned among the strictest church-goers and most zealous hymnbook verse singers.

The gigantic task of uniting all these varieties of Christians under one umbrella, or at least in one church, was undertaken by Dr Mücke from Berlin, who has settled here in South Australia. He has established a liberal or free congregation and is now pastor in Tanunda. Naturally he and Kavel are bitter enemies, since even though Dr Mücke does not contend against the other faith but simply for his own, that does not of course accord with the principles of the opposing party, and it is said that some edifying scenes have taken place. Dr Mücke is in a very difficult position, since he intends to carry out in a small way what would be a great blessing for humankind if it could be achieved on a grand scale, or at least a great step forward in its culture. He wants to meld into one a tangle of sects that head in all sorts of directions, and the result is sadly all too easy to prophesy. He will not succeed. For the one party he is not orthodox enough, even if they are not Old Lutherans – they recall with silent longing their old pastor in Germany, who vigorously laid down the law from his pulpit when they had done wrong. And heavens! Did he not know his Bible off pat, and what a voice he had! 'No matter how fast asleep we were, he woke us up with a start,' a Saxon confessed to me once.

And the other party – the liberals, the Deists – by God, that is a ticklish matter. They quite like now and then to be reminded, even from a pulpit, that they are right, and that one can also serve God 'in spirit and in truth' and without external ostentation, but that is about all. They do not feel any need to go to church any more, nor do they like to spend money on supporting a church and a preacher, and the result is the same, and they become indifferent.

The pastor who has dedicated himself to religion possesses not only the spirit applied to this purpose, but also a body which has to be clothed, protected against the weather, and a stomach that wishes to be satisfied, and the saying that 'Man does not live by bread alone' can just as easily be reversed and applied to the Holy Spirit.

But enough of the religious sects and circumstances of this little German locality, which represents and maintains its own interests in the midst of an English populace. From the church to the field is just one step, and I breathe more freely when I drink in fresh air again and all around and above me see the clear sunny skies.

Tanunda is above all a little farming community, and the land nearby is quite good. The populace is also hard-working and – the main thing in this business – persistent. Hundreds who came here with meagre means or none at all have already established small properties and live contentedly or at least free from care. German diligence, which even the English know to value, finds expression here in many situations, for example, when the Kavelite congregation on arrival rented or bought at a very high price land that was not at all good, where at least with more practical leadership and just a little more home-grown experience and a little bit less praying, better land could have been obtained at a lower price, and where the people had ships' debts to repay. Nonetheless they have not only worked off their debts in quite a short time but have even managed to save a little as well as acquiring stock and tools.

But I am totally opposed to the lease system, at least to a lease system over a long period. Although it may seem to offer advantages for the moment – since people who have few or no means to make a start are helped out until they can stay afloat – all the same there are so many disadvantages. A farmer who intends to establish a new home in a foreign country should be very cautious before entering into a long-term lease arrangement, especially one without a purchase option. I have seen examples in hundreds of places here where the tenants did indeed cultivate their fields, because after all they had to live and earn their rent, but otherwise made only the most necessary improvements – in fact they hesitated to hammer in a nail, because they would have to leave it behind for the owner when they eventually left. I have seen them living in huts that I would have been sorry to drive a dog into, and their excuse was: 'Well, for those couple of years we'll make do; in the end we have to leave anyway.' For precisely that reason no fruit trees are planted, and any improvements at all – to say nothing of embellishments – are left undone, because they would bring benefit only after a number of years.

But he must cultivate the fields – he has to pay rent on each – so he needs to make good use of each, and in so doing he naturally contributes to the cultivation of the whole area, and what would be to his advantage if he were the owner of even such a small property, becomes a disadvantage to him as soon as he eventually wants to buy land in the area. He himself is driving up the price of the land, and he has to seek out another region and start from the beginning again there. A tenant never feels at home on his land, he knows very well that he does not really belong there, and as soon as his lease contract runs out he has to move on; he is an alien on the soil which he has worked and harvested for years. But if a person has even the smallest piece of land as his own property, he works it with far greater enthusiasm and love. Everything he does he is doing for himself; he knows that he will harvest the fruit of every tree that he plants. In a word, the land is his home, and later it will be the home of his children.

The area around Tanunda is fertile enough, but because of the uncertain climate it is impossible to determine an average harvest yield. I have spoken to farmers who assured me that they have harvested 40 bushels of wheat per acre in one year and in the next fifteen; hot winds or damp weather speak a powerful word here, and taking the best possible precautions cannot achieve anything against that. The hot winds have already destroyed whole harvests, and in the Adelaide district they occur particularly frequently, but individual seasons can make a difference there. During such windstorms the air is said to be suffocating, and the dust whirls so fiercely that in Adelaide one can sometimes not see across the street, and in the rooms everything is covered with a layer of dust despite firmly closed doors and windows.

Wine-growing will eventually become a very significant industry for the country, just as in New South Wales, as thousands of acres that are not particularly suited to wheat or even grazing will make excellent vineyards. The grapes grown there are supposed to be superbly sweet and juicy, and the wine pressed from them, of which I sampled several varieties, is really excellent. The whole business is of course still in the early stages of development, and the wine-growers who have started proper cultivation are still at the stage of experimenting to establish which grapes will be most suitable for South Australia. Mr August Fiedler near Tanunda goes to great efforts in this regard, and has already grown several excellent varieties.[19] The most remarkable wine I tasted there was a liquor pressed from Muscatel grapes which had a striking pineapple flavour. He has also grown Rhine wine, Medoc and several other varieties, and most of them are of such a kind that they promise the best results for later years. I took a small bottle of this pineapple-flavoured wine with me to Germany, and although I had carried it around with me in a very hot climate, the wine retained all its goodness – only the pineapple flavour was lost when I opened it again after about a year.

There are tradesmen of every sort in Tanunda, and almost all are Germans: tradesmen get on fairly well in Australia on the whole, especially if they do not always, or at least at the start, insist on their trade alone, but will take up something else now and then until they find better prospects for their own trade once more. It is difficult to set down a standard for their wages, since on the one hand this often changes, and on the other hand the situation varies, as one cannot always count on getting work, and the labourer may earn quite a high wage one week but be idle the next. If he makes his calculations for the whole year according to the good wages, it is very possible that he miscalculates significantly. In Tanunda there are three German general stores, a German pharmacy, two German doctors and one-and-a-half German public houses. One-and-a-half, to the extent that the one, the Tanunda Hotel, is wholly run by Germans (the landlord's name is Müller). The other – the Alliance Hotel – is run by an Englishman named Johnson who speaks very good German and has a very pretty young German wife.

The next Monday there was a ball, a German ball, in Tanunda, and although I cannot myself dance, I was of course interested in being present. The musicians had been booked from Adelaide, but they were prevented from coming, so a few makeshift replacements had to be rounded up in the vicinity. A German ball like this in Tanunda is no minor affair, it does not just last from seven or eight in the evening until as late as people want to dance in the morning, but continues straight through the next day into the second night. They do not bother with anything under two days.

On the first evening, just as the dance was about to begin, I went with the German doctor, Dr Pabst,[20] out into the bush about 1½ miles from Tanunda, where he knew there was an Indian grave. I was keen to take home a complete skeleton of one of the Aborigines, and we had decided to open the grave. One always has to exercise a bit of caution in such a matter, although there had not been any blacks in the vicinity by day. But one has no idea how and where the black fellows creep around, and they could happen upon one just at the wrong time.

We found the grave and started our gruesome task – the soil was light sand and we made rapid progress. My spade soon struck something hard – the Indians do not bury their dead very deep – but it was not the skeleton. We arrived first at the wood with which they usually cover the body. The light of an ordinary lantern illuminated us, and the smell of mould that rose up from the damp earth we soon reached was disgusting. I threw out a piece of the wood and kept digging.

'The head must be here,' said the doctor, 'the wood stuck in here is the plate.' We dug for it but in vain, throwing all of the wood out of the grave and all the damp mouldy soil, until we reached the hard and apparently undisturbed subsoil. There were old leaves lying there, eaten away by the body that had previously lain on them and then rotted away. The blacks had already taken the body away and burnt it, as is the custom with some of the tribes, and we had been cheated. The doctor cursed the scoundrels: 'You can't trust them even in death', and I packed up the spades and the sack we had taken with us to put the bones in, my companion grabbed the lantern, and we wandered back to the nearby township, highly dissatisfied with the result of our nocturnal mission.

Cheerful sounds greeted us from there. Violin, trumpet and clarinet each in its own key played a rousing gallop, the couples whirled around in a circle, the hall was festively illuminated. From the grave to the ball – the contrast was too violent, and it really took me a few minutes to accustom myself to the transition into my new surroundings. But the gaily dressed and cheery host swung round in a circle to the terrible trio, swiftly and with shining eyes. In a cosy little side room I found another society gathered, honourable citizens enjoying the twofold pleasures of the music and the dancers' dust, to the accompaniment of a glass of Medoc. Here the dignitaries were assembled, doctor and pharmacist, pastor and schoolmaster, merchant. They are the dignitaries among us too, but we also include the mayor and the customs inspector as well. Here in this happy little township we knew of neither the one nor the other. Customs inspectors did not exist for the simple reason that the township lay in the middle of the country, and there were likewise no judicial institutions, not even a policeman, surely a highly unusual situation in a German township. But the inhabitants felt the same, and, as they assured me, they had petitioned earnestly to get a police station in Tanunda, which had been most graciously promised them, and the servants of justice were keenly awaited in the imminent future.

At the same time they had, by the way, also petitioned to have a court and a Justice of the Peace located in Tanunda, to which the town itself and the densely populated surroundings were fully entitled. Angas however had applied at the same time, and even though his district could by no means demonstrate so many souls, and certainly not concentrated at the one point, the courthouse was connected with the benefit to the colony, and Angas had rendered too much service to the colony (that is, to himself) not to earn preferential treatment in this matter.[21] Angas was to get the courthouse and Tanunda the policeman.

To the credit of the Tanundans it must also be said that apart from that which social intercourse brings with it in the normal course of events – people of the same educational level always know how to seek and find one another – there were no further distinctions on display between the dignitaries and

'Brother Tailor and Glovemakers'. A very friendly and sociable tone prevails among all ranks; in fact I found all the Germans here in Tanunda much friendlier to one another than in Adelaide itself. So it happened that we spent a very enjoyable evening, and even though I did not dance myself, I was happy watching the cheerful couples and the pretty smiling and blissfully happy faces of the young ladies and girls, of which Tanunda has a richly blessed gift from God to boast.

Just because everything has to be upside down in Australia, however, Tanunda did not want to be the exception, and the brawl that always takes place at the *conclusion* of popular balls in Germany, occurred here at the *beginning*.

Next morning, just as the sun rose over the nearby hills, I got up, got myself ready for departure and set off straight after breakfast, following a narrow forest path toward Gawlertown. Most Tanundans were still taking their brief rest, on the one hand to recover from the efforts of the previous evening, and on the other in preparation for the next. I reached the town at about 2 o'clock in the afternoon, but did not enter it, turning aside instead in order to make a little side trip to Buchsfelde, where the Schomburg brothers from Prussia – Richard Schomburg well-known on account of his previous travels with his elder brother – had settled.[22]

One of the brothers, Otto Schomburg, I had already got to know in Adelaide, and I was most heartily welcomed by the dear people.[23]

Buchsfelde lies on the Gawler River – a small stream that ceases to run in summer like practically all Australian streams – and is a real little German colony which the Schomburgs have named Buchsfelde in honour of the valiant Leopold von Buch.[24] But disunity prevailed already at that time among the various inhabitants, and it is said to have broken out even worse since then, no matter how much the Schomburgs themselves did to try to keep the peace between the people.

The Schomburgs have a section of land here, and although unaccustomed to the land itself and to hard labour, had to cope with a deal of misfortune at the start, poor harvest and sick stock. They now show what human will-power is capable of, once it is firmly directed toward a calmly considered and articulated goal. What they had previously done with outside help, and which had not been successful, they have now taken in hand themselves, and the crop looked excellent, their stock is in a superb state, a garden which Richard Schomburg has laid out on a large scale with immense toil and effort is now nearing completion, vines and fruit trees have been planted, several buildings that they have begun working on for the sake of greater comfort will most likely be completed already this winter, and they can well say that they have overcome the greatest difficulties of the foreign land since bidding farewell to their homeland. But it is still not their homeland, and for the educated man a wild continent can never offer that which it offers the labourer intent on his personal needs, and the former has lost many thousand times more. A turnip is much more easily transplanted than a rose; the one is pulled out of the soil just as it is and stuck in again somewhere else and pressed down. After the first rain or the first watering-can full it is at home again, but with the rose the thousands of roots and fibres which may not have been violently torn off when it was pulled out have to be cut off in order to make it fit the narrow housing intended for it, and that hurts the poor rose terribly, yet it sends out green shoots and blooms all the same, and in the following years at least produces the most beautiful buds and flowers.

If Richard Schomburg is an excellent gardener, his other brother Otto combines all three faculties in one, for apart from helping to cultivate field and garden himself and lending a helping hand as architect and veterinarian, he has a quite significant medical practice in the neighbourhood, particularly in obstetrics, has been nominated as Justice of the Peace for his little district, and will soon, when the Buchsfelder have built themselves a church which is currently in progress, preach there. That is what I call practical.

In order to characterise the Germans in Australia, I believe it would be remiss of me not to mention two incidents that occurred while I was there. It was right in the midst of the great excitement surrounding the elections, and in fact the district on the opposite side of the Gawler River was supposed to cast its votes the next day. We were sitting at our evening meal when one of the brothers was called away for a moment. He came back in laughing and told us what had been expected of him. A German from across the creek had just come across to ask him what was the meaning of the note he had received that afternoon. It was one of the usual papers put out by the local Justice of the Peace to inform the various voters of the time of the election and request their attendance.

'And do I have to go?' the German asked, meaning more or less, 'Is it commanded by the police?'

Mr Schomburg explained to him that he would not be compelled to go by the police, but that it was his duty as a citizen to give his vote for the election of a representative, so that the real opinion of the majority could be ascertained, and the minority according to public opinion would not be able to push through their choice just because they had been the 'more diligent'.

'Ah so', said the man, 'I'll see if I can go.' But he could not, as he spent the next day nicely at home. After all, he did not have to go.

The other German they told me about had played a very significant role in his little locality in the last German revolution; he had been a shining light, a star that many had looked up to and from whom they had expected an improvement in their situation.[25] He had to leave Germany in a hurry at that time I believe, and had narrowly escaped the danger of being arrested, or had suffered pecuniary losses. In short, he had found a hair in the soup in this regard. When he was challenged to participate in the election here he had stated decisively: 'Vote? I had my fingers burned in such an affair once, and never again. Sign a petition? No, I can't do it, the devil knows what they might do with it afterwards, and then we have the same old comedy once more.' He could not be persuaded.

Poor Germany.

Unfortunately I could not stay very long with this dear family, for if I were really to travel to Sydney and Manila with my intended ship I had no time to lose. I wanted to look around a little more in Adelaide and write a few letters. I set out at about 9 o'clock next morning in order to reach Gawlertown before evening, so I could travel on to Adelaide with the Mail at five the next morning.

I stumbled along in the dark – it was truly pitch dark – through the forest of gum trees and over an indeterminate number of fences after I lost the path beneath my feet, but I managed to stay on course as the stars shone brightly, and reached Gawlertown at about quarter past ten. I spent the night there and was in Adelaide next morning at 10 o'clock.

Nothing extraordinary happened en route apart from the fact that we had an old lady with us on the Mail who consumed a nobbler[26] of gin at every public house we stopped at, and we stopped at every one of them; and apart from her there were two men who wanted to go to the newly discovered Sydney gold mines, one of whom declared solemnly that he had been led to leave his previous good occupation, because this was the fulfilment of an age-old prophecy of Holy Scripture, and he was now beginning to be firmly convinced that Australia really was the 'promised' land of the chosen.

There is nothing which has ever been too insane for religious fanaticism.

In Adelaide a pleasant surprise awaited me: while I was in Tanunda my trunk had turned up, in fact with the same schooner that had been meant to bring it in the first place, and since then had already made the voyage a second time. You can imagine with what joy I greeted it.

8.

The Natives of Australia

I cannot put to sea again without providing the reader with the promised account of the Australian tribes – in it he is sure to find some things of interest.

On first impression the native inhabitants of Australia are indeed the people most neglected by the Creator, for it is difficult to imagine a race which is uglier or dirtier. Even on closer acquaintance one is unlikely to form closer bonds with them, or only in very rare and singular cases. Nevertheless, they do possess many more talents than one might believe possible on the basis of a fleeting acquaintance.

In earlier descriptions of this race, I have found, for example, that they have been accused of having no proper huts and not even the bow and arrow, a weapon possessed elsewhere by even the most primitive of native tribes, and yet this is clearly explicable in terms of their lifestyle and the land that they inhabit. The climate makes houses unnecessary, and their way of life makes them impractical, for being nomads, they roam from place to place as far as their hunting grounds extend. They keep out the rain with skilfully arranged pieces of bark, and their natural toughness makes them insensitive to the cold. They do not have bows and arrows because the wood of their forests is not flexible enough for bows, but, with the help of a throwing stick, they can throw their small, sharp spears so that they fly as sure and as far as an arrow. The natives of the pampas also have no bows, but there is little doubt that their bola is a more dangerous weapon.

The Australian race seems to be a mixture of the Negro and the South Sea

Islander, if not of the Negro and the Malayan, but their character is not the same throughout the entire Australian continent; in some instances their features are different, in others even their colour, which ranges from black to a copper brown. Their hair is jet black and sometimes straight, sometimes curly, but never woolly like that of the Negro, and they are particularly fond of smearing it with fat. Indeed fat plays a very important role for them, and kidney fat is the trophy they extract from enemies they have overcome. By rubbing themselves with it, they believe that the strength of their vanquished opponent will be transferred to them. Like the North American savage, who simply scalps the enemy he has thrown to the ground and often does not even kill him, I have heard many stories of blacks, and now and again also of whites, who, with bodies sliced open and robbed of this most valuable fat, have run some distance – blacks are said to have even swum across a river – but ultimately there was no escaping death.

Now, with Australia behind me, I am able to write with great equanimity about this unpleasant custom, which is the least one can say about it, but when I was proceeding down the Murray through the midst of these savage tribes, I felt very ill at ease, and I recall one morning carefully examining myself to see if my 'butter' was still there.[1]

It is quite extraordinary what a traveller needs to heed in different parts of the world, and how many different parts of his body he risks on leaving one country and entering another. As is well known, the North American Indians want his scalp, the Australians want his kidney fat, the Germans demand a certificate of origin, or they take the whole person; on the island of Luzon[2] the natives are after travellers' calves, some African tribes just take the cheeks, while the New Zealanders take the whole head. It is most confusing to be confronted with so many different needs.

As far as the appearance of these natives is concerned, I was perhaps a little spoilt, having just come from the South Sea Islands with a prejudice against these black, dirty tribes. Nevertheless, I do not believe that even the greatest flatterer could say of them that they were well-proportioned. Even if some, particularly the men, have a well-formed upper body and sometimes even a noble-looking head, their legs and arms are on the whole repulsively thin and emaciated, and similarly the women seldom have a good figure. It is possible to make an accurate judgment of this as they conceal none of their charms.

It is odd that the men can much more readily be persuaded to put on clothes than the women. The latter normally cast off everything again, and even in Adelaide, where they are not permitted to appear in public without clothing, they simply drape themselves in their possum-skin coats. While the men adjust easily to trousers and shirts, they do not like shoes and consider all footwear with profound contempt. Among the thousands of women I saw in the Australian forests, I do not believe that there were three pretty ones, or if there were, they had carefully and successfully hidden themselves behind a crust of dirt.

To gain a more exact knowledge of the manners and customs of these tribes, however, it would be necessary to spend many years among them and to have much more frequent contact. To do the former, I had no time, to do the latter, because of my 'butter', no inclination. In spite of that, I did, wherever possible, collect the most exact information about the tribes and sometimes learned more about their customs than I desired to know. I obtained the most interesting information in Adelaide from the Protector of the South Australian natives, Mr Moorhouse, who put the journal he had been keeping since 1839 at my disposal and permitted me to make notes from it.[3]

His observations are confined mainly to the Adelaide tribes and those from some parts of the Murray, from Lake Boni[4] downstream to Morrunda,[5] and as these were the places I also visited, they were of particular interest to me. The reader will perhaps find a short excerpt from the whole of some appeal; he will at least find some new information about these savage Aborigines, who are so little amenable to attempts to civilise them.

A compilation of information on their manners and customs will follow; here I will, for the most part, follow the journal.[6]

From the beginning the main difficulty in civilising the natives seems to have been to get them to give up their moveable habitations, to build proper houses, and to cultivate a piece of land. Had this occurred, all difficulties would have been overcome, for once the native has abandoned his old life and begun a new one, each step leads to the next, taking him further along that path. Despite the many experiments undertaken with them, this was something that the natives resolutely refused to do, and even if they were given food and clothing, they set to work with great reluctance, and only for as long as they were unable to avoid it.[7]

In 1839 there were around 540 Aborigines in the Adelaide area, belonging to five tribes. The first lived on Muliakki (the so-called Millner estate) and consisted of 20 souls, the second, the Wirra tribe, lived on the banks of the Para river and consisted of 120 souls, the third inhabited the district to the north of Adelaide up to Mount Tenible[8] and consisted of 80 souls, the fourth, the Patpunga, lived on the south coast from Mount Tenible to Rapid Bay and consisted of 90 souls. All of these spoke almost the same language. The fifth, the Ramong,[9] lived on the banks of Encounter Bay, on the upper reaches of Lake Alexandrina, and consisted of 230 souls. Half of these are afflicted with venereal diseases which are said to have come from the coast. They also suffer from inflammations, rheumatism and stomach complaints.[10]

The number of Murray natives in the district from Ponunda to the north-west bend, a distance of around 120 miles, is approximately 300.

1840, 25 Jan. Bob, the prisoner, has again returned to his Aboriginal ways. He is indolent and very impertinent – prison seems to have been a bad school for him. It is impossible to get him to do any work.

14 Febr. Mr Honock's shepherd was speared and killed by the Aborigines.[11]

A woman was brought before the court for infanticide but refused to answer any of the questions directed to her.

25 May. A large celebration in honour of Queen Victoria – 100 caps, 120 shirts, 100 dresses distributed, followed by examination of the children and later a festive dinner – 283 natives present.

To keep children at school, they are given some rice and biscuits, and when they can read and pronounce words properly, they receive a blanket and a dress. They are particularly fond of soup with fresh meat and peas.[12]

In the year 1840 the number of men (blacks) was 271, women 178, and children 183.[13]

As the natives lose their fear of firearms if they hear them discharged frequently without suffering any harm, a law was passed forbidding whites from firing firearms to frighten the natives, thus depriving shepherds living alone in remote areas of their last form of protection.

A native on the Murray gave his wife a wild dog to look after. A white man, Robert Gauger Esq., *Colonial Treasurer*,[14] for some reason, had the dog shot. The native returned home, and, finding the dog dead, thrust a spear into his wife's side, thereby causing her death.[15]

1841, 2 August. A stockman on the Lyth river found a calf missing and, suspecting the natives camped nearby, he went to their camp. On arriving there accompanied by two other whites, he saw something roasting on the fire, which he took to be his calf, and accused the native of stealing it. The latter hit him with his spear, whereupon the stockman shot him. The daughter of the murdered man declared that it was a kangaroo that was being roasted. The stockman's name was Roach.

Skirmish on Rufus creek involving 49 Europeans and 150 natives.[16]

On 20 Feb. in an area of 2,800 square miles there were 650 Aborigines, that is approximately 1 in every 4½ square miles.[17]

The blacks are vulnerable to certain diseases, in particular inflammations of all types and their consequences. Mostly it is the throat and lungs which are affected, probably a result of their constantly lying outside in the damp and cold. They have been ravaged by nguya or small pox and many still bear the scars.[18]

1843. In 1840 the number of blacks living in the town was 159
        1841   249
        1842   296
        1843   405

This number is to be found in an area 100 miles to the north, 60 to the south and 200 to the east to near where the Rufus meets the Murray. On the Murray the numbers of men and women are almost equal. In the Adelaide district there are 150 Aborigines, 70 men, 35 women and 41 children;[19] there are 200 Murray blacks in Adelaide; of these 85 are men, 53 women and 62 children.

8 July 1843. Many clashes with the blacks. The latter plundered many huts and tied and bound the hut keepers – but did not harm anyone.

The girls who have been educated by Europeans are, at a certain time, called on by the sorcerers to return to their tribe and threatened with death if they do not obey.

It appears that there are three stages in the natives' contact with Europeans. When they first see the latter, they are harmless and rarely present a threat to the whites. But soon this trust gives way to other feelings – which does not exactly speak in favour of the whites. They never go unarmed and are constantly on their guard; only after longer interaction with the whites do they lose this fear and lay down their weapons.

1844. Numbers of natives:

	Those in regular contact with whites:	Those at a distance, or with irregular contact with whites:
Adelaide District	300	---
Encounter Bay	230	100
Morunda[20]	300	200
Port Lincoln	60	340
Hull River	<u>30</u>	<u>40</u>
	920	680 = 1600

On the Queen's birthday[21] there were present:

1840	283 natives
1841	374 "
1842	400 "
1843	450 " [22]

The list of those attending school presents a strange contrast. Children have only been persuaded to attend school very irregularly, and adults even more seldom, but as soon as a festive dinner takes place, they are all there, and they are prevented from participating only if the distance is too great or they find out about the important day too late. The blacks are prodigious eaters and drinkers, and it is amazing how much food they can sometimes consume.

The news of such a feast must have spread particularly quickly in 1845, for on this day there were assembled in Adelaide 1041 Aborigines, 384 from the Adelaide tribe, 207 from Encounter Bay and 450 from Wellington, from Lake Alexandrina.

On this day 100 blankets were distributed to the parents who sent their children to school. On average, 9 boys and 10 girls frequented the school on a daily basis, but only ever for a short time, after which their place was taken by others.

Whites on the Murray killed several natives and then dug up their bodies and burned them in order to conceal the murder.

On 5 September 1845 a black boy was found starved.

In their native state, the natives, typically, do not have unhealthy teeth, but this changes after they have lived with the whites for five or six years.[23]

On 6 December 1845, Nancy, a girl working in government house, went away with her husband and could not be persuaded to return. The young man even refused a position he was offered with the mounted police. The woman is 19, the man 20 years old.

When the natives living outside the town heard that a Protector, who was passing through, wanted to visit them and take their children so that they could attend school, they took the children across the river, and the few whose parents could be persuaded to hand them over and whom he took with him, escaped again on route.

1846. On 30 March, the Protector attempted to bring children down from the Murray, but the savages hid them in the reeds. He only managed to collect two who followed him for five miles but then fled into the bush.

In May whooping cough raged amongst the children of the whites, but the blacks remained free of it and could not be infected.

On receiving dresses or blankets, the children passed them on immediately to their parents.

In hospital in 1847 there were: 86 suffering from influenza, 41 from skin rashes.

1848. On 27 January, the Deputy-Registrar joined a European called Thomas Adams and a black woman named Kudanoto, who belonged to the Flinders Range tribe, in marriage. This was the first case of its kind.[24]

The woman was given a selection of crown land (as encouragement for others keen to marry).[25]

A girl, 18 years old, left the school – she had lived for nine years among Europeans, had attended school for four years, spent one year with one of the missionaries, worked for two years as a servant in the town and two years in government house. She cast everything aside and ran away in order to resume her former life with her people in the bush.

Mr Younghusband had employed a Chinese as a shepherd, but in February he was killed by the blacks.

1849. Five Aborigines were found poisoned – a shepherd in Port Lincoln is suspected of having been responsible. The blacks had plundered his hut a number of times and stolen provisions, and it is thought that he left some out as bait and poisoned them.

Recently it seems that the numbers attending school have increased significantly. When I saw the school, there were at least between 30 and 40 children present, and most of them could make themselves understood in English. The teacher is greatly assisted by the differences existing between the tribes, whose children attend school, and the differences in the native languages, which although spoken in neighbouring districts, have no similarity with one another. As they do not understand the other native tongue, if the children of two such tribes want to talk to one another, they are forced to use English as a medium of communication.

9.

The Manners and Customs of the South Australian Tribes

As a result of greater familiarity with the language of these tribes, more has been learnt about their customs, and, contrary to what was previously believed or had been strongly disputed, it has been found that they do have territorial rights. Families own certain stretches of land which are passed on from father to son (never to daughters) with the same regularity as property in Europe or in any other civilised part of the world. They even go further than that, sometimes exchanging it with another family whose land is located more favourably or appears desirable as a result of marriages into other families, as in the case of King John, for example, who belonged to the district of Adelaide Glinely-Sturt River and Hurtlewale[1] and exchanged it for ngalinga and maitpunga.[2] In relation to land possession, it is noteworthy that some own extensive tracts of land, while others have none. They seem, however, to be unaware of the reason for this inequality – it has its origins in a time too long past and has not been passed on in their oral transmissions.[3]

As far as the food of these blacks is concerned, they are of course totally reliant on hunting – their more basic fare is, however, not restricted to hare, partridge or perhaps fieldfare, as it is in Germany, but includes caterpillars, larvae, worms, beetles, snakes, lizards, and goodness knows what else. I am convinced they eat anything they come across – whatever it is – at least the grown men. The women and minors are subject to certain laws that must be observed.

Children are given no vegetable matter as it is considered to be harmful to them. As long as it is still being suckled, an infant (and they retain this status for two to three years and sometimes even for longer) is permitted to eat the mangalya turlukka – a larva from the wattle tree; as soon as they have teeth, they may eat liver and mussels, and after they have been weaned, at an age of two to three years, they can eat vegetables and the lung and liver of animals.

During pregnancy women are not allowed to eat emu (the Australian cassowary) or possums, otherwise their children will become ill. In this state, women on the Murray are also not permitted to consume any type of fish.

At a certain age, young women and young men on the Murray are also not permitted to eat a fish called relabko, and children already able to eat meat are not able to consume a particular type of duck.

When women have passed child-bearing age, they are free to eat what they want, as are the men who have undergone the last ceremonies making them burkas or grown men. Until then, they too are forbidden to eat certain foods. Unmarried men, for example, may not eat: kangaroos which have been taken from the mother's pouch, the large intestines of animals, the red kangaroo, or in some districts just the front shoulders, the female kangaroo of any type and the wild dog. When they are married they can indulge in lung and liver and eat emu, and when they become burkas, they are allowed, as previously mentioned, to consume anything they come across.

They sometimes use nets to catch kangaroos and emus. These nets (which they, by the way, make in exactly the same way as the Europeans) are strung across the trail, and the animals, whose resting or grazing place they have established beforehand or already know, are driven into it. Wombats – a type of badger – are suffocated in their holes.

The preparation of their food is also very simple – like most savage tribes, they steam their meat and vegetables; only the larvae of insects are eaten raw.

They do not have intoxicating drinks, and the only drink they make themselves consists of the blossoms of the banksia which they soak in water so that the honey will be drawn out and dissolved – they then drink this water.

Their dwellings consist in part of bushes, in part of pieces of bark – the Australian trees can mostly be stripped very easily, particularly the gum trees – the bark is then laid in a semi-circle so that the tips meet at the top, and a single stick at the front supports the entire tent or roof. They make their fire close to the opening, and the bark is placed in such a way as to protect them from the wind. These dwellings can and must be easily moved as they are dependent on the food they find in the vicinity, and if the food becomes scarce in one area, they move on to another.

Weapons. The Adelaide tribes have a winda, which is a very large spear about 10 to 12 feet in length with a smooth point made of flint or glass or cut to shape. This spear is thrown a distance of 10 or 12 yards. The smaller or Raya-spear consists of two parts, is five to six feet long and sometimes also barbed with glass. The upper part is made of tea-tree or some other heavy material, the other from reeds or the stalk of the grass tree, and both are fastened to one another with gum and animal tendons. This spear is thrown 60–80 yards.[4]

The catta wirra is a two-edged piece of wood four feet long, round and chisel-pointed and is normally used in hand-to-hand combat. The wirra is two to three feet long, has a knob or butt and is used to bring down and kill game. The shield, which they use to protect themselves from the weapons of their enemies, is made of the bark of the gum tree, about two feet long, broad in the middle and tapering at the ends. In the middle are two holes through which a string or tendon is pulled to make a handle for the warrior.

Flint is used either as a knife or, when fastened with gum to a handle (the kandappe), as a hatchet or chisel. Sometimes shells are used instead of flint.

The Murray tribes do not have the kandappe, at least I have never seen one there. In close combat they have no weapons apart from the wirra and the club. But they also have shields which are mostly made of wood, sometimes with a carved handle, as the shield is thick in the middle but only wide enough to cover the hand. It is around two feet long and tapered at the end.

Apart from that, the tribes of the upper Murray have the boomerang, already mentioned, a bent, flat piece of wood about two inches wide and one and a half feet long and shaped like a sickle, which they throw and which, should it miss its target, makes a short arc and whirls back to the thrower.

Their needles are made from bone of the kangaroo or emu, which is sharpened with a stone. Their nets are made from animal tendons or plant fibres which are chewed and made into string by rubbing the hand on the thigh.

The skins intended for use as garments, or rather covers, are stretched out, held fast with small pegs and rubbed with ash and dust to remove the fat. The smaller skins are rubbed with smooth stones to make them soft and flexible. The garment, when finished, is nearly square, and is thrown over the left shoulder and fastened to the right so that the right arm remains free and unimpeded. The women throw it over the back and left shoulder, pull it around under the right arm, and the whole is held together with a string thrown over the garment and the back. This leaves a type of pouch on the back in which the children are always carried.[5]

To climb gum trees the natives use a wadna or climbing stick in the following manner. Firstly they cast off all of their garments and then make a notch in the bark with the wadna. The first is made about two feet from the ground and the small toes of the left foot are placed in it. Clasping the trunk with their left arm, they make another notch with the wadna, fixing it in the trunk so that they can use it to pull themselves up. The ball of the right big toe is placed in the second notch, while the wadna is released to make a third notch for the next step with the small toe of the left foot and so on.[6]

Insect larvae are discovered by the kudna (dung) found at the openings of their holes. Even when the insects have bored their way into the plant through the root, their presence is detected by the sickly appearance of the plant.

The grub hook is a special implement employed by them to extract larvae from the bark of gum trees. The hook consists of a normal twig about one foot in length and cut to shape. Larvae or pupae found in the earth are dug out with a kurko or small spade.[7]

This is also used to collect mussels on the banks of lakes or rivers.

The Australian natives are not at all as unsociable as descriptions of them would generally lead one to believe.[8] In spring and summer and sometimes in the autumn, tribes come together with various other tribes. In fact, they pay one another regular social visits, rather like coffee meetings.

Their gatherings have two different purposes, either festivity or war.

If they assemble for the former, the different groups still adopt a warlike stance – their bodies and shields are painted with chalk and each young man carries a spear. On approaching one another, they sit down on the ground. Newcomers are formally introduced and their family background and country described by the elders. In the evening each tribe takes turns to perform formal dances and pantomimes. The Adelaide tribes have the *kuri* and *palti*.

The kuri is performed by the men – the women and children sit on the ground in a half-circle, and in their midst a burka or old man crouches with two sticks in his hand, the wirri and the katta, beats them in time and sings. The young men stamp and dance in front of him. Bunches of bushes tied to their knees or belt help them to keep time with the music, and they adorn themselves with cockatoo feathers and ochre.

The palti is much noisier than the kuri. The women and children sit on the earth and with their hands beat tightly rolled kangaroo or possum skins which make a hollow sound, while the men dance and beat their wirris and kattas together or alternate with the women in singing.

If the tribes come together with hostile intent, on the evening before they have a kuri and palti, and at the break of the next day the battle begins – there is something quite chivalrous about this. Their battles are cold-blooded and cruel, and it seems almost as if they attack one another not to avenge past injuries, but to test the courage and agility of their young men. During the fight, which lasts for three to four hours, hardly a word is spoken and hardly a sound heard, apart from the occasional shrill cry if someone narrowly escapes a spear, and yet, with the women and children, there are often hundreds of spectators present.

Friendly tribes set up their camps quite close to one another, but they are always different in some respect and ordered in such a way that each is located in the direction from which they have come. There are often several families in one hut, but each family has its own fire.

The Murray tribes call their dance the korro-beri, and all of the dances I saw there were similar to the palti and kuri.

The government of the tribes rests entirely in the hands of the burkas or old men. At each stage of ageing they acquire additional knowledge and power, and each stage is marked with appropriate ceremonies. At each new stage of life young people acquire certain weapons, so that it is only the elders who are able to carry all of the implements required for war, hunting, sorcery and medicine.

The women and children are not permitted to see all of these sacred instruments, or those that have been declared sacred, such as the rock crystal with which the sorcerer can produce rain and blindness, or cause the water to turn foul, and the kadnomarngutta, a small oval piece of wood, through which a hole is bored and a string attached. When it is whirled rapidly it makes a rumbling noise that one can hear at a distance of half a mile. The young men and women know what this noise means.

Girls are betrothed when still infants and given to their husbands when they are about 12 years old. Close relatives, closer than cousins, are not allowed to marry one another, and sometimes even they are not permitted to marry. The oldest men usually have the youngest women and acquire them by exchanging their daughters for them. When a woman reaches the age of 35 or 40, she is cast off and given to a 26–30-year-old man. Young men under the age of 25 are seldom allowed to marry.[9]

Children are given their names in the order in which they are born, thus:

	If a boy	If a girl
The first	Rutameru	Rutanya
The second	Warritya	Warriato
Then	Rudnutya	Rudnarto
"	Monartya	Monarto
"	Milartya	Milarto
"	Marrutya	Marruarto
"	Wongutya	Wonguarto
"	Ngarlartya	Nagarlato
"	Pourna	

These are given to the children on birth, but afterwards another name is added, which is taken from a natural object, a plant or an animal. The child retains this name until it grows up, marries and has a child. The father then takes the name of the child and adds the word binna or tpinna, such as Kadli, the name of the child, Kadlitpinna, the father of Kadli. The mother is called Kadlingangki, from nganki, a woman. The name of father and mother is changed in this way on the birth of each child.

If a grey-headed man should still have children, he adds the title of burka instead of tpinna, such as Karkalla, the child, Karkalla burka, the (old) father of Karkalla. Should he have no more children, he acquires a permanent name which, like the names of our nobility, is the place which belongs to him, such as e.g. Muliaki burka, the owner of Muliaki.[10]

Promiscuity is common, the woman is considered to be the property of the man, and a man, who is able to meet all the requirements, can take up to four wives which he casts off again when they become old.[11]

As part of their marriage ceremonies, some tribes have very odd customs.

Ceremonies.[12] Male children have to pass through five stages. The first is that of the child from birth to the tenth year.

From here they pass to the second stage, or wilya kundarti, in which they are smeared with blood that has been taken from the arm of a grown man. Now they are permitted to carry a wirri, a small flat stick about two feet long, used for hunting birds, and also a karko, a small wooden spade with which they dig worms and grubs out of the ground. The third stage is that of circumcision, which is performed when they are around 14 years of age, and the ceremonies that take place are as follows:

On the morning of the day on which the circumcision is to occur, the boys to be circumcised are suddenly seized from behind, their eyes are covered, and they are taken to a place about half a mile away. Three of the Aborigines now begin to limp, to groan and to creep around until they come to someone they intend to seize. He attempts to leap away, jumps over the boys and tries everything possible to escape them. But finally he is caught, laid down near the other boys and covered with dust. After catching six boys in this manner, they seize the others and shake them, pull their ears and shout into them, believing the boys to have been enchanted. The others then form a long row and, with one in the lead, they perform a number of evolutions, sit down and jump up again. Finally the leader thrusts his spear into the ground. All take hold of it and throw themselves into a heap. Now those who are inspired rise up, throw the boys onto this human altar and perform the operation. The whole procedure takes seven hours, and the boys are then taken some distance away, around four miles, and are kept there out of sight of the women until they are completely healed. During the ceremony a man even stays in the camp to ensure the women and girls do not leave. The boys receive a covering, yutna, and their head is rubbed with grease and ochre, a band is bound around it and adorned with a tuft of feathers. Until they are completely healed, the young people are not permitted to consume any animal food.

The fourth stage, which is reached at the age of 20, is called wilyana. In this stage the back, shoulders, chest and arms of the young man are tattooed. During the operation he is called ngulta, when the wounds begin to fester, iellam bombatta, when they are just healed, tarkanje, when the incisions start to rise, mangkawitja, and when they have reached their highest point and are now the ornament of the grown man, bartanna. Each tribe has its own form of tattooing, some making incisions across the whole chest, others circles, some half-circles. Their manner of tattooing is as primitive as their lifestyle.

The fifth stage is burka – a grey-haired man.

Such a grey-headed man, if the blackguards would just keep themselves a little bit cleaner, sometimes looks imposing enough. They allow their hair and beards to grow freely, and they mostly have frizzy full beards that rather suit their black faces and lively eyes. I have seen a couple of old fellows on the Murray whose shoulders were covered with as much hair as their faces, and it looked as if they had thrown a grey fur, a type of hood, over their head and shoulders. But both in the men and the women, the arms and legs detract from their stature. The men in particular may sometimes have a well-formed upper body, but their legs are always thin and spindly. In fact, they very frequently do not have any flesh at all, but like a skeleton, the bare bones and the tendons attached to them are simply covered by back hide. The women also often have arms and legs that look as if they have shrivelled and died.

Strangely these tribes, at least as far as is known thus far, have no religion and no religious ceremonies.[13] They do not believe in a higher, or rather a benevolent creator. They seem little concerned about how the world and everything that surrounds them came into being. Some creatures created themselves and then created others – this will be what happened. But they do fear evil spirits who can exert a harmful influence over them, and they have sorcerers to protect themselves from them.

Before they can acquire any magic power, these sorcerers must partake in many ceremonies. In one period they are even required to eat the flesh of young children, in another that of old men. But it seems they must only sample each once and that this suffices for the rest of their lives. After they have undergone all that is required, they possess extensive powers such as the ability to heal diseases, make rain and hail, enchant rivers and transform themselves into other beings.

They believe in a soul or a spirit which lives separately from the body (itpe tukutya). After death the spirit journeys west to a deep chasm in which the souls of all people come together. When all are dead, the souls return to their previous abode, go to the graves of their abandoned bodies and ask, 'Are these the bodies that we formerly inhabited?' The bodies reply, 'We are not dead, we are still living.' But the souls and bodies are not reunited; the former live during the day in the trees, descending to the ground only at night where they eat grubs, lizards, frogs and kangaroo rats, but no vegetable matter. They never die again and remain the size of a boy of around eight years of age.

This belief explains their reluctance to leave their camp at night. They remain lying quietly by their fire, which they keep burning brightly to let evil spirits know that they are keeping watch.

On the Murray they call the devil toh, as they do, just as flatteringly, the white man (meru is a black man), and lutko means both shade and soul.

Some tribes do not seem too concerned about the nocturnal movements of spirits and the devil, at least not on moonlit nights. I recall that they often went out in the moonlight to hunt wombats – a small kind of badger – and I remember only too well how they sometimes came into my camp in the night. Further north, however, particularly towards Sidney, they would, under no circumstances, leave their huts after dark.

On the Murray the Boni blacks[14] are reputed among the other tribes to be able to make the weather by digging out and covering certain bushes with earth.

As for superstitions or beliefs – and who can really judge the difference between the two – of these they have many. The puingurru is a sacred bone which they sometimes use for letting blood. A type of relic, if placed in the fire and burnt to ashes, it is assumed to exert a mortal power over enemies. If two tribes are in conflict and one of them falls ill, it is commonly held that the sorcerer of the opposing tribe is responsible. If the puingurru is burnt, then death is inevitable.

They also believe in a type of monster of human appearance, but immense size. This supernatural being is said to have the power to fly through the air or through the earth from one side to the other. They are particularly frightened of it at night when it creeps around, keeping watch to see if a fire might have gone out here and there. To protect themselves, they attempt as far as possible to keep the fire stoked and blazing brightly.[15]

The curing of different diseases is entirely the province of the sorcerers.[16] Internal pains, whatever form they may take, are attributed to sorcery or paitya. Thus a sorcerer is the only person who can relieve them and he does so by applying his mouth to the seat of the pain – a type of live cupping glass – and sucking out the blood or the paitya. After this, gum leaves – which are a rich source of cajaput, a strong smelling medicinal oil – are placed over the spot, and the cure is complete, or is at least assumed to be complete.

For head or stomach pains they employ another method; they press and knead the sick part until the person suffering experiences some relief. To relieve headaches or release the build-up of pressure in the body, they sometimes let blood just as the Europeans do from the arm. The incision is made with a piece of crystal which is assumed to have additional supernatural powers.

They attribute deformation of the body to the stars – or to the mother who ate forbidden foods during pregnancy. Young girls believe that they become pregnant if they eat meat or plants forbidden to them at this stage of their life.

The sorcerers sometimes pretend to extract bones from the mouth of the sick person, which are supposed to contain the sickness, but often the origin of the illness removed in this fashion remains completely invisible and is burnt.

When a member of their tribe dies, the body is placed after a few days on the wirkatti or bier. The wirkatti, which is shaped like a wheel, is carried by five or six men over the places previously inhabited by the dead person. In that time one person walks under the bier, supposedly in conversation with the dead person, and asks him: 'Who killed you? – do you know him?' As soon as the corpse replies 'no one', this type of interrogation ceases, but if someone is named, the procession continues, moved, it is believed, by the dead person himself, who is influenced by Ruinyo (a spirit – death). The alleged murderer may be present, and if that is the case, one of the branches is made to touch him. A battle ensues either immediately or in one or two days.

After this the corpse is taken down from the bier and laid in a grave from four to six feet deep.

Children up to the age of four years are not buried for several months after their death. They are carefully wrapped up and carried on the mother's back during the day and at night serve her as a pillow. Only when they are totally dry and mummy-like are they buried or placed in a tree.

The dead are buried with their head toward the west. Two relatives then spring onto the grave, pulling their hair as if in a paroxysm of grief, and tearing and beating one another. – In our country the relatives only see one another in the funeral carriage and adorn their hats with flowers.

Several months after the burial, the women still sit at the graves and lament and lacerate their thighs and breasts with flint stones.

Still-born or very small children are mostly burnt. Some tribes dig up their dead after a certain time and burn the skeleton. In some places, as a sign of great veneration, they even dry the corpse and put it in a tree.

Their signs of mourning also differ from tribe to tribe.[17] The men cut off both their hair and their beard, and the women their hair. In some places they put hot ashes on their head in order to singe the hair to the roots. At the Rufus and in those areas of the Murray above and below the Rufus, the women make themselves a cap of white clay and kneaded grass, one and a half to two inches thick, which they put on their heads and allow to dry. White is the colour of mourning, and as a sign of grief, the men too sprinkle and paint themselves with white clay. When they are removed by the women, these caps or scalp lids, as they might more fittingly be called, are placed on the grave of the person mourned, which is then covered with bushes like a hut. Everyone passing throws a small bush or twig onto the hut as proof of their respect for the deceased, eventually creating a thick roof which provides shade and protection. It was these skullcaps, as they are called by the English, that led me to crawl into the grave hut on the Murray.

The cause of all the thousands upon thousands of fights and arguments that occur amongst the blacks, particularly on the Murray and the Murrumbidgee, is superstition, or rather the lack of belief in a natural death. Each death is attributed to the secret enchantment of an enemy and must be expiated with the blood of the enemy. The women sit around the dead person and lament, howl and scream and finally drive the men so far that they jump up in despair, seize their weapons and run out to shed blood for blood. Many a poor innocent devil from another tribe who has happened across their path or failed to keep watch at night has been killed in this way and had his kidney fat removed to his enemies', or perhaps not his enemies', but simply his neighbours' fires.

This unhappy custom does not seem to be practised by the Rufus tribes of Lake Victoria and Lake Boni,[18] or at least it takes another form which is less hostile.

At their funeral celebrations dances or a type of contest take place in which blood must flow, but only from a light wound, and that seems to appease the spirits of the dead in a more reasonable way.

They have another idea about life after death, which probably only arose after their acquaintance with the whites, unless we want to see it as a type of revelation, that on death the soul of the blacks passes to the bodies of the whites, who they consider to be superior beings, and that all white men were therefore once blacks.

Two missionaries, both Germans, have published several pamphlets in Adelaide on the manners and customs of the Aborigines of Encounter Bay and Port Lincoln.[19] Although they do differ slightly from those of the Adelaide and Murray tribes, the differences are not so substantial as to warrant a further account of the life and habits of these wild tribes which the reader might find tiresome. I will therefore only pass on information relating to their beliefs and legends, it being at least of some interest to follow the ideas and fantasies of such a strange people.

Of the Encounter Bay natives, Pastor Meier[20] says:

> There are but few diseases which they regard as the consequence of natural causes; in general they consider them to be the effects of enchantment which can be produced by means of two instruments, the plongge or the mokani.
>
> The plongge is a stick about two feet long, with a large knob at the end. They believe that if a person is tapped gently upon the breast with this instrument he will become ill or die, or if that does not occur, then the next wound he receives, be it ever so slight, will be mortal. The charming is generally performed at night when the person in danger is asleep; therefore, when several tribes are encamped near each other there is always someone keeping watch to prevent such enchantments occurring. Should a man have an enemy whom he wishes to enchant, and he can steal upon him while sleeping without being discovered, he believes that he can cause him to fall into a deeper sleep by lightly moving his hand before his face, as if he were holding a tuft of emu feathers in his hand that had previously been dipped in the putrescence of a rotting corpse. In this way he ensures that those nearby also sleep soundly, and then he gently touches the breast of his victim with the plongge.
>
> The mokani is a black stone, formed somewhat like an axe and bound between two pieces of wood, which serve as a handle. The sharp side of the

stone is used to exert a magical influence on men, the blunt side on women. Apart from that it is used just like the plongge.

The *ngatunge* is another instrument to cause illness and death. Enemies watch each other, and search diligently for places where they have eaten ducks, parrots, cockatoos, a kind of fish called *ponde*, &c. If anyone has eaten of either of these animals and neglected to burn all the bones, his enemy picks them up. But if the other has been too careful to enable him to do this, he has to find his own material. He kills one of these animals, cooks or roasts it, and offers it in a friendly manner to his intended victim – having previously taken from it a piece of bone. This he keeps carefully, and fixes with grass-tree resin upon the end of a small needle-shaped piece of kangaroo about three inches long. This is the ngadungage or ngadunge, which he places near the fire, in order to induce the illness and death of his victim.

There is something spiteful and malicious about these customs, and I truly believe that only the Australian savage is capable of such cowardly treachery. Is it not quite horrifying to imagine how the black wretch at first gives the appearance of being friendly, offering food to his chosen victim, while knowing all the while, or believing himself to be in possession of the latter's seed of death. And when the unsuspecting victim has eaten, he sits down in the still night by his fire and gloats as he uses the scorching bone to sap the other's juices and life force.

If a person is convinced that the death of a friend or relation has been caused by enchantment, and he suspects someone, then here too he attempts to obtain such a ngadunge and thrusts it into the thigh of the corpse. This is also supposed to bring about the slow and lingering death of the enemy.

If someone should die without his relatives being able to determine who caused his death, they attribute the cause to a particular type of enchantment called melapar. They also give this name to the Adelaide and more northern tribes and believe that they are able to transform themselves into birds, trees etc. Young and old alike fear these melapar and are therefore reluctant to leave their huts after sunset.

When they die, children are treated in much the same way as those of the Adelaide blacks that I have described earlier, but they have a special way of dealing with older people. As soon as old people die, their knees are drawn up to their chin – (this is also the custom of the northern tribes) – and their hands are pressed together between their thighs. The corpse is then placed between two fires so that it is exposed to the heat of both fires and to the sun. In a few days the skin loosens and is removed, after which the corpse is called a *grinkari*. This practice may explain why the name *grinkari* is also given to the Europeans whose skin colour, in the eyes of the blacks, is rather similar to that of a body mistreated in this manner. The blacks certainly do not flatter the whites with their appellations, comparing some with devils, others with skinned corpses.

After this, all of the openings of the body are sewn up and the whole body is rubbed down with fat and red earth. The person who does the needle work must, however, be sure that his needle-ware is in good order, for he sometimes runs a considerable risk. If the thread breaks, it is assumed that this is a sign from the deceased, indicating that the sewer was the person who enchanted him. Likewise, if his needle is not quite sharp and makes an indentation similar to that made by a blunt object when piercing the flesh, he is exposed as the guilty party.[21]

Their mythology and traditions are in many respects quite interesting.

They consider the sun to be a woman, who, when she sets, passes the dwelling places of the dead. When she approaches, the men assemble and divide into two groups, through which she passes. They invite her to stay with them, but she can only remain for a short time as she needs to prepare for the next stage of her journey. For any favour she grants she is given a red kangaroo skin and thus she appears in the morning in a red dress. The moon is also a woman, but not one like Diana – she spends much time consorting with the men and becomes thinner and thinner until she resembles a skeleton. In this state, Nurrunduri has her driven away. She flees and hides for a time, but in that time she busily searches for roots that are so nourishing that she is soon able to show herself again, becoming visibly fatter and fatter.[22]

The stars were formerly people and only leave their huts at night to do those things that they formerly did on the earth. Some are more important such as Pungngane, Waijungngari and their Ningarope. The first was born naturally, the others came into being in the following strange way. Ningarope, who had withdrawn for a natural reason, was so taken with her red excrement that she moulded it into the form of a man, and when she tickled it, it showed signs of life and laughed. Because of its colour, it thus became a Rainjani, and his mother took him into the bush with her and stayed with him.

Pungngane, his brother, had two wives and lived near the sea. Once, when he had stayed away from home for a long time, his two wives left the hut and found Waijungngari. When they approached him, he was still sleeping, and the two women returned to the hut, where they imitated the call of an emu. That woke him, and he seized his spear and jumped up to kill the emu, but when he came to the hut, the two women embraced him and asked him to remain with them as their husband. But Pungngan's mother was so enraged by this, that she told him what had happened. Pungngane, who was furious, hurried to the hut of his brother but found no one there as everyone had gone out to gather food. Extremely angry, he made a fire on the hut, but said as he did so 'Rundajan', which means something like to remain, not to burn straight away. Waijungngari returned home in the evening with his two wives, and after they lay down to sleep, the fire began to burn and soon after fell onto their covers. Waking up in fright, they cast off their covers and fled into the sea. Only here, out of danger, did Wainjungngari begin to think about how he could escape the wrath of his brother. He therefore took a spear and threw it into the sky, but it did not stick fast and fell back. Then he took a barbed spear and threw it with all his might into the sky, and this time it remained there. He used it to climb up, and his two wives followed. Pungngane, who saw his brother with his two wives in the heavens, immediately followed with his mother, and since that time they have remained there together.

To Pungngane and Waijungngari the natives also attribute their abundant supply of ponde fish and kangaroo. The former caught a ponde, tore it into small pieces and threw it back into the sea, where even the smallest piece grew into a new ponde. The latter did the same with the kangaroo.[23]

They also have a number of legends and stories about the stars. The Milky Way, they say, is a row of huts, and they claim to be able to distinguish between the ash and the rising smoke.

Unlike most other nations, they do not seem to have a story of the origin of the world. They believe that nearly all animals were once humans who performed some important act and then transformed themselves into animals or stones. On their coast the Kamingerar, for example, point out several large stones or rocks whose name and gender they identify. One rock, they say, is an old man called Lime, on which women and children are not allowed to tread. Old people, however, through their long acquaintance with him, ignore that. They claim to be able to distinguish his head, feet and hands, and also his hut and fire. The occasion on which he transformed himself was as follows: a friend of his, Palpangye, paid him a visit and brought him some *tinwarrar*, a river fish. Lime liked it very much and regretted that there was no river nearby. Palpangye, who was probably moved by this, went into the bush, fetched a large tree and thrust it into the ground in a number of places, thus creating the Inman and Hindmarsh rivers or creeks. As a sign of his gratitude, Lime gave him some kanmaris, which are small sea fish, and was so pleased that he transformed himself into a large rock in the neighbourhood of which, since then, there have always been shoals of these fish. Palpangye became a bird and is often to be found near these rivers.[24]

They tell a number of other stories about the origin of the sea, heat etc., but it will perhaps suffice here to mention the stories about the origin of rain and languages.

Near Geolina there lived an old man called Kortume with his two friends, Munkari and Waingilbe. The latter, who were much younger than Kortume, went fishing, and as they caught kuratje and kanmari, they set aside the kuratje, which were not as good, for Kortume and kept the kanmari for themselves. The old man, noticing this, began a song: *Annaitjeranangk rotjer tampatjeranangk* (in the Encounter Bay dialect it would be Ngnannangk Kuratje tampin 'for me they set aside the kuratje') whereupon it started to rain. Kortume then went into his hut and closed it with bushes so that, as punishment, Munkari and Waingilbe were forced to remain outside and get wet. The three were transformed into birds, and as soon as Kortume is to be heard, it is a sign that rain will follow.

Languages originated from a quarrelsome old woman. Long ago there lived in the east an old woman called Wurruri. She normally went out with a big stick which she used to scatter the fires while the others were sleeping. Eventually she died. The tribes, which were greatly pleased about her death, sent out messengers in all directions to spread the good news. Men, women and children came running, not to lament, but to rejoice. The Raminjerner were the first to fall upon the body and begin eating the flesh, after which they promptly began to speak intelligibly. For the other more eastern tribes, who arrived later, there was nothing left but the innards, the lung, liver etc. and they therefore spoke a slightly different language. The northern tribes, who arrived last, had to be content with the intestines and remains and therefore spoke a language that was very different from that of the Raminjerner.

All this occurred before the time of Nurunduri, on whose departure they lost the power to transform themselves and to make rivers, hills etc. As a new era commenced with Nurunduri, I will tell some of his story, in as far as it can be told.

He was an exceedingly big man who lived in the east and had two wives and several children. Once his wives ran away and he pursued them. Wherever he went, the tribes were filled with dread, as they were dwarfs in comparison. In the course of his pursuit, he came to what is now known as Freeman's Knob, where he stopped for a short while. The place was given the name Kainjenuar. Annoyed at not finding his wives, he cast two nets, called witty, into the sea. Immediately there arose two small rocky islands which are still called Wittungenggul. By stamping his feet and throwing his spear in various directions he created a number of other islands and rocky outcrops until he found his wives in Taggong. After receiving a thorough beating, the wives again managed to escape. Unwilling to embark on a second pursuit, Nurunduri ordered the sea to rise up and drown them. The two women were transformed into rocks and are still to be seen there when the tide is out.

Disgruntled and unhappy, he withdrew with his sons to the west, where he still lives, now a very old man. When he departed one of his children was sleeping and was left behind. On reaching his destination, Nurunduri noticed he was missing. Fastening a string to the end of his maralengk, he threw it back towards where he imagined his son to be. His son took hold of the maralengk and used it to find his way to his father.

This string is the line that still guides the dead to Nurunduri. When someone dies, Nurunduri's son throws the dead person the line that guided him, the dead person catches hold of it and is brought across in the same way. When he comes near, Nurunduri notices by the quivering of the line that someone is on his way and asks his son who is coming. If it is a man, the son calls all the men together and they rouse the half-conscious man with a lot of loud shouting. As soon as he comes around he sadly and silently approaches Nurunduri, who indicates where his future dwelling place will be.

If he belongs to the Encounter Bay or one of the Gortwin tribes, he is allowed to live in Nurunduri's hut, but if he is from another tribe, he is given a place further away. Before he proceeds to his allotted place, Nurunduri carefully observes his eyes. If tears flow only from one eye, it is a sign that he has left only one wife behind; if they flow from both eyes, then he has left two. If they stop flowing from one eye but continue to flow from the other, then he has left three, and Nurunduri provides him with the same number. In his company old people become young again and sick people well.[25]

The tribes of Port Lincoln have a number of other legends, but even though they have other names and events, they are all rather similar. What is evident from these various traditions is that all of these tribes believe in a life after death, even if they do not believe in reward or punishment for good or bad deeds. If they have some concept of a higher being above, then only of a benevolent one. Here on earth they maintain, in contrast, that if bad deeds are committed, punishment is quick to follow. If they die, however, no one asks how they have conducted themselves, but they are given the appropriate number of wives and can resume their old lives, just in a different place.

What all of their stories do reveal is their innate malice and treachery. Most of these legends are about murder and betrayal, and they seem faithfully to follow their example. This is not surprising given that the manner in which they marry makes it virtually impossible for them to develop a real family relationship – love is a word that they do not seem to know, even though they do have attachments. A girl is not asked if she loves the old man to whom she was promised 12 years ago; the man is not asked if he likes the old woman one of the burkas has passed on to him after living happily with her for some 20 years. The law speaks through the mouth of the elders, and the young must obey.

On my whole overland trip I heard only one story of real love between two young people, and that was something out of the ordinary. It caused quite a stir amongst the blacks, as it contravened not one, but two of their laws. A young man of the tribe of the Bameras from Lake Boni[26] had fallen in love with a girl from the Rengmutkos, one of the upper tribes, and as she shared his feelings, he fetched her one night in secret and took her downriver to his hunting grounds. But his tribe soon heard about it, and he was told to return the girl immediately to the enemy tribe. He could not disobey the orders of the burkas and therefore did what was demanded of him. He could not, however, bear being separated from the being he had grown to love even more, and two weeks later he again took her with him.

Now, however, the story took a serious turn. The elders came together to consult about what was to be done, and after thorough consideration, they agreed that such disobedience could, under no circumstances, be permitted, but that the young man, even this time, should not be punished if he followed the orders of the elders. A further transgression would, however, be punishable by death.

The two offenders were called before them and informed of their decision. The elders, having presented the enormity of the young man's offence in vivid colour and drawn his attention to the next degree of his punishment, ordered him to beat the foreign girl until she bled and chase her back to her own people.

That was a harsh sentence, and Rangan – being very fast, the young fellow was named after the emu – looked sadly at his Mattiatko. But she, knowing that he had to do as commanded, pulled her possum skin more tightly around her and fell down before him. He thereupon took his wirri and began to beat the poor woman who did not utter a word of complaint. His blows rained down on her head and shoulders and blood flowed from many places, until the elders themselves called on him to stop.

The girl was then driven from the camp and Rangan remained alone in his hut. That evening his tribe held a corrobery,[27] but he took no part in it, and the next day, when the young people went out to hunt emu, he stayed lying by his fire. When they called him to follow, he shook his head.

He remained lying there for three days, eating only what his brother brought him. On the morning of the third day, he went into the mallee hills from which he had a view of the Murray valley, or the Runneke as it is called by the Aborigines. Upstream, in the far distance, he saw two small pillars of smoke ascending – the fires from which they rose had been kept burning for him for three days.

Rangan threw his possum skin over his shoulder, took his spear and walked straight toward the smoke. With each step he sealed his fate irrevocably – when the elders of his tribe met for the third time to pass judgment on him, death was no longer a threat, but a certainty. He found his girl at the fires; the wounds caused by his wirri had not yet healed, and yet she had waited for him for three days alone by her fire. On hearing his steps, she hurried towards him and laid her head on his chest.

After everything he has heard previously, the reader may find this a bit too romantic, nevertheless it is true. The two young people left their tribes and were never heard of again.

10.

Sydney in August 1851

In Tanunda I had made the acquaintance of a Prussian ship's captain whose vessel, the *Wilhelmine*,[1] was ready to sail and bound for Manila via Sydney. Captain Franz Schmidt was a most amiable man, and, as I found out in Adelaide, we were to be in such excellent company on board that I made up my mind to travel on this ship to visit Sydney again and then to continue to Manila. From there I thought I would later have a good chance of getting to the Cape of Good Hope.

In Adelaide the gold rush had by now reached its peak; just for amusement we once set a false trail of brass cuttings for a few acquaintances, and I myself was truly shocked to see how blindly and madly people fell for it.

But the time for our departure drew closer, and on Thursday 17 July I took the so-called Mail Coach – nine-seated, two-wheeled vehicles, just like the real Mail Coaches – down to the Port. What a track! The distance is only five miles, and the whole stretch is flat. All goods have to be transported up to Adelaide on these dreadful roads, and everything exported from Adelaide has to be taken down to the Port. Traffic is also very heavy, and Adelaide still has not put in a railway line leading down there, indeed no one has even thought of one yet, and instead people make do with such tracks.

Often we got stuck in mud and water right up to the axle; for whole stretches the track was completely flooded, and in one of these spots the coachman once said very quietly, 'If I can manage to keep the left wheel out of this here hole, and if I am lucky enough to get past these tree stumps that are under water now, then I don't think we'll roll over.' That was comforting.

But we did not roll over; the coachmen have a kind of instinct that helps them to get round all the obstacles in their way, and even though we were terribly shaken up and almost all our fingernails had been ripped off – having had to grip our seats so tightly – we nevertheless reached the Port itself without any broken bones.

It is incidentally one of the most miserable ports that I have ever seen in the world, and even though ships can moor here quite safely, as at least there is no swell and they only have to contend with the wind that roars in off the plain, one can hardly imagine a dirtier and more insignificant dump than this Port Adelaide. In addition, large ships end up stuck in the mud at low tide, and if they are heavily laden and also not *very* strongly built, they can end up with a keepsake that they will never get rid of in their lifetime. What is more, Adelaide at that time only had one steam tug – I do not believe that there are any more in the meantime – and even that one was old and decrepit and constantly being repaired. There was also talk of building another port or rather a mooring place especially for larger ships further south, but as most businessmen in Adelaide also owned property in Port Adelaide, those plans still met with opposition.

After waiting for the steam tug for a number of days, we ourselves finally had to manoeuvre our way out to the open sea without it and indeed for miles, depending on how the wind blew and how we were able to use it. Once we reached the open sea, a glorious breeze favoured our voyage, which promised to be one of the most pleasant I have ever taken – and it kept its promise.

The captain was a fine, educated gentleman – and how seldom one can say that of German ships' captains – furthermore there was pleasant company among the passengers, also an excellent small library on board, chess, rubbers of whist ..., what more could we ask for?

At the beginning these pleasant times were, however, interrupted for a few days. From across the sea there came a howling gale, the waves got higher and most of our fellow passengers became increasingly pale, and their faces grew longer than would have been excusable under different circumstances. In a word, seasickness was swaying in the masts, grinning gleefully and scornfully down on the poor dismal souls creeping dejectedly across the deck.

On board we had a strange character, a miner, but the personified image of calmness and placidity – and, of course, as a necessary consequence fat and portly. On the second day the sea was still quite rough. After he had had a significant bout of seasickness, he nevertheless was audacious enough to come down for breakfast. But when he saw the greasy fried ham on the table and smelled the warm odour, he got up again very slowly and said in his low, slow voice, carefully choosing every word, 'I think I had better go back up again – otherwise I might behave indecently.'

Bodies lay in every corner, dead or half-dead, and only on the 24th, when the wind had considerably abated and the sea had calmed almost completely, because we were close to land, they came up again with their pale, exhausted faces, in order to breathe in some fresh air. But things improved very soon, and with the calmer weather, life on board also became happier and livelier.

My daily routine was quite regular. I wrote every morning until lunch; only on those days when there was a strong wind was I able to sit at my desk the whole day, because the captain had to be on deck too often near these dangerous coastlines, which did not allow him the peace and quiet for a game of chess, and, of course, I could not count on the other passengers. Once they had recovered a little, after lunch there was usually a game of chess, or we read, and in the evening we regularly sat at the whist table.

In this way time flew by, and even though we were not sailing at great speed, the last few days seemed to me more like hours, when we finally entered the beautiful Bay of Sydney (and on this occasion not during the night).

But how Sydney had changed during my short absence! When I left the place about four months previously, admittedly it was a busy city, but otherwise calm, to all appearances perfectly reasonable, a city in which not the slightest symptoms of any feverish unrest or hidden madness were discernible. Everything functioned in an orderly fashion, and even if now and then a few ambitious speakers in some anti-transportation meeting stirred up a small section of the population for a few hours, this momentary surge had already abated by tea-time in the evening, and by the next morning there was no trace of it. But what did I find now?

It will be difficult, dear reader, to give you a *clear* idea of the really incredible state of affairs in which people seemed to find themselves and how I myself felt. Have you ever found yourself, completely sober, in the company of some slightly inebriated, extremely jolly, high-spirited people, a company where everything was topsy-turvy, where the bottles lay under and the people on top of the tables, where there was singing and jubilation, where speeches were held and people yelled stories into each others' ears, without noticing that your neighbour was doing the same? Any newcomer was also expected to join in the merry-making just as merrily, and not only to work himself gradually into the highest frenzy without any preparation, but to launch himself straight into it. That is roughly how I felt on my return to Sydney. Like the witches on the Brocken mountain on Walpurgis Night dancing around the flames of the devil's light, so everyone here was dizzily, yet tirelessly, dancing around the glistening false God of the newly found gold. And the only reason why I did not think that everyone had gone mad, was because I knew why they were behaving in this way.

Wherever one turned, one heard of nothing in the whole world but dreadful stories of huge 'nuggets' (a word that was probably found with the gold and not yet in any dictionary), *cradles, licences, claims* and whatever other mysterious terms might be used.

All calculations were reduced to ounces and pennyweights, and one was not able to have a normal conversation with anyone.

'Dr, I don't know why, but I am not feeling well this morning,' I heard one of my friends say to his doctor.

'Have you heard about the huge nugget?' was the reply.

'Yes, of course, yes, of course, but do you think I have to take something?'

'Heavens no, 106 pounds Troy[2] it is said to weigh in pure gold.'

An orange vendor is pushing his cart along the street and up George Street, as if he wants to catch up with the Mail Coach.

'Hello old fellow – how much are the oranges?'

'Last load, last load, gentleman!' cries the fellow, stopping and wiping the sweat from his brow. 'Tomorrow I will be pushing something other than oranges up to Bathurst – eight for sixpence – bless your eyes, have you seen the nugget?' It is exasperating.

In George Street particularly the strangest crowds gathered. People were standing in front of jewellers' shops, marvelling at the extraordinary nuggets 40 and 50 ounces in weight, which had just been found in the Ophir Diggings and were now on display here.[3] The message was: 'Look, you can get a piece like this too – or maybe a little smaller – if you buy yourselves scales, shovels, pick-axes and all sorts of other torture tools immediately, move hundreds of miles to the mountains and start working there as if you wanted to dig yourself through to the Antipodes.

It got even better in front of the *Morning Herald* office.[4] The newspaper had just been posted there, where the newly found hundred-pound lump was described and some 20 people seemed totally unconcerned about what would happen to the rest of their bodies if they could just squash their heads into the veritable pyramid of skulls that the greedy readers of the golden report had formed around the newspaper hoarding. Whoever had not made up his mind by then, whether he should go up to the gold mines or not, was now persuaded by the three hundred pound lump and set off head over heels in order not to leave lying around the nuggets that had not yet been picked up.

Iron – who has claimed that iron has a magnetic power that allows it to have an effect across the globe? *Gold* is the magic power that is now pulsating like an evil, feverish dream across the globe, gold, the magnet to which at this moment the compass needles of the whole of Christendom are turning, and by which even the heathens have been affected, so that they leave their home and friends to suffer hardship and misery in foreign lands.

In the street it looked even livelier. Carts were being loaded in lots of places, barrels and crates at the bottom, washing and mercury equipment tied on top, and spades, shovels and pick-axes shoved in wherever there was a gap. There were always crowds of people standing around these carts; they marvelled at the equipment or envied those lucky enough who were already able to rush towards the Eldorado – the fortunate ones! Dray after dray, loaded with all sorts of useful and useless objects, pulled by emaciated oxen or horses and escorted by whole caravans of outrageously clad girls, moved up the street or stopped in front of the public houses in order to have yet another farewell drink.

But the largest crowd always gathered, when the mail, the Royal Mail, departed at 5 o'clock in the evening, packed to the gunnels with living freight. Among the crowds were not only those saying farewell (and they had a damn good reason to bid farewell to those who were putting their necks on the line on an Australian Royal Mail Coach) and well-wishers, but also throngs of the curious, who at least wanted to catch one last glimpse of those passengers who in twice 24 hours would already really be in those fabulous regions, compared with which Aladdin's lamp and Sinbad's cave were mere old armouries of discarded jewellers' work. When these people went back home afterwards, they usually did so with the firm resolution no longer literally to push their luck away, to give up any other occupation, no matter how profitable, and to set off themselves for the mines at the first opportunity.

In the meantime our ship had to undergo several repairs, which were likely to keep us here for a few weeks. For example, the foremast was to come out in order to have new bearings fitted, and the ship had to be hoisted onto the 'Patent Slip'[5] to fix a few copper plates which had come loose, because the anchor chains had become entangled. Otherwise the copper would have been scraped off even more during the voyage and would have required far more extensive repairs, apart from the fact that due to the loose copper the ship's progress would have been significantly slowed. Due to the most recent news of gold there was such a rush to the mines that the Mail, which left only three times a week – a trailer is unheard of – could not take all those who had made reservations, and people had to book their seats and pay for them up to eight to 12 days in advance.

The fare to Bathurst, approximately 138 English miles, had until now been 30 shillings or 1½ pounds sterling, but because of the hordes of passengers that wanted to be transported it rose to 2 pounds sterling 5 shillings, and when I did not immediately make a reservation on the day and came back again the next day, it had risen to 2 pounds sterling 10 shillings, and the luggage allowance was only 14 lbs. Moreover, because I had enough time here in Australia, and as I was determined to see the mines at least once and get an impression of them, I did not wish to tarry any longer and reserved a seat for the Wednesday of the following week, and so now had to bide my time until my turn came.

Meanwhile, my time in Sydney was passing quickly enough. Firstly, I had to catch up a great deal on my reports, as I had got extremely behind because of the long journey overland, during which it had been quite impossible to write even a page. And here in Sydney I was given such a warm welcome by the Germans and some English families as well that the days literally flew past.

So Wednesday came; at 5 o'clock in the evening I was in the appointed place, mindful of my earlier journey to Albury. I climbed straight up to the top of the coach, where we were sixteen adult passengers, and with the shout *All's right*, even though no one had yet secured a seat, the horses set off, and by and by we were jostled into each other.

The stagecoach, a beautiful, handsome vehicle, goes as far as Parramatta, which is 15 miles. From there to Penrith, about 18 miles further, you catch a kind of omnibus, still covered, but after that the open wagons start. The horses were awful, and the wagons likewise, and the whole journey in the cold night was a miserable affair. It was pitch dark, and so, of course, we could not see much of the surrounding area, but everywhere we saw the campfires of people walking towards the mines with provisions and equipment, sometimes clusters of five to six fires, and several times we overtook people on foot, pressing on with determination in the middle of the night and seemingly unable to wait for daylight to reach the mines – the gold.

At about 9 o'clock the next morning we met four men returning from the mines – they were having a short break in the same house where we were having breakfast. My fellow passengers pounced on them eagerly in order to coax out of them an honest account of the Eldorado. Their answers were monosyllabic, but they hinted that there was a lot of gold up there, and whoever was prepared to work hard could earn plenty of money. The money-hungry were completely satisfied with that – work, bah, what is that, that goes without saying – only gold matters. To me it sounded just like California, and I was looking forward to the result – 'Keep calm, old fellow.'

On that same morning we reached Mount Victoria, and this was the first place in Australia where I have seen real scenery of a quite impressive nature. Mount Victoria is itself a fairly significant mountain, rugged and picturesque, sloping down into a depression that surrounds it on three sides, forming a wide, deep, densely wooded valley. The vegetation is, however, the same in all other parts of Australia that I have seen so far. Gum trees, nothing but gum trees, which makes all the remaining countryside so terribly monotonous. But here, where the extensive and distant mountain ranges offer a more expansive panorama, the layers forming the backdrop all the way round take on various hues, and in this way, my friends, the gum trees are given an honourable place within the whole picture; you forget momentarily that their brothers in the distance have only decorated themselves with the sunlight and have draped themselves in colourful, misty veils, in order to give them a different and mysterious aura, but that in reality they are also just plain, dun-coloured gum trees, all with the same leaves.

The track that here crosses a deep ravine to a rocky outcrop on the other side divides the two valleys into two apparently almost equal halves. From these, down to the right, there is a pleasing view onto small scattered white houses, the homes of busy people, while on the left, the pristine, unspoilt bush stretches out in all its glorious vastness.

Did I say unspoilt? The coachman told us an anecdote of Mount Victoria that made my blood curdle. We were just passing the highest crest, which with its steep and rugged rock-face juts out far over the forest rustling below it, when he pointed to the highest peak and turning round to us said: 'That's the peak where back then the young lad threw himself off.' 'And why?' nearly everyone asked. 'Oh, it was said he wasn't quite right in the head,' remarked one of the passengers, who had been in the country for some 20 years and was more familiar with the conditions than he himself perhaps cared to admit. It was at the time when they were building the road here, and they had a young lad who was always depressed and did not want to mix with the others. Of course, they were all in shackles, deportees who had to do public work. None of them liked the young lad, he did not fit in, and the foreman sometimes gave him a few lashes when he, as he said, had his black mood, 'that hung in shreds off his back'. One morning, when he had done something wrong, I cannot remember what, and had had his due portion of lashes, he suddenly disappeared, and just where we are now, where people were working down here on the track, they suddenly saw the young man standing up there on the rocky peak. The foreman, of course, immediately called up to him to come down and start working, otherwise he would get another thrashing. The 'madman', for he certainly had to have been mad, slowly shook his head, raised his hands above his head and cried out loudly, so that we could all hear it clearly: 'God save my soul – God bless you all', threw himself off and hit the ground immediately like a sack of wool!

'And was he dead?' enquired someone.

'Dead?' the narrator said, and a great shudder went through the rough fellow's body, as in his mind's eye he probably saw again the broken body of the miserable soul.

'A while ago, two fellows fell down from this bridge here as well,' said the coachman, to let us also enjoy the second pleasant tale.

'Over the railings?' Yes – there, quite close to the railings where you can see those small bushes, the two were walking to Bathurst. Along the way they started to quarrel, and right here they began to box and wrestle with each other, until they both fell off the cliff, and one was dead right away, and the other, I believe, had only broken an arm and a leg. But he probably died later, too.

'No,' said one of the passengers, a pale, gloomy looking fellow, 'that was me.'

We all looked at the man, but at that moment the coachman whipped the horses, the track went steeply downhill, and at full gallop the animals pulled the heavy vehicle behind them down the hill, so that I thought that we would at any moment tumble head over heels down the steep slope, and then I would not have bet a single penny for our lives. But we were lucky, arrived at the bottom unscathed and changed horses in the valley.

The track now resembled a road through a fair – wagons everywhere, now drawn by horses, now by oxen, but everywhere heavily laden with luggage and with droves of people in front and behind, strolling towards the mines and thus, as they thought, towards their fortune. Here and there we still found campfires along the track, where the caravans had not left early, or individual drovers had gone into the forests to muster the scattered animals. In other spots the burnt out fires were still smouldering, and on the way we met and overtook hordes of heavily burdened men and often women, even some with children on their backs. The weather was fine and clear; people seemed to be in the best of moods and full of the highest hopes.

In the afternoon, when we hit a stretch of the track that was very bad, with the two right wheels we ran over a root sticking up in the middle of the ruts, and something on the vehicle cracked. The coachman got off and checked the wheels and springs, but everything seemed to be in good order, or rather it was so covered with dirt that nothing was visible. He got back on again, whipped the horses, and we galloped down the steep, bumpy mountain. When we reached the bottom, the shaft fell off the crossbar – which had probably buckled when we ran over the aforementioned root and had only held so long to do us a favour, and we now had to walk almost to the next stagecoach stop. Had it fallen off along the way on the mountain slope, we would have broken arms and legs.

In the evening some time after sunset we reached Bathurst and put up at the Royal Hotel with Mrs Black. There was hardly a room to be had; all the inns were full. I heard, too, that the Mail Coach that was going up to the mines the next morning was also fully booked, and I soon decided to walk the rest of the way – only about 28 miles.

The conversations in the hotel in Bathurst were exclusively about the gold that had been and was still to be found, and however much I was disgusted by the subject matter, at the same time, the often genuinely crazy opinions of individuals were of interest to me. I was particularly interested in an English Jew, who in the most mysterious manner talked about veritable mountains of gold that he had himself discovered and that were unknown to anyone else, and around which he could simply pick up diamonds and other precious stones.

Those around him listened to him with open mouths in the true sense of the word, and he crowned his whole tale with a few pieces of gold that he passed around. These people were not just talking about ounces and pounds, but of hundredweights, and the best thing of all was that everyone took it seriously.

I took my glass of brandy hot and afterwards went quietly to bed. I had a considerable journey on foot ahead of me the next day and knew only too well what sort of exertions and discomfort awaited me. But I was also determined to stay up there as long as it took me to gain an overview of the whole business and not to get bogged down in work again, as indeed I had done in California.

With two of my fellow passengers on the Royal Mail – I should really call them my fellow sufferers – I set off for the mines the next morning; the track was bleak and there was little traffic, because the main and nearest track to the mines in the interior did not go via Bathurst. Nevertheless we overtook many heavily laden drays heading to the mountains, and we could have reached the Turon soon enough, had my two companions not been such dreadfully bad walkers. One of them in particular was a fat little man, and no matter how quickly his own weight propelled him downhill, with him always sighing deeply, he lagged behind all the more whenever the track was barely even. When the track went uphill again, the two of us had to wait for up to a quarter of an hour time and time again before he reappeared. Later we left him behind completely, and I never saw him again.

Similarly my other companion at first seemed rather corpulent with just a somewhat lean face. His forehead, however, was constantly covered in large beads of sweat, and he suddenly announced he could not walk any further until he had taken off 'a few of his shirts'. A few of his shirts? I looked at the fellow in amazement, but he was being quite serious, threw down a couple of thick blankets he was carrying tightly rolled up on his back, and took off three – and I mean three – woollen shirts, while he still, as he assured me, kept on only two, a woollen over-shirt and a flannel shirt (probably with a few more vests underneath). Of his trousers, of which he was wearing three woollen pairs and a pair of underpants, he did not want to remove any, in order not to catch cold, but he took off a few pairs of stockings and socks and only kept on a pair of woollen stockings and a pair of cotton ones. He also took off the woollen scarf he had been wearing round his neck. The man started to get really thin, and I am quite convinced that, if he took off the rest of the quarter and half dozen shirts and trousers as well, he would no longer have cast a shadow.

That night we camped in the mountains, where we found only a few invariably muddy waterholes here and there and not one single flowing creek, in order to brew at least a quart-size pot of tea from a small puddle. The next morning soon after dawn we reached the Turon.[6]

We had already passed a few small, deep creeks in which I heard the rattle of gold-panning equipment, but they did not contain any running water either, only stagnant waterholes. I did not want to waste any time climbing down into them and decided to do so on my return. What is more, when I descended the last slope that still separated me from the Turon, I found all my expectations fulfilled and all my fears confirmed. It was the same hustle and bustle, the same searching and grabbing, the same success and the same delusions as in California, only the countryside was more desolate and the difficulties in panning and working even greater, as it appeared to me then.

So this was the Turon, towards which thousands of people were feverishly heading as if to an Eldorado. This was the place that seemed bathed in a golden light to all those running around there, the place where their boldest dreams and expectations were to be fulfilled? You poor people, I felt extremely sorry for you at that moment, and I walked down the mountain with much lighter steps, because I was not one of you and would be able to bid farewell to this dreadful place soon, indeed very soon.

But it cannot have been all that promising with this Eldorado, for to my amazement I saw veritable droves of 'miners', with their scales and tools on their backs, making their way down the Turon, and as some of them I talked to told me, they were heading for other newly discovered mines. 'But along the Turon the mines are said to be so productive,' I responded. 'Yes, certain spots are quite good,' came the answer, 'and some have made good money here, but too many are coming here, and in many places there is too much water, in others too little. You don't want to do *such* work just for a meagre day's wage, and we just want to find out if it's any better at the "World's End".'[7]

For the new diggings are in a place that is funnily enough called 'the World's End', and I saw hundreds streaming there in the strangest and also sometimes the drabbest outfits in order truly to find there finally the fortune which they had looked for in vain on the Turon. They may indeed find it at the end of the world.

Now it is actually the same in California; people there also move tirelessly from one gully to the next. Where 50 people arrive, they most certainly also meet 50 who are leaving, until everyone has found the spot where he believes his work will pay off, so that he can finally leave the mines again. Here, however, it seemed a little premature to me, for the newspapers – oh, the newspapers! – had said people up there were not content even when they found one ounce a day. *Only* an ounce! I had been in California too long not to know what it means to find an ounce a day and how few people are capable of doing that for weeks. I also found out very soon that I had not been in the least wrong in my expectations regarding the local mines, and that they did not at all deserve, just like the Californian ones, those descriptions and tales of the Thousand-and-One-Nights variety.

As in California, it was certainly hard work and the reward uncertain, and the number of unhappy people infinitely outweighed the number of happy ones. However, there are a very few points along the Turon that pay those working there extremely well. At the so-called '*golden point*' individual parties have literally panned their fortunes. Although individual parties have done extremely well, and their fortune was of course trumpeted around the world by very interested merchants and traders, others in contrast – and they were in the vast majority – worked close by and barely earned their daily wage, while hundreds move up and down the river, starting and stopping again here and there, because they cannot earn their daily wage at all or only barely. After all, they had not come here to live like dogs and to earn the same as they would have if they had stayed in Sydney and thereby had a decent life. Many simply made up their minds to go back to Sydney, while there was still time and work was in demand there. Others assured me that they were going to continue watching the situation, 'they hoped they would at some point make a lucky strike', and others in contrast said that they would under no circumstances return to their old life until they had at least extracted as much as they had brought with them or had borrowed. That is how much they had lowered their expectations. All of this is *not* reported in the Australian newspapers; they only highlight the positive elements of the picture and their purpose and goal is easily recognisable. They want people to come to Australia, *workers*, and those that could not be enticed by the pamphlets on emigration that had hitherto been distributed by the English; it was to those that the gold was supposed to give the final coup de grâce. Without fail they will reach their goal, immigrants will arrive in droves, and not only will and must labour become cheaper, but they can also bring over in masses the workers that are so much in demand now. But will *these people* later be *contented?* Australians, however, are not interested in that; they need shepherds and watchmen for buildings and cattle, herdsmen and winegrowers, gardeners, farmers and road builders, and it stands to reason that they will use the opportunity to bring such people here. The Government, of course, supports that as much as it can, because it holds the purse strings and draws a huge and always secure income from its licences. The more workers the Government gets into the mines, the more workers have to pay it 30 shillings a month. And even if those are worked into the ground or leave the mines totally exhausted, there is a constant supply of good workers. 'The worker bees have to work,' say the Russians, and those who have hitherto worked as miners, if they do not want to starve as soon as they are unable to earn any more in the mines, also have to work as shepherds and the like, and then, when all the jobs are taken, for any wage at all.

A certain Mr Hargreaves,[8] who discovered the gold in Australia, is now travelling all over the country and is looking for and also finding new places. In this way the mines and the imagination of the gold addicts are kept in constant excitement. The wildest rumours cannot be exciting enough; people believe them, and, to top it all, the whole picture is then enhanced with fabulous veins of gold in quartzite, with diamonds, rubies and platinum. Even up in the mines, in feverish excitement they whisper mysterious hints to each other, steal off under cover of darkness with their tools and provisions, walk and climb across the steep mountains, panting as they go, to begin the same work, perhaps with the same success, in a different mountain valley.

And do the mines really yield as much as reported? asks the reader. Yes and no. Isolated spots do indeed, but on the whole the gold lies too scattered, and panning it is more difficult and less rewarding than in equally rich areas in California. For the gold is not to be found just under a shallow layer of earth, on rocks and on clay like in California, or in the lower layers of soil, which are mixed with clay and gravel, but it is found at the top, even in loose topsoil, albeit mostly in quantities too small to make panning worthwhile. Up there from the summit of the mountain ridge I saw people digging up the earth to a depth of six to seven inches and dragging it to the nearest water, which was enough to earn a day's wage. This sounds very encouraging to someone who is not sufficiently familiar with the work involved, however, the big drawback is that the gold is too scattered, and it is not worth panning *all* of the soil in order to extract the little amount of gold in it. Incidentally, this also seems to be proof of the young age of the country: the heavy gold has not had time, as in California, to settle in the ground and lies scattered throughout all of the light soil. It is certain that there are isolated spots, and those are mainly found in the river bars and probably in the riverbeds themselves, which are very rich in gold, and from which even later a great deal of gold can be extracted. Some individuals will still strike it lucky there and make their fortune in a short time, but how many thousands will try their luck and will draw blanks! How many thousands leave their homes and businesses to try their luck at gold panning and do not even earn enough to manage to get back to their home and business? No, whoever wants to emigrate here for the sake of gold panning, should say from the beginning: 'I am still young and want to live an adventurous life for a few years, even if in the worst case I do very badly and I cannot earn anything; *perhaps* I will still strike it lucky and get to see a little of the world to boot.' A *young* man may risk it in *this* sense, but somebody who does not have many more years to waste should really think about it very carefully, before he tries his luck or misfortune in the mines.

But enough, more than enough, about who should go digging or not. Everything that has been said about this with reference to California applies here as well. And if it really were not to tire the reader – I do not believe it would – to hear the whole story again, I can completely assure him, I would dig for another month – and I do not normally commit myself so easily – before I would repeat all the advice and arguments from the beginning, even if only fleetingly.

I will only mention how the Australian mines differ from the Californian ones, because such small characteristics always present various interesting details.

The reader will forgive me for not describing the mines themselves, tents, shops, panning sites etc. I described all that when I was in California, and there is no significant difference here. English flags fly above a few shop-tents instead of the 'Stars and Stripes' in California, and on the whole there you see more blue woollen shirts than red ones. Otherwise it was the same old hustle and bustle, and yet in some respect, especially regarding personalities, it was so different from the latter that at first sight one could almost not help shouting out: these here are the English, those are the Americans.

There is a very sensible law for the mines, which, by the way, lends the campsites quite a different character than in California, where the very drinking tents form the inner core of all the small mining towns. A law which here in Australia totally prohibits the sale of liquor forbids the setting up of gaming tables, which in California have led to such infinite misery and to so much bloodshed. Of course, this law, at least the first, is dealt with in the same way as those that are only passed by some government – they are breached, and there are said to be many places where liquor is sold secretly. However, once the liquor is in people's heads, it can no longer be kept secret very easily and thus, particularly on Sundays, a group of drunks or at least tipsy men stagger around, in whom the effect is easily recognisable, but the source is not

Sydney in August 1851

revealed. To the horror of the clergy and the *pious* Englishmen generally, a most annoying incident had taken place the previous Sunday. While a clergyman had a small flock of his *sheep* congregated around him near Oakey Creek and was preaching 'God's Word in the Desert' to them, close by, a very large herd of rams gathered around two prize fighters, who were merrily punching each other. Later, small private disputes brought the Sunday diversions to an end.

A lot more wheeling and dealing goes on with the gold itself up here in the mines; people are more nervous about it here than in the mountains of California. There is hardly any form of currency other than the gold dust itself. Anything you buy is paid for in original gold, and every Real, equivalent to sixpence here, is thrown onto the scales and is weighed, whereby a great deal of the gold is lost. Here the miner very rarely has his own scales, which in California can be found in almost every tent, but he goes to the shop and has the gold that he found weighed there, and if he wants to buy something, he first *sells* his gold for cash and then pays for the goods with the money.

Another thing that the Californian dealer rejects struck me here: the breaking up of the smallest pieces, which were thought to contain only the tiniest amount of quartzite. The dealers put the gold on a large weight or a piece of iron and smash it with a hammer, so that the quartzite sprays out of it. Of course, in this way many fine gold slivers are lost to the miner, and that means they land in the dealer's pocket, because he can later wash out the soil on the tent floor around the piece of iron and can retrieve them all.

I met several acquaintances in the mines, fellow passengers from Adelaide, most of whom had been up here for a week, but nobody had found anything significant or had even been paid for his work, while several of them talked about going back soon; some had in fact already left and were on the way to Sydney.

A number of these individuals were also attracted by the newly discovered and highly praised mines at World's End, but I tried to dissuade them as best as I could. I assured them that, based on my experience in California, they would very shortly hear of newly discovered, extremely rich mines, here and there, and if they were always to follow each lead immediately, then they would simply be moving back and forth across the country, and if they really earned something in one spot, they would surely lose it again on the next venture. Some of them I managed to dissuade, because however uncertain the work in the mines is, someone who duly sticks to one place and works day after day can indeed expect at least an average yield. Others, however, could not be talked out of believing that the fortune destined for them was located at the 'World's End' and set off. I am convinced that on that one day more than three hundred people left the Turon with all their belongings, in order to go on to Louise's Creek, as the area at the end of the world is known. But a few sold all their tools and left the mines altogether.

The next morning I walked a bit further up the creek and was particularly interested in the peculiar method of processing in these mines, where in many places people carried soil from the summit of the hills down to the water and panned it there. But that was a rather tiring activity and, as everybody told me, did not yield a day's wage.

At any rate the government derives the greatest benefits from these mines. First of all, in spite of the much praised Australian honesty, people do not consider the streets to be entirely safe, because almost all the gold is transported to Sydney under police cover. On that matter, the government covers any loss, except, oddly enough, when the mail is held up and robbed, which, however, would be an extremely audacious and dangerous undertaking, given the strong protection and the busy roads. Secondly, the government gets its enormous revenue from the digging permits. Thirdly, the most important and permanent advantage of all is the considerable immigration, which must in the end prove to be a blessing for the country, no matter how the gold yield turns out.

The licence costs 30 shillings a month. A month starts, however, on the first day, and when workers arrive at the mines on the 10th, 15th or even 20th of a month, they still have to pay the whole amount even for the few working days, unless they want to be idle for one or two weeks and then want to live off the same amount as the licence would cost. That is indeed grossly unfair. But even more power lies in the hands of the Commissioner, who seems to have unlimited authority here. The miner may be able to work anywhere with this licence, but if he chooses a spot on the bank of a little river or creek, it is again at the discretion of the Commissioner how many feet up or down the creek he allocates to the miner – because in the direction of the hills the miner can go up as far as he likes. The norm is six feet per man, but in more productive spots – and whoever has worked in the mines knows how unreliable the term is – the Commissioner allows only four feet, in other less productive ones, eight and ten. It is completely up to him to favour those to whom he is well disposed, and that can only be at the neighbours' expense. I hope that in time these arbitrary practices will be changed.

In California it was similar, with digging permits being issued, and the money for these was also collected by government officials. But there the whole business was not policed to the same extent as it was here, and indeed there was not so much concern about trifles, such as the Commissioner on the Turon, for example, personally hauling back fellows who wanted to avoid paying by absconding. Nevertheless, here again no distinction was made between Englishmen and 'foreigners', which in California had been and still is the cause of so much trouble. Here *everyone* who wanted to dig for precious metals was equal in the eyes of the law, that is, the Government took its 30 shillings from *everyone* without exception.

There were, incidentally, not many foreigners here at all, and at first glance one was able to recognise the entirely English and Irish population, among whom only a few Germans and French were the exceptions, and there were no Americans at all, I believe. I saw a large number of ghoulish faces gathered here, the likes of which I have truly never seen in any other place in the world, not even in California, which says a great deal. And yet that mixture of nationalities, which made life in the Californian goldfields so interesting, was completely missing here, while in the same way the scant tree cover, namely the dull, green gum trees, did not serve to lend the whole a livelier ambience.

The English, meanwhile, constantly tried to emphasise honesty and order, which according to them existed here in Australia in contrast to California, where at precisely that time the *Vigilance Committee* had formed.[9] It was reported everywhere in the newspapers that 'it was so safe that one could leave whatever one wanted outside the tent during the night'. I have nothing against that, but the question is whether one would find it again in the morning. Even then there were thefts, which seemed to have increased to such an extent that even the Australian newspapers are discussing the possibility of introducing an anti-lynching law.

Even during the short time that I was in the goldfields, a German trader and gold merchant had his tent slit open just after dark, and an amount of approximately 600 pounds sterling in gold, silver and banknotes was taken. In several places equipment and articles of clothing were stolen, so that several miners I talked to decided not to leave their tents unattended while they were at work, but to leave a hut keeper or guard there. That was never necessary in any place I visited in California, and I saw quite a large number of the mines there. There is something else that does not support the so highly praised Australian honesty either. The merchants who take the gold from the mines to the city earn a significant percentage from it, because the roads are dangerous, and therefore a large number of armed policemen always accompany the gold transports, as individuals do not dare to carry the gold with them. In California the gold in the most remote mines has the same value as in San Francisco, and it does not occur to anybody to spend money on a safe transport of gold to the city.

But I soon got tired of the whole thing, rolled up my blanket and walked back in the direction of Sydney, happy to have escaped the awful, messy business of the mines so quickly. Before that I visited some of the neighbouring creeks, none of which had water running in them, but where the miners panned at individual waterholes and had to carry the soil down to them to do so. Here and there they climbed over the rocks to look for small pieces of gold in between, and some of them would have made a tidy profit from it on the whole, but it is a highly insecure occupation. Many also left these creeks and either went over to the Turon or moved on into the hills to find other mines.

On the same day I left the mines, I made it to Bathurst, and the bush up here in the hills looked somewhat friendlier in some places, as the bushes were starting to flower. In particular the pleasant smelling yellow wattle, a type of acacia, made some areas look more garden-like. Although I walked at a brisk pace, I only reached the small Bathurst River about an hour after sunset, in other words in total darkness. The river is fairly shallow in a few places but also has deep holes in others, and as I had soon lost the road, which branched off in various directions when it came down into the valley, and as I was able to keep my direction only with the help of the lights of Bathurst shining through the darkness, I was, of course, not able to find a ford in this pitch-black darkness. I crawled back and forth along the very steep banks – almost falling down twice – until I finally grew annoyed, and my increasing hunger did not help matters. Taking my chances, I jumped down into the dark river. I had become rather immune to being wet, as I had lain in the rain all night. Now I was fully expecting that I would have to swim, but I found myself in only three feet of water and reached the other side safely. Here I shook off the water and was soon sitting in the Royal Hotel in front of a good dinner. Here I heard the good news that there was not a seat left on the Mail Coach to Sydney in the next two weeks, and I was faced with the prospect of having to walk the whole dreadful way.

But it turned out to be not as bad as I feared. Luckily on the Mail Coach the following day there was a seat that had been reserved but not paid for. I availed myself of it immediately, and the next morning I was already rattling toward the distant capital. I will only mention here in passing that about four or six miles from Penrith, and luckily in a sandy spot, for otherwise we would all have broken our neck, we rolled over. Missing only a coat, stolen from the coach in Penrith while I was taking one of the passengers injured in the accident into a house, I arrived back in Sydney the next morning.

In Sydney the *Wilhelmine*'s foremast had been removed, and the ship looked more like a wreck than a brave, seaworthy vessel. Therefore there was no chance at all of sailing within the next fourteen days. Moreover, the ship's destination had been altered; there was very bad news from Manila regarding the sugar crop. The news from Batavia, however, was much better, and as Captain Smith[10] was free to take the ship wherever he thought best, he decided to head for the latter port. To me it did not matter at all, indeed it was preferable to Manila, firstly because I knew that there would be letters from home waiting for me in Batavia, and secondly, it would also shorten my later voyage to the Cape by about 40 degrees of latitude, not insignificant. I did not mind staying longer in Sydney either – I had found many dear friends there, and the altogether exciting life, which at that time affected the whole of Australia, was most appealing to the foreigner.

At that time the still fermenting enmity – and probably also envy – against North America was once more erupting in Sydney. Only a few days earlier a ship from there had arrived, and its captain, a Mr Harris, published an explosive article in the *Morning Herald*, in which he urged England to declare war on the Americans *via California*. It concerned the anti-lynching law, in particular the *Vigilance Committee*, which the Americans had again put into practice against individual *'Sidney coves'* and under which *'poor Capt. Harris'*, as he was soon referred to all over the city, had had to suffer quite innocently.

During the most recent fire[11] this English captain, according to his account, left his ship in order to help save lives and extinguish the fire; at the market he had, however, called on a Yankee, who was lazily strolling about, to work, and perhaps the captain's tone was slightly harsh. This Yankee answered him rudely and hinted that the foreigner, whom he may have recognised as an Englishman because of his accent, was ultimately himself to blame for the fire and for that very reason was now helping. These words ignited the soul of the bystanders; once the rumour had reached the third person, he no longer knew what it was all about and what had happened, he only heard that somebody was being accused of arson – perhaps all his belongings had at this very moment been reduced to ashes – and the Englishman suddenly found himself seized and dragged away. Where to? The crowd was watching the excitement and hearing only that one of the arsonists had been apprehended, naturally shouted, 'string him up on the nearest lamp-post', because they felt their own necks were safe enough in all of this. And it stands to reason that in such times, especially when there was a fire in the city, such a suspected villain was not given much opportunity for defending himself. The 'charming rabble' is not any better in American states than in any others. The *Vigilance Committee*, however, took the man into their custody, once the more sensible ones had gained the upper hand, and, of course, allowed him to have a proper interrogation, during which it quickly emerged that he had been erroneously apprehended. He was immediately released and assured of every possible compensation currently available. The Californian newspapers, however, for fear of the *Vigilance Committee* did not want to publish this letter, at least that is what Captain Harris claimed, and that would, of course, reflect badly on the free American press. Who knows what further details had been added to the story, and naturally Captain Harris told the story from *his* point of view.

Captain Harris now presented his story in chapter and verse to the Australian newspapers, which immediately made a real hue and cry about it and above all emphasised one fact, which again gave the whole affair a rather comical touch. For when he was seized by the rabble and dragged before the court, he maintained that he had either lost his watch or had been robbed thereof. Finally acquitted, he had demanded a replacement for his watch, but the one they offered him cannot have been as good as his own, or he had also asked for compensation – one could not quite make head or tail of the whole story. In brief, he emerged without a watch, and the *Morning Herald* made a real song and dance about it and demanded of England that it view the affair as a *casus belli* and equip and send an expedition to America, so that honour would be restored to England and the watch to Captain Harris.

The excitement regarding all Americans was so dreadful that I would not have wished to advise any of them to show their face in the Australian goldfields, because their life would have been at risk. People here were really appalled by the lynching law and the Californians, who for their part had not paid any compliments to the Sydney-siders when they implemented it. In fact, they all showed the delightful inclination to follow their example. It would surprise me if that had not already happened.

One simply cannot accept with cold detachment the view of people who take such measures and who in the end, when pushed to the limit, assume the right to defend themselves and to crush under their feet the enemy, with whom they could not deal in any other way. One has to consider the permanent state of agitation in which the inhabitants of San Francisco found themselves due to the constant fire alarms and ultimately the conflagrations themselves, which each time reduced half the city to ashes. I know myself the kind of nervous state I found myself in when there was a fire alarm in the evening when I was in San Francisco, and I had nothing to lose. I am convinced I would then without the slightest hesitation have given my consent to such a lynching verdict against a captured murderer and incendiary – and would do so even now.

The citizens of San Francisco were only able to rid themselves illegally of the judges whom they had recognised as incompetent, so as to control the increasing number of misdeeds such as arson and robberies. But when they could no longer bear the circumstances they were in, and for once an illegal act *had* to be committed, then it was also better to attack the evil at its root and to show this unworthy lot that they could no longer count on corrupt judges and rogue lawyers to protect them from a well deserved punishment. I am also convinced that a few such extempore courts will be much more beneficial for the peace and safety of the city than 20 criminals legally incarcerated for any number of years.

The Americans, incidentally, must not only blame the English or preferably the Australians to have sent masses of criminals and rotten characters to California. The worst riff-raff in the whole of California are the public gamblers, and they are *all* American, with the exception of a few Spaniards. This is a gang of criminals who have all moved from the Mississippi and the southern states – Arkansas, Louisiana and Texas – to California, where they have procured rich takings from their deeds. These characters were never short of travel money, for when they were not able to procure it legally or did not already have it, no means were disreputable enough to procure it. With these principles in mind, they went to California, determined to strike it rich there, with no regard to the way they obtained it, as long as it did not involve hard, honest work.

The Americans are right not to be happy about the influx of this sort of people, who were also sent over from Australia, as the English thieves most certainly tried particularly hard to keep up with their American brothers in pursuing their business. But there is still enough of the riff-raff here in Australia. By the way, later, when I was already back in Germany, I had the opportunity of talking to several German members of the *Vigilance Committee*. Regarding the special case of Captain Harris, they informed me that the man had been found in a place where he should not have been, and it seemed that he was a little under the influence, but also that his accent had suggested he was an Englishman, and he had been taken unfairly for one of the arsonists by the ever suspicious crowd, whereas he later turned out to have bravely helped to extinguish the fire. The rabble, however, had taken him prisoner and might even have hanged him, if the *Vigilance Committee* had not fortunately turned up and freed him.[12]

At this time we had the most peculiar situation in Sydney, when actors took their leave of the audience, as it were, not in order to take up another engagement or to leave the stage altogether, but in fact to go up to the goldfields. For the farewell performance of these actors, the final appearance of Messrs F. and J. Howson and Hydes and the performance of the opera *The Enchantress* by Balfe[13] was announced in the Royal Victorian Theatre '*under the distinguished patronage of His Excellency the Governor General, General Sir Charles Augustus FitzRoy K.C.H. and the Honourable Mrs Keith Steward*', as the programme stated.[14]

The performance on this evening was particularly ceremonious due to the presence of the Governor-General and his charming daughter, Mrs Keith Stewart, and as both of them entered their box, the whole of the so-called dress circle rose; the ladies were in ball dresses, and the orchestra began to play *God Save the Queen*. After the first verse, which was also sung by many from the stalls, the audience sat down, the curtain rose, all the actors were on stage in costume, and three female singers sang the whole anthem, each time accompanied by the entire choir.

As strange as the custom is to give such a loyal demonstration in costume before a performance – especially when the members of the company, as in this case, are almost all portraying pirates – every national anthem, particularly the English anthem, has a deep but also painful effect on me.

There is something beautiful, something solemn about a national song, where an entire nation expresses its unity and its strength in *one* pure chord. The American *Yankee Doodle* moved and gripped me in the same way, even if its melody sounds wild and cheeky, even absurd and tasteless to some people. It is after all the national anthem of a powerful nation, whose forefathers went into battle full of enthusiasm to the tune of this same *Yankee Doodle*, in order to fight for freedom and human rights for themselves and their children. Even the Russian anthem would have the same effect on me, if I heard it sung jubilantly by the people, but it is only with the English anthem that I am overcome by a melancholy feeling that a *German*, Haydn, composed it.[15] Not for Germany, no, he wrote this sacred melody for a foreign nation – we Germans do not need a national anthem – after all, we are not a nation, and it really is a reason to despair that we have to envy even the Chinese for the highest good – that of having a Fatherland.

The opera itself went very well, although surprisingly we do not yet find it in German theatres, for it has very pretty arias and choruses. Admittedly some pieces were dreadfully mistreated, but the main part, the 'enchantress' herself, was sung by a Miss Sarah Flower, and so outstandingly that she would cause a sensation in the top theatres in Germany.[16] Miss Flower had a wonderful alto voice, which admittedly was said to have suffered a little from – brandy. There were really some charming anecdotes told about her. On one occasion at a large social gathering, after some artistic excitement, she is said to have lain down on a sofa full of ladies' hats and to have squashed their shape 'into the middle of next week', which is quite believable given her robust figure and her healthy complexion. The horror of the ladies may have been extreme. Be that as it may, she sings beautifully, and on stage she is very pleasant to look at.

Before I conclude my account of the theatre, I cannot help giving the reader a brief outline of the 'Freischutz', as was to be read in the English programme, which spurned the 'ü'; we would not be German, if we were not interested in the 'Freischütz' and, what is more, particularly the 'Freischütz in Australia'.[17]

'Thursday, 7 August, Der Freischutz!' The reader can imagine that I was looking forward to the evening. How long had it been since I had heard a

German opera! And now I was to find it again here in the Antipodes. The Captain of the *Wilhelmine*, F. Schmidt, and I went early enough in order not to miss the overture, and the orchestra started to play just as we had taken our seats. But how sad! The most glorious overture was being maltreated in a truly blasphemous, Samielian[18] manner, and a few times I could hardly recognise the melody. At last the curtain rose. There was a target set up on the stage, all the marksmen were positioned on the left. Max was the first to take aim and missed, then two other huntsmen and finally Kilian, upon which something fell from the target, and so he had made the masterly shot. Max, by the way, wandered cheerfully among them, until finally the mocking choir annoyed him etc.

Max's and Caspar's arias (I have to mention here in passing that the names had also been changed: Max was called Rodolph, Agathe was called Linda, and Annchen was called Rose), in other words, Rodolph's and Caspar's arias went quite well, and I became rather emotional. The dear old melodies evoked such old and familiar memories in me, and I could have listened to the familiar tunes for hours. It was Samiel who first brought me back to the Australian stage; during Max's aria he appeared close behind him in a flash of Bengal fireworks – even if Max did not really see him, he should have smelled him – but disappeared at the exclamation: 'Is there no God?', at which Max carefully knelt down in such a charming manner that I was really surprised. For he threw himself to the ground and immediately disappeared into it. The hole in the stage was covered with grey material, and through a slit in this he flung himself out of sight in a flash.

Except for a few insignificant changes, the second act began in the same manner as in Germany. Agathe and Annchen sang and played their roles fairly well. Only one thing annoyed me a little at the beginning of their songs: Annchen, although gifted with quite a pleasant voice, always came in half a beat late in the ensembles and in her solos, but the orchestra soon adapted to her and we simply finished a little later. But before Max appeared, Kilian approached the young ladies (Kilian was more of a jester and ran about throughout the whole play) and told them jokingly that not Max, but *he* himself had made the masterly shot. They were most astonished about this, and Kilian went off. Now came Agathe's famous aria, which she sang quite well, but the orchestra's accompaniment was miserable. 'It is he, it is he, let the banner of love fly!' Max entered; hearty welcome, abundant joy on both sides. The orchestra plays a few passages never before heard in the *Freischütz*, Max takes Agathe's hand and leads her to the front, and – 'was it perhaps once, was it perhaps twice, was it perhaps once or twice, that you were unfaithful, my bonny sweetheart, please think about this a wee bit!' I felt as if somebody had poured a bucket of cold water over my head without warning. 'The Viennese in Berlin!' shouted the Captain, 'Upon my oath!' And he looked at me with such a comical, melancholy expression that I could no longer contain myself; I burst out laughing and had to leave the box in order to somehow pull myself together again outside.

The Wolf's Glen[19] was done quite well, and I have seen it done much worse in many smaller and larger theatres in Germany. The only problem was that the devils made such a loud noise that Caspar was only able to cast six magic bullets; in any case, immediately after the sixth bullet the curtain fell, and I assume that he cast the seventh afterwards.

The audience, by the way, was delighted, and in the next interval a very lively discussion developed between the upper circle and the stalls, conducted partly with the help of gesticulations and half-articulated screams, partly with orange peels.

After the Wolf's Glen came a most peculiar scene. Unless I am greatly mistaken, the moralising Christian sense of the English has been introduced into this demoniacal German spectre in a piously childish manner. The head forester, Caspar, Kilian and the other huntsmen are sitting in the hall. Just like Punch in the Punch and Judy show, Kilian keeps trying to tell a long story, which begins with, 'Once upon a time there was a King', but is not allowed to continue. The head forester now announces that he can only remember *one* such night like the previous one, and it was the one in which once upon a time a godless young hunter had cast seven magic bullets with Satan. He still remembered the way the hunter looked the next morning: pale cheeks, hollow eyes. He looks at Caspar and recoils in horror; the same dreadful person is standing before him! Caspar becomes furious, but the head forester calms him down, reminds him of how kindly disposed he has always been towards him and then kneels down in front of him and pleads with him to become a good person again in the name of God. Caspar is moved and allows his gun to be taken from him. At this moment Samiel appears among them, but this time without the Bengal fireworks, and reports to Caspar that he is hopelessly devoted to him. Nevertheless, once Samiel has disappeared again, Caspar wants to make one last desperate attempt, and with the old head forester goes toward the chapel, which is now open in the background. However, on its threshold the enemy re-appears and, laughing scornfully, pushes him back. Caspar is *'a gone chicken'*.

Then comes the scene with Caspar and Max. But, amazingly, Max has two bullets left and hands them to Caspar. Then Max sings a very jolly hunting song, which ends with a chorus from the hunting choir; then the hunting choir sings on its own, and after that comes the test shot. Agathe then appears before the shot but does not assure us that she is the dove, and altogether there is such dreadful confusion that I certainly would not have been able to make head or tail of it all, if I had not already known the plot.

After the shot Caspar entered and collapsed but recovered immediately and took a great deal of interest in Agathe, shown by his singing sincerely with the choir, 'She lives', in spite of his bullet wound and still lying on the ground. But Samiel at once put an end to all of this. He came on, went up to Caspar, seized him by the chest, dragged him to the nearest hole in the stage and disappeared with him. Incidentally there was no hermit; Max simply declared that Caspar had led him astray in the whole business, and it was in no way his fault, and since everyone believed his every word, there was nothing to prevent him from immediately becoming engaged to Agathe or Linda.

In the meantime the weather had changed, and it had begun to rain in earnest, and soon after that there was news from the goldfields that there were a few inches of snow up there, that the tracks were bogged, and that business for the miners was bad at the moment. Nevertheless there was still a constant stream of people going to the mines, and every new piece of gold that was found also claimed new victims.

Meanwhile the *Wilhelmine* was to take on board 40 cattle after mast and rigging were back in working order; ballast and hay also had to be loaded, and it goes without saying that the men were very busy from morning to night. Every now and then in the evening they went ashore and on such occasions had the captain pay them small amounts of their due wages. They also had been treated very well on the ship, both by the captain and the officers, from whom I had not once throughout the whole voyage heard a rough word. The food left nothing to be desired either, so that it did not seem likely that they would leave such a good ship in order to rush up to the goldfields, particularly at this time of year. But gold is a powerful magnet, and one morning – it was a Monday and we thought we would be ready to sail in four to five days – the steward came into the cabin early and announced: 'The entire crew has run away.'

In fact the entire crew was *not* gone, for individuals such as the carpenter, the cook and two of the men had stayed behind, but nine of them had in fact done a runner during the night from Sunday to Monday and had left us high and dry. The captain immediately reported it to the 'harbour constabulary' and offered a reward for recapturing the men. The officers assured him that he would get his men back soon, as none of them spoke any English, and they would all easily be betrayed by the innkeepers, into whose hands they were bound to fall. That was all that could be done, and the chances of setting sail soon had diminished considerably, as sailors could hardly be found and, if they were, only at a very high price.

The only thing left for me was to make the best use of my time in Sydney and to see whatever there was to see of everyday life there.

The city itself was quite interesting, mainly because of the gold. The main streets had taken on quite a different character, and the shops had changed their appearance in an almost miraculous way. In the haberdasheries there used to be colourful materials, tastefully arranged into ladies' dresses, ribbons, laces and the like, and so elaborately displayed that they offered the greatest

Sydney in August 1851

possible overview of all manner of things, especially designed for female eyes. Of all that there was suddenly nothing to be seen; grey and blue woollen trousers and skirts, even hobnailed shoes, woollen scarves and vests, woollen blankets and stockings seemed to have forced cotton and muslin back into a past era. Here and there horrible stuffed figures in complete miners' outfits stood outside various shops, dressed in a blue working shirt with a straw hat on the head, carrying a pick-axe, with a weather-beaten mask for a face – often with a terrible expression and contorted limbs.

In the ironmongers' there was almost nothing but pick-axes and shovels, perforated sheet metal for machines and little hatchets; every shop endeavoured to display at the front whatever could be used in the mines in any possible fashion. And in front of all this stood crowds of people, discussing the advantages and disadvantages of the various objects, and purchasing and loading themselves with things which up in the hills they would have liked to flog again at cost price, if only someone wanted them.

As far as Sydney is concerned, it is, of course, laid out according to English taste. The streets are wide almost everywhere, equipped with pavements and gaslights, and the main streets are adorned with the kind of beautiful and tastefully decorated shops as any important city in the old world has to offer.

Only the enormous number of public houses is striking, and, with few exceptions, there is one on every street corner of the city, except for those that are in the middle of the rows of houses. The state, however, gets huge revenue from them, but they also contribute terribly to the ruin of the lower classes, and in no other place in the world have I seen so many drunks in the evening, and *particularly* drunk females, as in the streets of Sydney.

I had an excellent opportunity to visit most of these places. On 12 September an employee of the harbour constabulary notified us that they had caught one of our men and that they were on the trail of the others. A thorough search was to take place that evening, and so a few members of the harbour constabulary were planning to come on board in disguise that evening, to take the first officer with them, and with his help to search some of the most notorious establishments, where they hoped to catch the fellows one by one. Of course I joined the group and we roamed the streets until midnight and visited about 20 of the roughest places in those rough areas, one after the other. Unfortunately we did not find any of the men we were looking for there, but for me the search was interesting enough, and I did not tire of entering den after den. There is music in most of them and dancing in some; others put on small performances, similar to the *café chantants* in San Francisco, where they put on skits and sing obscene songs.

That evening I counted seventeen totally drunk persons (naturally not counting those who were still on their feet), and of these seventeen, *fourteen* were women.

The famous honesty in Sydney is not all it is made out to be, for hardly a night passes without burglaries being attempted or carried out, and the Australian newspapers are full of such reports.

At this time an expedition was due to start from Moreton Bay, which was meant to explore the fate of our unfortunate countryman, Dr. Leichhardt. He had started his second dangerous journey, and people at least wanted certainty as to whether, where and how he had perished, for it was almost beyond doubt that he had become a victim of his own audacity.[20] Most recently, however, news has come in – but I am not sure how reliable – that bones and a watch key had been found en route. But *that* would still not indicate the demise of the whole expedition. In any case the latest expedition is said to have returned empty-handed, as I have heard here. This can be explained quite easily, for few people are enterprising and courageous enough to follow Leichhardt's trails.

Much as the population of Sydney had taken an interest in Leichhardt's fate on my first visit to Sydney, when actual meetings were held to explore and find out what had become of him, now gold had superseded almost any other thought – gold, gold – the talk was all of gold.

On Saturday the 13th in the evening two more sailors were caught, who had foolishly shown their faces in the city. The people who ran the rooming house they went to betrayed them themselves in order to earn the blood money. But much as we needed sailors, much as I really wished to depart from here, and even much as I myself was trying to find out about the fugitives, I still felt sorry for the poor devils, once I knew they had been apprehended and were now in prison.

Many of the people running the 'doss houses', as they are called by German sailors in the coastal towns, who take in mainly sailors, make a real business out of cheating the poor devils by taking money from both parties, while also appearing totally justified in doing so, unless by chance the matter comes to light. First of all of course they persuade the sailors, if possible by meeting them face to face and making tempting promises, to desert their ships. They may even promise to help them secretly with a boat, so that they can bring all their clothing with them, which later, of course, becomes the property of the landlord. Once they have extorted all the items that they could get from them and have hidden them in another place as long as possible, until a good reward had been set for their capture, then they themselves approach the harbour constabulary, who in turn make a profit from it all and are usually in cahoots with the landlords. These mock the people they have taken in and not only get rid of them in such a way as to avoid conveniently any unpleasant discussions, but they also pocket the blood money from those they have betrayed, so that they can start the same game all over again the same day, since they now have free beds again.

On the 18th we had finally reached the point of there being a good chance that we would be able to set sail in a few days. In addition to those who had been re-captured, the captain had taken on three English sailors, and the main task now was to get the cattle on board. But that was accomplished far more easily than I could ever have imagined.

First of all they were driven close to the ship on the wharf and were surrounded there by a quickly erected fence of poles and boards. Then one of the men hired for this purpose came and fastened a rope around the cows' horns. He did this in the clumsiest possible way with a long pole, on the end of which a kind of lasso was attached, so that the cow pulled back to avoid the dreaded pole each time the man came close with it. Once the rope was finally slung around its head or its horns, the animal was pulled by the men standing by toward a block close to the ship. Here it could no longer move, until a further rope to take it on board had also been slung around its horns, or, if it did not have any, as was the case with many of the cows in this shipment, around its neck and one of its front legs. The cow, struggling with all its strength, soon found itself suspended between heaven and earth, but who cared about its kicking – the sailors standing by pulled it by its tail over the large hatch and with a '*lower away*' the animal then slid down to where everything was in readiness for it, and there it soon found itself in its future berth, tightly tied to a sturdy pole.

In addition we also took on board a few kangaroo dogs, which the captain had bought for himself and which, it was said, would fetch a good price in Batavia.

Monday the 22nd was finally the day set for our departure to Java. Only someone who in similar circumstances has had itchy feet and wanted to get away can imagine the impatience which had tormented me, not only in the last few days, no, but in the last few *weeks,* for we had again been waiting here in Sydney for seven whole *weeks* – all those days had been stolen from our being at home.

And yet, in the end, my leave-taking from Sydney, no matter how strange that may sound, was hard – that is, not from Sydney itself, but from very dear, dear friends I had made there. Among them were in particular an English and a German family, the Rickards and the Hötzers,[21] at whose homes both the captain of the *Wilhelmine* and I took turns in spending all our evenings. Also Herr Dreutler,[22] as well as Dr. MacKellar had welcomed me most heartily and I had become as fond of Mrs Rickard's children, as I used to imagine one could only be of one's own children.[23]

There is something quite awful and painful in the world about saying farewell, when it is time to leave dear friends, to whom one has felt drawn, and in whose company we have felt comfortable and at ease; you pull yourself together and stay calm on the outside, but it pulls at your heartstrings and penetrates every fibre of your being. I believe a whole month in the open, in the rain and cold, does not affect your body as much as a single farewell from dear friends – and for most of my life I have done little else but lived in the open and said farewell. I must be blessed with a strong, sturdy constitution.

11.

Voyage through Torres Strait

Our ship lay at anchor in the harbour, sails reefed, but ready to run out to sea at the moment the wind became even a little more favourable. Until that point, however, the prisoners remained behind bars so that there was no danger of losing them once more. It was decided that when the ship was to weigh anchor, the water police would board one more time and would bring the prisoners with them.

In the prison there were also three Prussians from the English vessel *Sarah* who would gladly have joined us, but Captains Aymers of the *Sarah* did not wish to release them unless our captain paid the enormous indemnity of 72 pounds sterling.[1] Almost the entire crew of the *Sarah* was in prison, because at sea they had refused to work, that is, they had not performed their duties, with the result that the captain placed them in irons and on reaching port delivered them to the courts. When the matter was investigated, however, it was established that the captain had mistreated his people disgracefully during the voyage, often in a state of drunkenness. Nonetheless, the courts had to convict the sailors, because they had refused to work while still at sea and thereby had exposed all other persons on board, and the ship itself, to grave danger.

On the morning of Tuesday the 30th the Prussian flag fluttered from the tallest mast as a sign to the water police that the ship was ready to weigh anchor and leave port. A water-boat in the meantime drew alongside to refill the empty barrels once more before departure. The second anchor, which had been deployed during the night when the winds had picked up, was now raised, and the pilot approached in his little boat. The perfect wind was blowing – a strong westerly breeze – and when we were ready we were able to run out of the harbour. However, we were still without the people who were supposed to arrive with the water police, and in their absence we struggled hard to raise one of the anchors. Then the boat appeared from behind the end of the fort and approached rapidly; shortly thereafter the four prisoners climbed aboard, sullen and ashamed.

At this point the water police inspected the ship from top to bottom to ensure that some runaway sailors had not hidden themselves aboard; they shone a light or crawled into every nook and cranny and then finally, hot and bothered, returned to the deck after one last visit to our 'cow shed'.

Rather than having more help at hand with the arrival of the imprisoned sailors, there was simply more trouble. To be precise, the men refused to work and were locked in the forecastle. Just at that time the policemen were completing their inspection of the ship and reviewing the people on board. In one case they caused difficulties with a sailor from the *Sarah*, who had not refused to work, and who appeared to have secured his release from that vessel, but on the basis of a verbal agreement from the captain rather than a written discharge. As our vessel had such a small crew, our captain could not simply let this man go, and so although our departure was favoured by the most magnificent breeze, he returned to the *Sarah*, which was moored close to the town, to solicit a written discharge from Captain Aymers.

In order then not to waste any more time, the pilot decided to make for the open sea and gave the order to weigh anchor. Although we were lightly crewed we set to work and began hauling in the anchor chain to the 15-fathom mark, where the depth was 12 fathoms. As the ship began to move, the foremast sail and the large topsail were unfurled. The jib helped us to keep clear of the next ship as we edged toward it with our anchor still swinging, and with our maximum exertion we now had to haul the heavy anchor on its 15-fathom chain out of the mud, even as we travelled for some 2 miles through the water.

At this time one of the boys, the most useless of all on board, had sneaked out of the forecastle, and as we steered toward a headland wanted to jump overboard. When he found, however, that all of us favoured such an action, he thought better of it and was surely glad to find himself safely once more inside the forecastle.

In the meantime mad confusion reigned on board, the pilot barking and screaming a muddle of commands. The handful of crew were to heave up the anchor, then set or brace the sails, and the crew started to complain and said that if the other four did not want to work then they should not go to sea in the first place. Nonetheless we finally raised the anchor and got clear of the other ships and soon found ourselves in deep water, where we could sail back and forth without danger until the captain returned. A short time later we saw his small sail darting across the bay. He came on board; the pilot signalled to his boat to collect him and return him to Sydney. With the sails set to run before the wind, we glided with the aid of a splendid breeze out into the open sea.

The first priority was now to persuade the captured sailors to return to work, and that occurred in a manner as simple as it was quick. The captain explained to them that whoever did not work on his ship would receive nothing to eat, and to prove the point they were made to watch while the others took their breakfast. Now they knew all too well that Captain Schmidt would not allow them to starve, but at the same time they were aware that if they remained stubborn then they would be imprisoned once more in Batavia for as long as the ship was at anchor there, and Batavia was an unhealthy place; to sit in jail there posed a serious threat. Soon they sent a deputation, and when the captain promised to forget their earlier misdemeanour if they behaved well, they first of all launched themselves at the breakfast and then, as if nothing had happened, went back to work with the others.

The wind was excellent, but it became ever stronger, with the result that toward evening we brought down the topgallant sail and reefed the topsails. The wind drove us on an east-north-east course to put some distance between us and the land, so that later, when the expected trade winds set in, we would have more room to manoeuvre at sea.

On the 24th there was a magnificent breeze; topgallant and lee sails were set to follow a north-east course, with the wind still blowing from behind us. The breeze remained favourable, until at about the latitude of Moreton Bay a few days of calm threatened to slow our journey. However a storm one evening delivered us the splendid south-east trade wind, and with bulging sails we pursued a northerly course.

We would soon be in a latitude with reefs, and it was time for us to prepare for the perils of the Torres Strait.

However, before I follow our journey further, it will be necessary to provide the reader with at least a brief geographical overview of this strait, of which it is perhaps likely that he has not heard even once in his entire life, and yet which has cost many a human life and many a good ship.

In northern Australia, if the reader takes his map in hand, he will see running north toward New Guinea a rather pointed looking stretch of land, which is many miles wide. Its furthest extremity and sharpest point is Cape York, and the remaining stretch of water separating New Guinea or Papua from Australia is called the Torres Strait. This strait, however, offers by no means a smooth and open channel comparable with, for example, the even narrower English Channel between France and England. On the contrary, it is peppered with small and large islands, reefs, sandbanks and cliffs, and the entrance to it on the Pacific side is blocked by a veritable wall of reefs comprising the so-called Barrier Reef. Forming a solid and perilous wall, it curves upward from the Australian continent to the New Guinea mainland. Only particular, narrow passages, which are highly dangerous because of the strong north-western current, lead into the centre of the reef, where the ship cannot even contemplate steering a course determined by a compass, but rather every evening or even afternoon on its first approach it must drop anchor and remain in that one place until the next morning sun illuminates the channel once more.

Particularly noteworthy is the formation of the Barrier Reef, which in a distinctive fashion arises almost perpendicularly from the vast depths of the ocean to the surface, and although the surf relentlessly thunders against it, it has held firm for centuries. On the outside of the reefs, no more than 30 and often barely 10 feet away from them, the water not uncommonly has a depth of 600 to 1200 or 1300 feet, while immediately adjacent to it the white comb of the coral becomes visible. It is not easy to explain how the mass of coral is able to resist the constant rush of water; it remains one of the most marvellous of nature's mysteries how the little coral insect, to which most people attribute the formation of the coral, is able to build the fragile cells ever higher, so that the awesome power of the sea is overcome. The sea appears to encounter little resistance, yet it crashes and thunders against the coral in vain.

As I just mentioned, most scientists believed – and indeed this appears the most plausible explanation – that the coral banks which surround almost all the islands of the Pacific and Indian oceans, and which above all build wonderful walls around the islands of the South Pacific, are the creations of a small insect. Over a rapid succession of generations the insects build a rock-hard nest from a particular substance derived from their own bodies and lay their eggs in it, so that nest is constructed upon nest, colony set upon colony, until the huge structure grows to the surface of the ocean and thereby reaches its limit, because salt water is necessary for its creation as well as for its continued existence.

Others consider coral to be a marine organism in its own right, whose cells are merely used by the coral insect as a place in which to lay its eggs and to set up a living space inside it. I must myself confess that this theory is the more plausible one; moreover it has the endless charm of being the more poetic interpretation, while a number of important factors speak in its favour. Just as polyps represent the transition from the plant to the animal world, so coral provides a medium or transition between the plant and the mineral world, and across the entire globe we encounter such gentle transitions between types and species. Almost nothing is separated strictly and sharply from everything else. Like all other sea creatures, the coral, according to this theory, would slowly but surely grow upwards, and its entire appearance – part tree and part sponge – seems to a large degree to support this supposition. We cannot dismiss the possibility that these tiny insects are capable of building around themselves a mass which would harden in water and take on the firmness of granite. If this were the case, we would also have to attribute to them the ability to lay the very first foundations of a structure on a massive scale, many millions of times larger than the insects themselves, and to take into account over time the pressure exerted by great masses of water. More plausible, however, is the notion that coral is a combination of stone and plant, which by its nature anchors itself in the ground so as to protect itself from greater pressure. The coral plants which are most exposed to the elements always have the strongest roots, and the stone-plant would form a colossal whole, while the mass formed by the insect would consist of millions of small but individual parts.

Whatever the case may be, only narrow passages led into this Barrier Reef; one could almost call them channels, while inside the reef, that is, in the area immediately between Australia and New Guinea, ships are able to anchor in depths of 5 to 15 fathoms almost everywhere. Apart from the *right* channels, however, that is, those which really have sufficient water to allow a large ship to make a safe entry, there are also 'false passages', that is, those which from outside seem equivalent to an entrance and which sometimes seduce vessels into trusting them, but which then suddenly present them with a wall of reefs running across them and threaten the ship's demise. Even immediately before them there is no prospect of anchoring, while the wind and current drive the vessel toward its rocky fate with no hope of rescue.

The reader will soon become more familiar with this region, and it is in any case the most interesting voyage which one could possibly make among this veritable jumble of reefs and islands.

The prevailing winds here are quite closely connected with the Indian monsoons, so that for 5 or 6 months of the year they blow from the south-east, and in the other months – apart from a neutral transition period – they blow from the north-west. The passage is of course entirely determined by this, because the current follows the wind. For example, in a north-west monsoon it would be an utter impossibility for a ship to sail from the Pacific to the Indian Ocean via the Torres Strait, because with the wind and current against it, it would soon be stuck in the narrow channel and be lost. We ourselves arrived there quite late in the season, and usually September is the last month in which one would venture from here into the strait, because sometimes the northwest monsoon begins as early as the middle of October. Moreover, a voyage undertaken during the monsoonal change is doubly dangerous, because not only sudden storms but also thick fog occur commonly. A vessel then of course has no escape from waters where one cannot rely at all on the compass but must steer entirely according to what can be seen in the way of rocks and shallows around the ship from the topgallant yard. The most important things, however, on a voyage of this kind – which ships have been making for just a few years – are courage and coolness, providing the captain has a good grasp of his job. All of us were convinced that there was no danger; for us the Torres Strait was a distraction from the usual monotony of life at sea, and for that reason I can say that I welcomed it with open arms.

On the 4th of the month foggy weather, which seemed to commence here, meant that we were unable to make observations. On the 5th, however, at about midday the sun shone brightly, and we found ourselves so close to the reefs that we did not even dare to remain at anchor in that position. At 8 in the evening, with reefed topsails and a stay-sail, we moved away from that position and then turned around once more at 4 in the morning so as to make our way back to the same position as we had been at 8 the previous evening, and then we maintained a course sailing right before the wind toward where, in the captain's calculation, our destination Raines Island should be.[2]

The captain had been absolutely correct. At about 9 in the morning from the topgallant yard I saw the surf at the first bank, and both the captain and the mate came up to observe it also. We maintained our course for some half an hour, when suddenly ahead of us on the horizon two dark dots came into view, which on closer approach proved to be the Raines Island beacon and a ship, which was either sailing very close to it or was at anchor. Our jib boom was pointing directly toward the beacon.

This passage south of Raines Island is a good entrance to Torres Strait. The channel between this island and the large reef to its south is about four English miles in width, and the water is blue and deep right up to the reef, reportedly some 300 fathoms or more. As we approached, we could clearly identify the reefs by a high, foaming line of waves, which dashed against the coral in an unbroken surf.

As we came closer we found that the ship which we had sighted at the same time as the island's beacon or tower was by no means sailing or even lying at anchor. Rather it was lodged firmly on rocks, and indeed had been lifted by a mighty surge of the sea over a reef and was now wedged fast, with no prospect of rescue, amid the seething masses of water. It was a brig, painted black, with white trimmings and high topgallant stays, the fore-topsail was flying, the mainsail was loose, and the topgallant stays and yards were set in such a way that it seemed almost as if the vessel had on this very morning arrived at its desperate situation. In any case, it would lie here just a few more days. There was no sign of human life, no flag was raised, no sign was given, and as another English ship, the *Bank of England*, had passed through the strait just a short time before, one could imagine that it would have picked up the shipwrecked survivors. The brig lay about one English mile from the small sandy island on which the beacon stood.

From a distance this beacon resembles one of the standard, wide lighthouses, yet it appears, at least as far as we could discern, to consist entirely of pieces of lath, for we could see the light shine through. It did, however, provide a splendid landmark by which one could find one's bearings, and because of its height and breadth can be seen from quite a distance. The island on which it stands will be little more than one English mile in length and consists of sand, covered by patches of vegetation. Only at its western end, where on the leeward side there is a good place to land a boat, we saw two low-set huts, possibly constructed by the crew of the brig or by those who built the beacon. Next to the beacon one could also make out with a telescope a low-set object in the shape of a house, but there was not even a trace of human or any kind of living creature, except for the seagulls. No cloth or flag fluttered, not a soul stirred or appeared on the white sand, where even with the naked eye we would have been able to see a dog.

As was established later, the *Bank of England* had found not a soul on board, and the possibility exists that the ship's crew managed to make it to dry land, where, however, they would not be able to remain for any length of time but would have had to make their way westward to one of the Indian islands. This north Australian coast is inhabited by wild and vicious tribes, and in any case the shores are so lacking in fresh water as to provide only a wretched place to stay.

On entering such dangerous waters it is by no means pleasant to find such a wreck, whose crew no doubt had reached the Barrier Reef with the same high hopes as we had. A glance at the chart strengthens this feeling, when one sees the most remarkable examples of individual rocks amid deep waters. For example, the chart indicates at latitude 12° 15' a place where a ship ran onto rocks in waters with a depth of between 160 and 138 fathoms. Reportedly the bow lodged on a reef, while at the stern even the long plumbline could not reach the bottom, which must have had a depth of more than 235 fathoms. Incidentally, we had beautiful weather, a favourable breeze and good instruments, and our captain was quite confident in his actions.

Immediately beneath Raines Island we ran toward the so-called 'big bank', as if we intended to sail right up onto it, but then we came to a halt some hundred paces short of it. On both sides the surf thundered and foamed, and while we passed a few places with very green water, where there were rocks just below the surface, we had the entrance, the most dangerous point, happily behind us. Half an hour later we sighted Ashmore reef to our left, a short and narrow strip of sand.[3] On our right was the middle reef, an ugly combination of sand and rocks forming a long, sea-green strip, which in patches rose up above the water's surface.

Before us lay now the barren higher land, Hardys Island, two small and barren islands which we passed to our south, as we made toward the northern reefs of the Cockburn Islands.[4] These are three islands surrounded by an expansive bank of reefs, and we could hardly have strayed from our course if the sun had not already made its way westward. However, as we had to steer toward the west, the blinding, glistening vision of the sun lay right before us, casting wide stripes onto the water, and now it seemed that the entire sea was laced with reefs and banks. As a result we held back a little too far, while the current sent us further to the north, so that suddenly we found ourselves in light-green water. The chart indicated that the middle of the channel had a depth of 6 fathoms, but the captain wanted to proceed with caution. Deploying a stay-sail we ran back a distance and then came to a halt close to the wind, as far south as we could, between the Hardy and Cockburn Islands, entering a bay stretching eastward from the Cockburn Islands. If the wind were to pick up during the night, we would be protected there from reefs in 15 fathoms of war. Accordingly we hauled in the sails, dropped anchor and soon lay calmly on a gently rippling surface – to dream away our first night in Torres Strait.

The mate also took measures to defend the ship against a possible attack by blacks, even though there was not the slightest danger here. Both cannons, which peered unmovingly onto the quarterdeck from behind a couple of embrasures, were loaded but not yet primed. The idea was not to fire straight away in the case of an attack, but the crewman on watch took a loaded gun with him on deck. Because of the lightness of the breeze it was extremely hot below decks, so that soon the entire crew was strewn across the deck in a deep slumber.

As it happened, through the day we had caught a number of excellent fish of a pike-like variety. While we travelled at speed they snapped greedily at a red cloth attached to a hook, and a few times they were so large that they broke the strong line with a single tug. Fresh fish are good on land, but at sea, and particularly in a hot climate where one cannot store much fresh fish, they are a true delicacy.

On the morning of the 7th at about 7 o'clock we weighed anchor and set sail with a light breeze. Hopefully we already had the most dangerous waters behind us, and the channel between rocks and reefs was relatively broad here. In any case, in such a favourable breeze it was possible to identify all obstacles from the topgallant yard and to steer clear of them in good time.

The islands and reefs we could see offered little or nothing of interest. Here and there were small patches with low-growing bushes, surrounded by expansive coral reefs. Sometimes they were covered by light-green sea water, and sometimes they emerged starkly from surrounding sandbanks. To our left were Arthur's Islands, in front of us the three small Hannibal Islands. Then there appeared on our right the flat, bush-covered Boydong-Cays and behind them Bufhy Island.[5] Directly before us lay the Cairncross Islands, and there we found once more a good site to drop anchor for the night.[6] In fact we had hoped to reach that site early in the afternoon so as to go on land, but the wind disappeared almost entirely, and the sun set before we could drop anchor. It was dark before we could fasten the sails. Nonetheless the mate Köhler and I decided to land so as to see what there really was on the island. The boat was launched, and we rowed toward the shore barely one English mile distant.

From a distance, and in the pale moonlight, the little island appeared sufficiently picturesque – the dense green vegetation surrounded by white sand and coral banks and reefs, the wonderfully coloured sky hanging above, and the gently lapping sea over which we rapidly glided. The background setting of fires glowing in the darkness of the Australian mainland strengthened the sense of the barrenness and distinctiveness of the entire place. Yet reality did not permit me to abandon myself to dreams and fantasies. Immediately before us a steep sandbank rose from the water, which seemed deep enough here for a landing-place. The boat made toward it, and soon thereafter its bow buried itself in the soft sand.

The mate had come with me primarily to gather shells, but what interested me most was the vegetation on the island, and so I set about making myself a path through the thicket of vines and briers.

What a noise there was! It cooed and surred and whistled and flapped – thousands of birds lived among the trees and branches, and everywhere they fluttered from the roosts where they had settled for the night, frightened by the dreadful spectacle I had created in the undergrowth, and sought for themselves a safer and quieter place of rest. At the same time, and at the other end of the island, some waterbirds, presumably some kind of crane, produced a groaning sound of the most dreadful kind, and the whole place seemed to be alive with pigeons. Of course I had my gun with me, for there was no way of knowing if Aborigines might have arrived here from the mainland, but I did not fire a single shot, because the bushes were so thick and impenetrable.

After I had crawled around in the bushes for about half an hour by myself and had established to my satisfaction that there was nothing more to be achieved than to have my shirt ripped from my body by the branches, I headed back toward the shore, and with my hunting knife I cut some branches from the various bushes, in order to inspect them the next morning by the clear light of day.

The mate was looking for shells, and now I joined him in his efforts, but it was too dark. I took with me only what I could gather together in the way of some small samples, but because it had already become so late, we set off home. The next morning we aimed to set out again just as soon as the day allowed, so that we would still be able to reach our next mooring point – a rather large island – in good time.

'Humans do the thinking, but it is God who pulls the strings', is an old saying whose wisdom was soon to be proved. The next morning the wind was rather weak. Nonetheless at daybreak, expecting that the breeze might freshen at any moment, the sails were set and the crew began to weigh anchor. It was a job which, in fifteen fathoms of water and with 50 fathoms of chain released, should have taken no more than half an hour. For as long as the loose chain was being hauled in, things went well, but suddenly it all came to a halt. One of the anchor's flukes must have become wedged in a piece of coral, and the trick now was to break it off. We tried to do so with all our might. For a good hour we worked, using all our strength, without being able to raise more than perhaps one or two feet of the anchor chain. Finally it gave way slightly, just an insignificant amount, and breakfast time was approaching, by which point we had hoped to have a few miles behind us. After breakfast we set to our task once more and with renewed vigour. There was no one on board from the captain down, and of course not excluding me, who was not attached to the anchor winch, but by 9 o'clock we had not managed to haul in even two fathoms.

By this stage the anchor could not have been sitting behind a rock, because the chain was hanging straight up and down, and we were drifting. The channel was quite wide here, and thus there was no pressing danger. Nonetheless, to be drifting between reefs and banks, of which only a few have been properly examined, is an undesirable situation, and so we doubled our efforts to raise the anchor, which we thought must surely now be free.

But it did not come, and now there could be no doubt that it must have hooked onto something, and with the best will in the world we could not free it. What could we do?

To leave the anchor and 15 fathoms of chain behind was not a good option, and in the meantime we continued to drift, the anchor not stopping us. So we made one last effort. The few fathoms of chain we had gained by the sweat of our labour were to be sacrificed, and an attempt was made one more time to loosen the anchor with a sudden tug, in the hope that the anchor would break away from whatever it was it on which it might have hooked itself.

The tug was felt through the entire ship, but it failed to bring the desired result, and our work had to begin anew. Inch by inch we strained to raise the enormous weight, and when the anchor was lifted from the sea floor, the captain dropped the other one so that it would hold us long enough to complete the job. Inch by inch, hour by hour, we proceeded, even if at times it appeared that the anchor was determined that under no circumstances would it budge even the slightest bit more. Who knew what was weighing on the anchor, and if it was perhaps some malicious old man of the sea and his whole family holding it down? We began to believe it must be hooked on another anchor with its chain. Eventually though it would have to come to the surface, and it did, but ever so slowly, so that not until 11 o'clock did we gain the first glimpse of what was being hauled from the depths. In the end I was not so far off the mark with the idea of an old man of the sea, because something white, which might have been his beard, could be recognised in the green depths, as we struggled once again to pull it to the surface.

And what was finally the result of our huge fishing efforts? A colossal rock made of shells, so hard that even with a heavy sledge-hammer we were unable to knock off even a single piece. It was so firmly wedged on one arm of the anchor that we did not know how to dislodge it. At last, and after many attempts, a chain was tied around one of the flukes, the rock hanging from the other, and fastened to the deck. When the chain was then loosened some distance, the anchor turned over and the weight of the rock forced the anchor to turn over and release the rock. With one great cry of 'Hurrah!' the old man of the sea, who just beneath the surface had transformed himself into this clump of shells, returned to the deep to the accompaniment of our blessings. Whatever our feelings about him might earlier have been, with our spirits now revived we were quite unable to wish him ill.

The breeze, which during the morning had been quite good, had now dropped off, and midday was upon us. As it is not advisable to travel during the afternoon because of the setting sun, and as we would not have been able to reach a mooring site before evening, at any rate not a safe one, the captain decided we should remain where we were and leave early the following morning.

That suited me all the better, because it gave me the opportunity to go on land once more and to inspect the island in daylight. The captain did not wish to leave the ship, so I went with the mate and four sailors, and when we arrived there we went our separate ways in search of shells, of which we found fewer than we had hoped or even expected.

The Cairncross Islands consist of two small islands. One of them has barely a quarter of an acre of space, the other has a circumference of perhaps one-and-a-half English miles, and perhaps not even that. They are pure coral islands, with sand made of shells and covered with a layer of earth created by decomposed vegetation. Although they lie at such a high degree of latitude, they have very few tropical plants, if one excludes a magnolia-like tree bearing a plum-like fruit. The fruit itself in both shape and size looks exactly like our common German plums. Good Lord, they would have been ripe at this time, and once again I was missing out! These ones, however, are drier, though just as sweet, and in taste they more closely resemble dates. The tree is by no means a form of palm but rather in its foliage and even in the shape and colour of the wood it bears a similarity with the American magnolia. That was the only fruit to be seen, at least in this season. However, the island offered something different in a truly incredible quantity, and that was a wonderfully pretty white dove with black lines and spots in its feathers, here and there with a touch of yellow much like a cockatoo. The mixture of white and yellow appears to be taken from the same palette. They build their nests in the simplest and apparently crudest fashion, by merely laying a few twigs over each other, so that from below it is possible to see if there are any eggs or chicks. This is no doubt because of the heat, to ensure that the young are not deprived of the essential flow of air. They must hatch the eggs there in the nest, otherwise the young would not be there. I shot a number of them, and we found them extremely tasty.

By the way, curiously not a drop of fresh water is to be found on the island, and the doves must be able to do without it in the same way as the seabirds.

We found masses of seabird eggs, always two or three at a time, and always with the pointier ends touching one another in the hot sand or in the crumbling coral, entire banks of which are eroded here by the sea. The task of incubation is entrusted to the sun.

Apart from a few other plants, which I am unable to name for lack of botanical expertise, I found casuarinas (known in English also as sheoaks) and an unusual species of tree with fleshy green leaves. All the leaves grew in a circle around the stem, were quite round in shape and ran upward to a somewhat pointed end. The tree's branches, in the manner of banyan trees, deposited little shoots in the ground, where they took root. As a result the main trunk, as if held in place by ropes on several sides, could withstand even the fiercest storm. I found such trees only in the immediate vicinity of water, and the shoots they sent out did not run straight down but rather at an angle away from the tree and were thin and elastic.

Toward evening, when the sun was no longer as hot and scorching as during the day, we bathed. It was such a delight to swim in the cool, heaving sea, in the crystal clear water. In the wonderful twilight we swam around above the jagged branches of the coral trees reaching upward from below. How I was drawn downward with an irresistible urge into the secret, dark passageways of the deep, flashing curious glances into the wonders of a world still unknown to us. Alas, my breath ran out – I am no amphibian after all – before I had been introduced to the monsters of the deep. These voracious creatures make no distinction between the genuine lover of the sea and the merely curious, so I commenced a rapid ascent to the surface, filled my lungs with air and swam around for a while among a bank of shells. Carried by a fresh breeze, we were back on board the ship by sunset.

At 9 o'clock in the morning the anchor was weighed easily and quickly, and just as the sun peered over the horizon to check that all was as it should be, our topgallant sails billowed, as soon did the others, and with the aid of a favourable breeze we slid smoothly and speedily across the calm, lightly ruffled sea.

Today we stuck quite closely to the mainland, as we approached the northernmost point of the Australian continent. For most of the time the captain himself was on the topgallant yard with his special chart and telescope; this is the only way to guide a ship safely here because of the strong and capricious currents. I was there beside him the best part of the day, and indeed there is nothing more interesting for the layman than to observe how to sail through such an archipelago of islands, cliffs and reefs, and in doing so follow the constantly changing procession of old and new. The sense of danger only heightens the attraction, and on such a passage danger is ever-present, as is proved by the many wrecks encountered. As a consequence one remains in a state of mild, certainly very healthy, and in any case extremely pleasant agitation. In my opinion, some danger is one of the essential ingredients of travel. If it is absent then the scenery would need to be sufficiently spectacular to compensate.

From high on the yard one could also see a number of interesting sights, apart from the coastline itself, as we slid along it, sights which one could not see from the deck. Every fish in the crystalline water around the ship is visible from above, and often we saw fish darting past, or lazy turtles making their way slowly and sleepily through the clear sea. Even large snakes with very pretty yellow and brown markings swam by many times to break what was otherwise the monotony of the sea. The most remarkable thing of all I saw from above appeared on the very first morning in the Barrier Reef. It was a fish which, when I observed it, was lying right in front of our bow, and then, frightened by the ship, it rapidly swam toward the reef, where there was a foaming surf. In shape and colour the fish very much resembled a bat, and from the tip of one wing or flipper to the other many have had a span of four to five feet, with a length of perhaps two-and-a-half feet. On its head a couple of protrusions stood out, and while it swam it used the full breadth of its flippers, giving the appearance that it was flying through the air.[7] What monsters does the deep conceal, of which we have no idea! Strangely, here in the vicinity of the land, despite my hopes we did not see a single bonito,[8] only very few flying fish, and even fewer sharks. These creatures seem to prefer and to seek out deeper water.

In the evening we intended to anchor at the island of Mount Adolphus,[9] either in or at the entrance to Blackwood Bay, and as early as about 2 o'clock in the afternoon we were close enough as to be able to see through the telescope smoke and soon thereafter blacks, who were descending from the hills toward a small yellow sand or coral bank.

The island itself was rather large, with a 500-foot-tall hill and a rather wide and spacious bay. Beyond that it appeared to have the same vegetation as Cairncross Island, with no palms to be discovered anywhere.

To the right, and in the vicinity of a bank some six miles away, we could see a canoe, which at first was fishing there and then was making its way back toward the mainland. At the headland, too, there was a canoe. It is certainly conceivable that these Indians did not live here permanently, at least not for the entire year, but came over from the Australian continent to catch fish.

At 3 o'clock the anchor dropped, rattling down into about eight fathoms of water. The sails were fastened, the boat was launched, and the mate and I rowed, along with the second mate and three sailors, this time well-armed, toward the shore, to be more precise toward the headland, where we could see that the Indians were already awaiting us.

As far as we could distinguish from a distance, the Indians carried spears, but when we approached they had laid them aside somewhere or hidden them, and they beckoned to us with green bushes, held up pieces of tortoiseshell, and waved and made quite a racket – all in the friendliest and most welcoming manner.

'That's a nice invitation,' said an English sailor who was with us in the boat. 'These fellows carry a club in one hand and a peace offering in the form of a bush in the other. What are we to believe?' Most of them, however, bore no weapon at all, and I saw no reason at all to fear making a landing. In order, however, to guarantee our safety, before we reached the farthest extremity of the headland, an old Indian jumped into the water, swam out to us and climbed into the boat, while all the time telling us a long story in a half-screaming voice. He appeared to consider himself a kind of hostage, and he remained peacefully on board until we had reached the shore.

Frankly it was quite unnecessary for the good fellow to do this, because with my shotgun and my old hunting knife I would have been able to make good an escape if the worst transpired. But this was in any case preferable, and after a few minutes we were all the best of friends in the world, and the blacks even went so far as to call over their women and children and to introduce them to us with a lengthy recitation of their names and of their place in the tribe. We became acquainted with the entire delightful family.

Some of them brought us the plum-like fruits we had found on Cairncross, others brought shells, while another gestured to our guns and gave us to understand that further inland there was game to be had. We followed him, and I also saw in the distance the same sort of white doves we had shot on Cairncross Island. However, the low ground here was almost impassable, consisting entirely of swamp and the curved, interlocking roots of the trees of the kind found on Cairncross. A meal of doves did not seem to me sufficient reward for spending a few hours in the mud struggling through such neck-breaking obstacles. Moreover, it was probably also inadvisable to grant the Indians the possibility of taking advantage of us; trust is one thing, but opportunity can turn the honest man into a thief. Besides, we did not have so much time today. The sun would shine for at most two more hours, and we wanted to be back on board by sunset at the very latest. Thus I preferred to explore the surrounding territory so as to learn more about the character of the island. In order to avoid all risk, we left the second mate behind in the boat with the sailors, so that only the first mate, who was as well armed as I was, and I spent time among the Aborigines.

The trees were of the same kind as on the earlier island, though I could not see any casuarinas, at least not from where I was. On the other hand, the pandanus palm grows here, even though the Indians do not appear to know how to make use of its bright yellow fruit, from which the inhabitants of the South Sea islands make their most significant ornaments. The soil was entirely volcanic, with coral growing onto it around the periphery.

At one place on the mainland, below Escape River, we had observed with the aid of a telescope something on the shore, but we had not been able to make it out clearly. It looked like broken-off tree stumps, and yet they seemed too yellow and pointed. At one place in particular they were as thick as tree trunks in a field being prepared for cultivation, while in others they were widely dispersed; in the hills there were none to be seen, or at least I could not recognise any. Here again I saw these amazing things on the shore, and now I had the opportunity to inspect them. They were solid mounds of earth, and the Indians, when they saw me stand before one, very soon gave me a very detailed description of them. What a pity that I did not understand a single word of what they said, because their language bears not the slightest similarity to those of the southern tribes. In any case, the earth mounds were the work of ants and were mostly four feet tall and had a diameter of about one-and-a-half feet at the base. A piece I broke off showed clearly the cells inside, and the earth was hard and loamy as if mixed together with a certain amount of moisture. It appeared however from marks all over the earth that the Indians had burnt out the ants, perhaps to consume them, because the southern tribes also eat them.

Above all else I now wanted to find out if they had fresh water on the island, because only with that would a longer stay be possible here. However, I had barely begun to communicate what I wanted when they understood me immediately, and with their cries of 'Kirri, Kirri, Kirri' they tried to show me the precise direction and distance where water could be found. To them this 'Kirri, Kirri' means the way to be taken and the distance to be covered. 'Kirri' seems to mean just a short distance, 'Kirri Kirri' somewhat further, and the total length is proportionate to the number of times the word is repeated.

As we followed them and reached the bare hills once more, a few young ladies came toward us. A rather handsome looking Burka (old man) with grey hair presented himself as the father of the one young girl, and he also, probably to cast himself in the best possible light, brought forth the girl's two brothers, both of them upright, broad-shouldered fellows, whom he introduced to us as 'his own flesh and blood' with the aid of a very funny pantomime.

He really did have cause to be proud of his daughter, because she was the most beautiful Australian Indian girl I had seen, even during my long march through the inland. She was perhaps 12 or 14 years of age but was quite mature physically, though small and slender, and – as is very rare among these wild people – clean. Her clothing could hardly have been simpler – she wore a loin cloth made of grass, perhaps four inches in width, and a hair braid which stretched from her right shoulder to beneath her left arm.

At the same time she had a number of genuinely Australian features. Her hair was curly without being woolly, her lips a little upturned, the nose a little flattened, but barely noticeably, and her eyes were dark but had a shy, coy expression which suited her extremely well.

I decided incidentally at this point to acquire a sample of this clothing. For the purpose of making an exchange with these savages, I had brought with me, among other minor items, a few shirts, and I pulled one of these out of my game bag and dressed the young beauty in it. This was an unusual situation in which to find myself as a married man, but necessity forced my hand, because among the Indians there was no one who knew how to handle articles of clothing, and the mate, too, was married, so I could hardly ask him to do it with a clear conscience.

The little one liked it very much and now regarded herself as fully dressed. The braided hair she was wearing I later exchanged for a fishing line and a few fish hooks.

Shortly thereafter we reached the water sources. They were located at the southern end of the bay, quite close to the sea, and they were not running. They consisted of two natural stone receptacles, into each of which a spring seeped with sufficient strength to keep the receptacle quite full. About a hundred paces to the east there was a further, somewhat smaller source of the same kind. Next to the largest there was a large shell for drinking, which I replaced with another and kept as a souvenir.

At this point I would have gladly visited their camp-site also, but it appeared that it was at the other end of the island, and their six or seven-fold utterance of 'Kirri' suggested a rather long way away. The sun was already quite low in the sky, and I did not wish to be the cause of the boat remaining here beyond sunset. Moreover the ship lay at too great a distance for me to contemplate using the canoe, which rested on the shore here, to reach the ship the following morning. If the wind had picked up, I would have had no choice but to content myself with remaining behind on Mount Adolphus.

Before we left the island, however, I wanted to leave them a souvenir, which might perhaps later be of some use to them. I had brought with me from the ship a few lemons and oranges and I now planted them on the southern side of the island in the presence and to the utter astonishment of the Aborigines, who, it seemed, had never encountered such fruits in their lives. I retained one orange so that I might give it to them to taste, and I cut it into several pieces, but the man who took a piece would not pass the remainder onto the others, who could only extract them from him with some use of force.

On the north side of Cairncross Island, where the thick vegetation commences on a slight rise, I also planted two oranges and two lemons. It would give me great joy, if I were to hear some time in the future that they had grown and borne fruit.

After these efforts we lay down for a while in the shade to cool off before bathing and returning to the ship, and while doing so we made further exchanges with the Aborigines, acquiring a few fish spears and a small throwing stick. Among the things I had taken with me I found also a few papers containing vermilion, and I opened one of them to apply as make-up to the members of the tribes camped around us. I took to the oldest and roughest fellows first, but because I did not have enough pigment to colour their entire faces, I contented myself, as I had done earlier on the Murray, with covering their noses with a clean, carbuncle-red hue. These chaps looked a treat, their noses glowing like fire on their dark faces. Once the old ones had received their share, the young ones also approached, and even the women did not wish to keep their distance and their black noses on this happy occasion. Fortunately I was able to keep everyone happy, and even my small girl in her blue dress approached and pressed her little nose forward. It pained me to disfigure her neat face in this manner, but she expressed her desire for it, and in matters of their appearance ladies are said to have the most reliable judgment. Thus she, too, received a red nose, and as a token of her appreciation she passed me three shells.

In the meantime the second mate had granted himself the pleasure of firing his rifle a few times. With each shot the whole group ducked, as if they had to protect their heads from a stone that had been thrown. Afterwards they laughed with remarkable good humour. In general these people do not appear to have a nasty bone in their bodies, and I am firmly convinced that the primary cause of all hostility, indeed of all acts of cruelty toward the savage tribes, is the white man himself. Acts of dishonesty or jealousy committed by one or the other were always the trigger, and when provoked the savage is quick to hate and not easily appeased.

It was now time to return on board. The sun was about to set, and the women and children had already commenced their march back to the camp. I jumped one more time into the sea to bathe, as the boat was pushed out, and with a good breeze filling the sails we glided quickly and contentedly before the wind back toward the ship, from whose gaff the Prussian flag was fluttering happily in the wind. It was the first Prussian flag to pass through the Torres Strait, and I believe indeed the first to wave in *Australia*, and, oh, with what joy I would have cheered it, had it only been black, red and gold.[10]

I could easily have suffered a slight accident on reboarding. The mate carried a needle pistol, which went off just as we steadied ourselves in the boat, and the bullet struck the shotgun I was holding in my hand. Fortunately no one came to any harm.

The following morning, 10 October, we weighed anchor at daybreak and unfurled the sails. While that was occurring, however, a canoe set off from the land, and the Indians in it cried out and once more held tortoiseshell and woven baskets into the air but were wary of approaching right to the ship. Eventually I waved to them with a bush from Cairncross Island we had taken on board, and now they began to row toward us, even setting a small sail made of woven bulrushes or grass. However the current was strongly against them, and our anchor was nearly up. I was able to recognise them clearly in their canoe, but at this point the sail on the foremast and then the mainsail were set, and the ship began to move through the water, and the poor savages, who had hoped to exchange some tobacco for items which they would certainly have regarded as extremely valuable, were left far behind.

Their canoe was made of light wood, some fifteen or sixteen feet in length, and equipped with so-called outriggers on both sides. These outriggers consist of light rails, much like those on a sled, and run some four feet along both sides of the canoe and parallel to it, slightly raised at the front. The outriggers on the South Sea Island canoes, which are on one side only, were set up in such a way that they rested on the water, while these sat so that on land or in calm water neither side was touching the land or the water. Across the middle of the canoe were laid poles or sticks, on which the Indians themselves sat, while others sat for or aft and rowed. In high seas these outriggers of course serve to prevent the canoe from capsizing.

Aided by a favourable breeze, we chose the middle passage, which is allegedly safer than the Endeavour Strait leading off to the south, and set course for Wednesday Island, which we passed close by on our port side.[11] At one point here the channel is barely two English miles wide, and on our left low rocks jutted from the water, while on our right was a bank, barely visible through the green water. It would almost certainly be fatal during bad weather. Fortunately we managed to pass through and now had the worst behind us and the last rock, a small island by the name of Booby Island, in front of us.[12]

Behind us a sail came into sight, but as it was running directly before the wind, we were unable at first to identify what it actually was.

Booby Island incidentally is such an important feature in these seas to warrant a more detailed description. This tiny island, with barely an acre of space, derives its name from the great number of sea-birds which make their home here, and it consists of volcanic rocks. It is situated, if one approaches from the east, at the exit of the Torres Strait, which is so dangerous for sailors, and contains a network of caves. This island, which is not visited by the Indians because it is too far from the mainland, is used by the English as a depot for provisions for shipwrecked sailors – and as a post office. Passing ships land here, take with them the letters or notices they find, and leave behind either letters or a report of where they have been and where they are heading. To the west is then open water, and it is no longer necessary to drop anchor during the night.

Captain Schmidt also sent his boat on land here. While he stood off the island and slowly allowed it to pass by with the current, I had the opportunity to visit the island.

The post office is as simple as a post office could possibly be, and, apart from its location, is set up more conveniently for the public than any other such office I have seen. One can find there pen, paper, ink and wafers, and one can be one's own postal official.

The building itself consists of roughly hewn stones piled to form walls about four feet high; in front is an open room some five feet in length and three-and-a-half feet wide. On top a small angled roof has been constructed of split planks, so-called clapboards, which are held together at the front by a rail running across them, and at the back they rest on the low wall. In the middle of this building sits a box with a high, coffin-like lid on top, into which are inscribed the words, 'Post Office – Provisions and water in a cave S.E. end of the island'.

Diagonally behind it is a flag-stick placed in the ground, or at least thrust between the stones, and presumably an English flag once waved from it. The wind and weather have blown it mercilessly apart, so that now only a few pale rags hang from the pole.

Here and there on the island stand a few green bushes with foliage much like that of a pear-tree; a few tiny white and yellow flowers struggled to eke out an existence among the rocks covered with a thin layer of guano. At various shady places vines twisted their way along, struggling over crevices and steep cliffs. The rigid, guano-covered rocks appear strange and not at all inviting.

Of interest, too, is the cave on the south-east side. It has a height of some fourteen to sixteen feet, reaching a peak at the top, and runs deep into the island. Inside it has a strange and wild appearance, because there are colourful piles of provisions here which have been landed by English ships for the desperate survivors of shipwrecks. Barrels of water and meat, potatoes and boxes of bread are all over the place. Part of the meat was already spoilt, and two barrels had completely dried out, but since that time fresh provisions had been brought, and sailors suffering misfortune could pass the days here quite easily until a passing ship picked them up. From what I hear, many a life has already been saved in this way, and the English have earned the praise of other seafaring nations, who cannot be grateful enough, not only because of the exploration and precise charting of the strait – and the most recent chart is excellent – but also because of this practical, humanitarian gift.

After I had made a fleeting sketch of those two locations in the brief time I had available – so that I would at least be able to take a souvenir with me – we boarded the boat and had soon reached our ship. The sails were braced and lee sails set on both sides so that we could run downwind with a magnificent breeze toward the west in the direction of our next destination, Batavia.

In the meantime the ship behind us had come closer and bore a light sail so as to send a boat onto the island. It was a barque, but we could not make out its signals. From Booby Island the magnificent breeze drove us far into the Indian Ocean and into safe waters, and we gorged ourselves on the fruits which we had taken with us from the last island. They look exactly like our long plums but taste almost like fresh dates and contain irregular seeds much like those of Chinese loquats. Some have just the one, others two, three, or even four. The tree would be an adornment to a greenhouse, so I gathered quite a collection of the seeds with the aim of disseminating them later across the various places I would visit. They could not have been very well known, because even the director of the botanical garden in Java, Mr Teismann, who has in his charge what is certainly the most beautiful botanical garden in the world, knew neither the seeds nor the tree.[13]

Our wind was not to remain good for much longer. It began to be inconsistent and then to drop off, and finally turned into a dead calm, at which point our cows, in the hot space beneath the deck, suffered most of all.

We lost relatively few of them to the heat, and some thirteen or fourteen of them had had calves, but when the hot weather arrived and water was in short supply, they were still-born and made a delicious meal for the sharks. We ourselves were not disadvantaged, because the cows not only continued to produce sufficient milk for coffee and tea, but we were able to enjoy one day after the next the fabulous luxury at sea of drinking thick milk.

Despite the calm the sea remained lively enough, with particularly large numbers of tortoises and sea snakes. There was no many-headed hydra among them, just the usual decent-looking yellow snakes, not more than four feet in length, with bright brown stripes and the tales of eels. They slithered across the water as if they were on land, and sometimes they raised their heads above the surface as if to listen. When frightened they dive down vertically into the deep, as far as the eye is able to follow them in the crystal clear water. As straight as a die they shoot downward, using their flat tails in the same way as a rudder is used to manoeuvre a boat.

On the 17th and 18th dead calm. After shipwreck and lack of water that is the saddest thing one can encounter at sea. Better a wild storm than to be becalmed upon a lethargic, barely stirring sea.

Today a shark visited us, and we threw out a hook with a piece of bacon on it. He approached and smelled the bacon, which is supposed to be his favourite food. Perhaps he had an upset stomach, or perhaps it was too warm for him to eat fatty food, in any case he chose to ignore it. Once again we saw sea snakes and crabs, which danced from side to side in the water and seemed to amuse themselves greatly in doing so.

A weak breeze every now and again allowed us to draw level with Timor.

On one day the sea displayed wonderful, splendid colours. The depth could hardly have been more than 40 fathoms, and so the colour, for the most part under a clear sky, remained a light sky-blue, against the background of which the silver-white foam looked enchanting as it dissolved in the sunshine. The most wonderful colours in such a sea, however, danced across its lightly moving surface at sunset. All the colours melted into one another, and under the cover of blue sometimes a wide, glowing net of sparkling bronze swims upon the splashing water. Like the sun it sets in the west, colours itself ever more faintly, until finally with a pale lead-glow it covers the entire surface of the ocean.

On this evening the sea had the most beautiful, or perhaps the most peculiar, colouring I had ever seen. A combination of the sea floor and the breaking-up of the sun's rays in the water produced a pure, deep-green colour, and the foam thrown up at the bow lay like a solid mass against this sombre background, set against it in the most magnificent way. 'The sea is boring', say many, 'always the same sky and water'. But I have spent many a day on it, and I can pass endless hours staring out onto the constantly changing waters. I will never grow weary of them. Yet there are also people who can study the most beautiful painting and still see nothing but 'faces and trees', and for them the sea, too, is dull and nothing more than 'sky and water'.

On the 20th we received a light breeze, and when the haze lying across the water lifted somewhat, the island of Timor came into view. With its high mountain ranges and deep, shady valleys, on which the last rays of the sun shone, it stretched before us like a picture. There is a land with heights and valleys and endless attractions, yet I cannot go there. I have to sail on by, as if it had nothing to do with me. And if indeed we could sail past it, that would not be so bad, but no, once again there is a dead calm, not a breath of air stirs the sails hanging limply from the masts. The sea is as smooth as marble, and even its normally steady heaving is barely noticeable. From over there the fires of the Malayans flash across to us, light clouds rise from the mysterious valleys which I shall never visit, and from the promontory which juts far out into the sea the tall coconut palms look out at us against the background of the setting sun, nod to us with their proudly crowned heads and bid us good night.

Well may they say good night, and they may immediately add good morning, because the next morning we still lay there, and it was thanks only to the current that we had moved even a short distance to the west.

On the 23rd the sun had reached the zenith; with no wind the thermometer recorded 84° at 7 o'clock in the morning and 91° at midday. In the space below decks, where the cows were, it was 106° at 9 o'clock in the morning. On the 26th the temperature climbed to 92°, and that was the maximum, but it was recorded up in the rather well ventilated cabin. Through all that not a drop of rain fell, and we found our water supplies so stretched that we could not give the cows more than two buckets over the course of the day, and they would easily have emptied 10. Three more of them soon met their ends, one after the other.

The sea here was also quite lifeless. Some dolphins swam up to the ship, but not within throwing distance, and in the evening came an enormous shark. The second mate, a dry, strange character, dangled the hook with bacon over board, at which the shark sniffed but did not wish to take a bite. Eventually he hauled the line back on board and said that he 'wanted to let the shark go hungry for a few days, then he would come of his own accord'.

Monday 3 November – calm, calm, and more calm. I am beginning to recognise that our German language has some deficiencies after all. When we become really impatient and want to swear, we say '*Donnerwetter* – thunderstorm', but that is a long way wide of the mark and gives expression to just a small part of what we really wanted to say. '*Windstille* – calm', is what we should say. 'Calm' is a frightful term, and it triggers in me such horrible thoughts, that if I were to be as delicate in my expression as most Englishmen and Americans, then from this point forth I would never write the word 'calm' but would replace it with a '–'.

On the afternoon of the 4th – after we had been becalmed in the most appalling way for a full 14 days – there stirred once more a weak breeze, which grew stronger and stronger. Early on the morning of the 7th off the starboard bow the shady green heights of Java greeted us, and the prospect of a happy new life presented itself in all its tropical glory to the sea-weary traveller.

Afterword

Friedrich Gerstäcker's Australia

Friedrich Gerstäcker's *Australien* is a snapshot of Australia right in the middle of the nineteenth century. As he travelled through the continent for about half of 1851, Gerstäcker collected and recorded his impressions at a watershed moment. In Sydney the 'convict stain' had not yet been removed, in and around Adelaide the presence of his fellow Germans could not be overlooked, and as he paddled down the Murray in his canoe and then walked the Murray Valley, the vexed state of race relations in colonial Australia was on full display. With the talents of one of the great travel writers of his age, Gerstäcker committed his observations to paper and shared them with the wider world. Unknown numbers of readers in Germany and elsewhere gathered their knowledge of Australia from Friedrich Gerstäcker.

Who, then, was this peripatetic German?[1] Friedrich Gerstäcker was born in Hamburg on 10 May 1816, the son of the opera singer Samuel Friedrich Gerstäcker and his wife Luise Friederike Gerstäcker, née Herz, an artist who also found work as an opera singer. After the death of his father, when Friedrich was just nine years of age, he and his sister Molly lived with their uncle in Braunschweig (Brunswick). Friedrich abandoned a commercial apprenticeship within a few months of commencing it to walk all the way to Leipzig, where his mother lived, to break to her the news that he planned to emigrate to the United States. A passion to see the world had been awakened, it seems, by reading Daniel Defoe's *Robinson Crusoe* and the early works of James Fenimore Cooper. His mother may well have been taken aback by her son's intention to make his future in such a distant land, but she at least persuaded him to prepare for life in the New World by undertaking agricultural training on an estate at Döben in Saxony. If he was to desert his homeland, so her logic ran, then he should at least acquire the skills he would need to make a go of it.

Friedrich Gerstäcker did indeed travel to the United States, in 1837. However, he did not become a farmer there, though during a sojourn of several years farming was one of several jobs he held – along with steamboat fireman, silversmith, hunter, deckhand and merchant. When he returned to Germany in 1843, he discovered that he had unwittingly begun to establish a reputation in quite a different profession – as a writer. He had sent the diary of his adventures in North America to his mother, who had managed to have parts of it published in a periodical. When Gerstäcker himself finally arrived home, he needed little encouragement to continue writing, drawing from the vast reservoir of material he had collected during his travels. Some of it was worked into fictional form, so that in the following years he published his most successful novels, *Die Regulatoren in Arkansas* (1845, published in English under the title *The Regulators of Arkansas*) and *Die Flusspiraten des Mississippi* (1848, *Mississippi River Pirates*). With the income from his fictional works supplemented by the earnings he made from various translations from English, Gerstäcker found that he could make a decent living from his pen.

Confident that he had stumbled upon his true calling, Gerstäcker married Anna Aurora Sauer in 1845 and began a family. Yet his days of travelling were by no means over. With a sufficiently reliable income from his writing to secure his young family's well-being, he left them behind to travel the world once more, indeed to travel all the way around it. His plan was that he would collect such a wealth of adventures and experiences, that on his return home he would be able to write about them for years to come.

In 1848 there were revolutions in many parts of Europe, including Saxony, where Gerstäcker had settled. An outcome of that political upheaval was the establishment of a parliament in Frankfurt am Main; its members dreamed of creating a liberal, democratic and united Germany. Sensing an opportunity, Gerstäcker wrote to the Minister for Trade in the new government, Arnold

Afterword: Friedrich Gerstäcker's Australia

Duckwitz, requesting support for his proposed travels by touting his talents as an observer of the wider world. He received the answer he wanted. The minister wrote that he was inclined to grant Gerstäcker support 'because your request presents the opportunity of acquiring information about distant parts of the world and the circumstances of the Germans there, which would be of use in providing assistance to emigrants, one of the basic rights of the German people'.[2] Such was the reputation Gerstäcker had built for himself by this time that he was also able to secure funding from the Stuttgart-based publishing house J.G. Cotta.[3]

The relationship with Cotta was a productive and long-lasting one. True to his word, Gerstäcker wrote accounts of his travels around the world, and Cotta kept its part of the deal by publishing them. As for the Frankfurt parliament, by June 1849 it was no more, and with it evaporated the dreams of a united and liberal Germany. That was a matter of some regret for Gerstäcker, not least because one of his precious sources of funding dried up overnight in the course of his travels.

Travels around the world

It was on 18 March 1849 that Gerstäcker commenced his journey. The *Talisman* sailed from Bremen carrying a number of emigrants bound for California. Gerstäcker's destination, however, was Rio de Janeiro, which he reached on 13 May. From there he sailed via another vessel to Buenos Aires, where he could begin his expedition by land to the Chilean port of Valparaiso – crossing the Andes on the way. From Valparaiso he sailed to California, where he was able to see for himself the hives of activity that were the goldfields. And from there, in November of 1850, he sailed across the Pacific to Hawaii, and then to Tahiti in a whaler. This was new territory for Gerstäcker, and yet the island was not entirely unfamiliar to him – one of the works he had translated earlier in his career was Hermann Melville's *Omoo*.[4]

His next port of call was Sydney. As the reader will discover, he arrived there in March of 1851. The reader will also learn that Gerstäcker's finances by this stage were in a parlous state. More than ever before, he had to rely on his wits and on long-honed skills in surviving on the smell of an oily rag. At the same time, he was not prepared to compromise his goal of making his way west to the colony of South Australia. There was no longer a parliament to which to report, but Gerstäcker was eager to see with his own eyes how successfully the Germans of South Australia had managed to create new lives for themselves in the Antipodes. He could hardly have been more parsimonious in his choice of modes of transport – mail coach to Albury, then by a canoe he made himself down an uncharted section of the Murray, until the canoe sank, followed by a trek of several hundred kilometres to Adelaide. It was one of the great travel adventures of colonial Australia.

Gerstäcker's arrival in Adelaide was not entirely unexpected there. Word was out that a German was making his way down the Murray. The topic provoked some excitement, as many South Australians wondered whether the Murray would provide them with a means of transport and communication with the east. In eager anticipation the *South Australian Register* reported in its 'Overland News' at the end of May that Gerstäcker had launched his canoe at Albury, 'trusting to Providence for the bulk of his food during a journey so dreary and arduous in the estimation of ordinary humanity'.[5]

Having finally reached his goal, Gerstäcker spent time in both Adelaide and the Barossa Valley. These weeks were in many regards the climax of his Australian tour. He knew very well that it was here that he would find the greatest concentration of Germans among the settlers, and neither in the capital nor in the townships of the Barossa was he disappointed. The knowledge he gained here would, he knew, be of great interest to many back in Germany. He would be able to provide a rare assessment of German settlements a decade or so after they were established, and he would be able to let prospective emigrants and authorities back home know if the long and perilous voyage was likely to be worth their while.

It was not only his fellow-Germans who were keen to hear from him on his arrival in South Australia. The question of the navigability of the Murray was one that piqued the curiosity of the then governor Sir Henry Young, who arranged to meet with the visiting German and to introduce him to the most famous of the colony's explorers of the time, Charles Sturt.[6] More than 20 years earlier Sturt, too, had explored the Murray by boat, but only downstream from the Murrumbidgee. To satisfy the curiosity of his host and of many others regarding the state of the river, Gerstäcker wrote a newspaper report on the question of the Murray's navigability, offering his readers a sanguine view. There were many obstacles to overcome – not least the countless snags and low water levels downstream from Albury – but the clearing of the river for navigation, he predicted, would bring huge benefits to the settlers of that region.[7]

The German settlers he encountered in South Australia were by no means a homogeneous group. In Adelaide there were craftsmen and professional people; others were involved in commercial activities of various kinds. There were the so-called '48ers', that is, Germans who, like Gerstäcker himself, had supported the ideals of the 1848 liberal revolution. When that failed, a mixture of despair, pragmatism and thwarted idealism had persuaded them to leave Germany and attempt to rebuild their lives in South Australia. Gerstäcker was to meet and befriend two of the most prominent representatives of that group, namely the Schomburgk brothers Otto and Richard, who were developing a property at Buchsfelde near Gawler. The Schomburgks, like the Germans who settled in Adelaide, were among those who assimilated quickly and, with few exceptions, soon felt at home in this 'paradise of dissent'.

The story of the country Germans was quite a different one. If Gerstäcker sought a compelling recreation of a piece of his homeland, rural South Australia was the place to look. It was to the east and north-east of Adelaide, and especially in the Barossa Valley, that German Lutherans had established communities in which their language, culture and beliefs were faithfully preserved. Religious rather than political persecution had driven the so-called 'Old Lutherans' to seek refuge in South Australia, thus avoiding the Prussian king's insistence that there be a single, state-ordained Protestant church with a universally adopted prayer book. Having climbed across the Andes, sailed across the Pacific, paddled down the Murray and trekked through the Australian bush, Gerstäcker could not help but record his astonishment at how faithfully these pious Lutherans had rebuilt lives not only in the spirit but in the form of those they had left behind.

From Adelaide Gerstäcker returned to Sydney by sea, sailing in the Prussian vessel *Wilhelmine*, with whose captain he had struck up a friendship in Adelaide. The atmosphere in Sydney, he soon noticed, was vastly different from before his departure in April. Gold had been discovered, and would-be miners were drawn to the goldfields of Bathurst like moths to the flame. Such was the attraction that it became difficult to crew vessels, and the *Wilhelmine* was no exception. Gerstäcker had no choice but to cool his heels for a time, so characteristically he made the most of the enforced delay by paying a quick visit to the gold diggings around Bathurst. There he could observe for himself the frenzy of activity – and the scale of the disillusionment – that was taking place. When sufficient crew members were retrieved, *Wilhelmine* departed Sydney harbour on 23 September 1851.

The continent was not yet entirely behind Gerstäcker, because the *Wilhelmine* flirted with the Great Barrier Reef and then negotiated a tricky passage through the Torres Strait, during which Gerstäcker landed on several islands. With those dangers behind him, he could proceed to complete his voyage around the world, spending time in Java, and then setting a course for his native Hamburg, where he arrived in 1852.

Gerstäcker would never see Australia again. Nonetheless, as he had hoped, Australia occupied him as a writer for many years. The main outcome of that preoccupation is the original German edition of this book, *Australien*, published in 1854 in accordance with the terms of his agreement with his publisher, and available now for the first time in English. It was the fourth of Gerstäcker's five-volume series of travel books *Reisen* (travels).[8] At a similar time Gerstäcker also published for a British and an American readership a volume titled *Narrative of a Journey Round the World*.[9] The best part of that is devoted to his travels through the Americas, but a sizeable section relates his adventures in Australia. That section is a relatively brief (some 120 pages) version of the English edition of *Australien*, but strictly speaking it is not an abbreviation or abridgement. Rather, Gerstäcker wrote his narrative in English, a language

Afterword: Friedrich Gerstäcker's Australia

he had long mastered, describing many of the scenes and episodes found in *Australien*.

Gerstäcker's literary output was prodigious. His Australian material alone led to multiple publications, long and short, fictional and non-fictional, and some translations as well, over a number of years. Many were published in the popular German journals of the day, such as *Die Gartenlaube*, *Ausland* and *Fliegende Blätter*.[10] Some were targeted at readers in their adolescent years, drawn in large numbers to his accounts of worlds far away. There were two longer fictional books which, like the shorter works, were closely based on his own first-hand experiences. The novel *Die beiden Sträflinge* (1856, appearing in translation in 1857 as *The Two Convicts*) was an adventurous story of a noble bushranger, while *Im Busch* (1864, In the Bush) was set in gold diggings near Sydney.[11] Here as elsewhere in Gerstäcker's writings, the distinction between fact and fiction was often blurry.

After a period of characteristically frenetic literary activity in Germany, the travel bug bit Gerstäcker once more. In 1860 he set off again for South America; in 1862 there followed another expedition, this time to Egypt. Between those two journeys his wife died. His second marriage in 1863, to the nineteen-year-old Dutchwoman Marie Luise Fischer van Gaasbeek, did as little as the first to curb his *Wanderlust*. In 1867 Gerstäcker travelled yet again to North America, and from there via Mexico to the West Indies and Venezuela. After that he seemed to settle down, purchasing a property in Brunswick. But with the outbreak of the Franco–Prussian war in 1870 he could not resist travelling, albeit much closer to home, in order to report from the battlefields. As he prepared for a journey to Asia in 1872, he suffered a lethal stroke.

Gerstäcker's *Australien*

Gerstäcker wrote for a living. To find a mass readership, as he managed to do with great success, he was well aware that he had to entertain his readers. In nineteenth Germany there was a large market for fictional and non-fictional works set in exotic locations, providing they were composed in an engaging style. Most famously Karl May, who hailed from provincial Ernstthal in Saxony, gained a legion of loyal fans by writing novels of cowboys and Indians, all of them set in a 'Wild West' which May himself never saw. His best-known characters, Winnetou and Old Shatterhand, were pure fiction.

Friedrich Gerstäcker, at least, had seen all the places of which he wrote, yet like May he wrote above all to entertain. Even in his non-fictional works he sometimes adopted the narrative strategies of the novelist to widen his appeal, and *Australien* is no exception. Gerstäcker works hard to heighten the sense of the exotic, and as the narrator of his own story he seeks to build a sense of suspense leading to crisis and resolution. Nowhere is this clearer than in his account of his travels though sparsely populated regions along the Murray. An atmosphere of danger is conjured through reports of murders and atrocities committed by Aborigines; as he treks through unknown territory, the narrator is permanently on tenterhooks, fearing an attack by a 'treacherous' black at any moment, and with it the attempt to remove his 'kidney fat'.

At the same time Gerstäcker seeks to inform, even to educate. He stakes a powerful claim to authenticity, assuring his reader in *Australien* and his other travel writings that everything he reports he has viewed with his own eyes. He seeks to establish himself as a reliable recorder of the world as he saw it, providing a wealth of detail, expressing scepticism where appropriate, occasionally citing the views and expert opinions of others.

In one particular regard Gerstäcker took his educational role very seriously. As one of millions of Germans who contemplated emigration in the nineteenth century, he had a keen and sincere interest in the fate of those who packed up their belongings and moved to another part of the world. It was a role he took so seriously as to join in July 1848 the newly founded National Association for German Emigration.[12] A German nationalist long before there was a unified Germany, Gerstäcker wanted not only to understand what drove his countrymen to cross the seas, he also wanted to issue sound advice to prepare them for their new lives. And before the premature demise of the Frankfurt parliament in which he had invested so much hope, he even wondered whether Germany might acquire some colonies of its own – albeit in the south seas rather than in North America or Australia.[13]

In America, both North and South, Gerstäcker came across countless examples of the German diaspora, and for that very reason was no starry-eyed emigration enthusiast. On the contrary, Gerstäcker established himself as an emigration sceptic who earnestly countered the often extravagant claims made by those with vested interests. As he well knew, the lot of the German emigrant was not always a happy one. This was not to say that he opposed emigration, but he believed that intending emigrants should make their choices on the basis of well-established facts and the authentic, lived experiences of those who had already taken the plunge. Given the difficulties of reversing a poor decision once an ocean or two had been crossed, Gerstäcker was careful to ensure that the images he projected of other parts of the world did not merely flatter or deceive.

Australia was a case in point. Well before he sailed into Sydney Harbour, he had written at some length about Australia in a book titled *Nord- und Süd-Australien. Ein Handbuch für Auswanderer* (1849, 'North and South Australia: A Handbook for Emigrants').[14] At that time there was a dearth of such guides to 'the fifth continent' in German, and what existed was not always particularly helpful or reliable. Though he might not have been conscious of it as he prepared it, Gerstäcker's handbook was part of a growing trend. Most German emigrants looked across the Atlantic for their future homes, but a significant minority were contemplating Australia and were keen to inform themselves about it. In 1849 alone, apart from Gerstäcker's handbook, numerous other books on Australia hit the German market.[15] The trend continued in the following years, boosted by the discovery of gold and the promise that Australia could bestow great riches upon its immigrants.[16] That meant that when Gerstäcker's *Australien* was published in 1854, accompanied by its claim to report what the author had seen with his own eyes, it was received by a readership wanting to be both entertained and educated.

The erudite adventurer
Much of the appeal of *Australien* and Gerstäcker's other travelogues derives from their authenticity, their solid grounding in the author's observations

and his skill in transforming them into a carefully crafted text. We also know, however, that Gerstäcker was an erudite traveller and that for him Australia was no blank slate. In preparing his 1849 handbook *Nord- und Süd-Australien* he drew unashamedly on existing literature. With a dearth of works by German authors, Gerstäcker turned to English-language sources, favouring those written by authors who – unlike himself at that time – had gathered direct experience of life and work in Australia. Without doubt they not only provided him with the foundations of his 1849 handbook, they also inspired him as he planned his own travels.

He names five of them.[17] The first is David Mackenzie, a Scotsman who in 1834 was recruited by the Reverend John Dunmore Lang to teach at Lang's Australian College in Sydney. Over a number of years Mackenzie acquired an intimate knowledge not just of Sydney but also of rural New South Wales, knowledge which he gathered in his 1844 book *The Emigrant's Guide; or Ten Years' Practical Experience in Australia*.[18] The second was the Irish-born Joseph Charles Byrne, who provided a very popular record of his very wide-ranging peregrinations in his book *Twelve Years' Wanderings in the British Colonies*. In 1839 Byrne and two companions managed to drove some 1000 sheep along the Murrumbidgee and the Murray to Adelaide, foreshadowing to some extent Gerstäcker's journey twelve years later.[19]

Then there was G.F. Davidson, whose travels took him through Asia to Australia, where he spent the years 1836 to 1838. The best part of that time was spent in the Hunter Valley, which Gerstäcker, too, would visit years later. On his return home Davidson wrote an account intended initially as a kind of travelogue for friends, but which gave sage advice to those contemplating a future in the Antipodes.[20] By contrast Charles Rowcroft, the fourth of Gerstäcker's British sources, had little connection with the parts of Australia Gerstäcker would visit. Rowcroft had lived in Hobart for several, mainly miserable years in the 1820s, and Gerstäcker never managed to cross Bass Strait. Nonetheless Gerstäcker appears to have admired Rowcroft's ability to convert his experience of Australia into entertaining popular fiction.[21] So much did Gerstäcker enjoy two of Rowcroft's early books, namely *Tales of*

Afterword: Friedrich Gerstäcker's Australia

the Colonies (1843) and *The Bushranger of Van Diemen's Land* (1846) that he translated them into German.[22]

Last, but by no means least, Gerstäcker drew on the work of George Blakiston Wilkinson, the author of not just one but two handbooks tailored to the needs of 'the working man' considering a new life in South Australia.[23] They contained precisely the kind of practical information that Gerstäcker was keen to pass on to the readers of his own book, and it also helps to explain why Gerstäcker was so eager to visit South Australia. While Wilkinson's advice was designed for British readers, his practical tips on how to go about acquiring and working land in the one colony devoid of the 'convict stain' could benefit Germans as well.

Apart from these British authors, Gerstäcker makes passing reference to the unnamed work of just one German, namely Eduard Delius. Delius was a Bremen-based emigration agent, responsible for arranging the migration of hundreds of Germans to South Australia and Victoria in the 1840s. Not surprisingly, Delius was inclined to promote a rosy view of the immigrants' prospects in Australia. To this end he included in his work a letter, reproduced in Gerstäcker's handbook, in which a German migrant by the name of August Klaehn wrote glowingly of the new life he had made for himself in the Barossa Valley. For the independent worker, Klaehn proclaimed, whatever his trade, South Australia was a 'genuine paradise'.[24]

We do not know what else Gerstäcker might have managed to read about Australia before arriving here in 1851 to check for himself the veracity of such claims. By the time his *Nord- und Süd-Australien* was published, he was already embarking on his voyage around the world, with little prospect of accessing the sort of literature allowing him to expand and update his knowledge of Australia. Of course, once he set foot in Sydney in March 1851 the situation changed, and he was in a position to complement his first-hand experiences of Australian life with whatever literature he was able to digest during his journey.

Alas, *Australien* contains neither notes nor a bibliography, so some element of mystery regarding the full range of Gerstäcker's reading remains. There is one part of the book, though, where it is clear that Gerstäcker went to some effort to inform himself in greater depth, and that concerns indigenous Australia. Chapters 8 and 9 contain an abundance of ethnographic observation based in very large part on Gerstäcker's reading of works by others and indeed consisting in large parts of unacknowledged 'borrowing' from them.

The topic was not entirely new to him, since the last chapter of *Nord- und Süd-Australien* provided prospective immigrants with some preliminary insights into what might be expected of the continent's indigenous inhabitants. In *Australien*, however, Gerstäcker goes into much more detail, a close reading of which reveals a deep indebtedness to several sources he must have consulted when he was in Australia.

The first of them comprises the journals which the explorer Edward John Eyre published in 1845. They describe Eyre's two expeditions north from Adelaide to the Flinders Ranges and west across the Nullarbor.[25] Importantly for Gerstäcker, the second volume also contains a lengthy section bearing the title 'An Account of the Manners and Customs of the Aborigines and the State of Their Relations with Europeans'. It was based in large part on the experiences Eyre had gathered while serving from 1841 to 1844 as resident magistrate and protector of Aborigines at Moorundie on the Murray.[26] It was an area with which, a decade later, Gerstäcker too would become familiar.

The other major source of ethnographic information, and one which is mentioned by name in *Australien*, was Matthew Moorhouse. By background Moorhouse was a medical practitioner; in 1839 he had arrived in South Australia to take up a Crown appointment as protector of Aborigines. In performing his duties Moorhouse kept a journal with quite extensive ethnographic notes. Gerstäcker tells us in Chapter 8 of *Australien* that he 'obtained the most interesting information in Adelaide from the protector of the South Australian natives, Mr Moorhouse, who put the journal he had been keeping since 1839 at my disposal and permitted me to make notes from it'. Gerstäcker also drew on the annual reports produced by Moorhouse in his capacity as protector, along with statistics he collected in collaboration with the German missionary Christian Teichelmann.[27]

Afterword: Friedrich Gerstäcker's Australia

There was one other German missionary whose work Gerstäcker used, and that was Heinrich August Eduard Meyer, whom Gerstäcker mentions – misspelling his name as Meier – in Chapter 7. Like Teichelmann, Meyer was sent to South Australia by the Dresden Mission Society. He performed missionary work at Encounter Bay south of Adelaide for eight years to 1848 and was then pastor of the Bethany congregation in the Barossa Valley. And like Teichelmann he was deeply interested in indigenous languages, leading him to publish work both on Aboriginal grammar and vocabulary.[28] The work that was of most interest to Gerstäcker though – to the extent that Gerstäcker borrowed from it at some length – was Meyer's *Manners and Customs of the Aborigines of the Encounter Bay Tribe*.[29]

When he was back in Germany, and working feverishly to complete both the English and the much longer German account of his travels around the world, Gerstäcker was able to consult further books about Australia. By this time there were other works by German authors, and he certainly became familiar with Albert Heising's *Die Deutschen in Australien* (The Germans in Australia) published in 1853.[30] Another work which he seems to have digested, at least according to a note in one of his journals, was Mrs Robert Lee's *Adventures in Australia*.[31] Beyond those works, however, it is hard to know what else he might have absorbed, but it is hard to imagine that it would have exceeded the copious quantities of text he was writing about his adventures in many parts of the world.

Legacy

When Gerstäcker departed Australia via the Torres Strait in late 1851, the country was gripped in a state of profound and irreversible change. Gold had been discovered, and Gerstäcker had witnessed the frenetic first stages of the rush that followed. He was better positioned to understand what was occurring than most, since he had been in California as the gold rush consumed that part of the world. The Australia he was leaving behind would within a matter of just a few short years be vastly different from the one he had entered so modestly at the beginning of that year. It was a great blessing, then, that Gerstäcker was about to make a detailed record of Australia just as the gold rushes were about to change everything forever.

Among the thousands who would now make their way to Australia from many parts of the world in the hope of finding fantastic wealth were Germans who imagined making new lives for themselves far from their homeland. If they had read their Gerstäcker, they could hardly have overlooked his scepticism. In *Australien* he makes it clear that the treks to the goldfields were doomed to lead to deep disappointment, if not misery. Most, as Gerstäcker well knew, would return from the fields worse off than when they embarked on their adventures, and in the meantime would have been shamelessly swindled and exploited. Gerstäcker sensed a grand, nefarious scheme in which the Australian press was complicit. The newspapers' enthusiasm, he confided in a letter to an Adelaide friend, was designed to entice more workers to Australia, already groaning under a shortage of labour in the post-convict era.[32]

Australien was true to Gerstäcker's intentions. Its liveliness, its humour and its wealth of anecdote engaged its readers, yet it painted Australia neither as a land of milk and honey nor as a dystopian hell-hole. For any of his countrymen who might have contemplated moving there, it advised of its advantages, but it pointed frankly to its drawbacks and perils as well. The truth was that once the word had spread that untold riches were on offer in Australia, then no level of scepticism would curb the enthusiasm of the gullible and the greedy. When the discovery of gold was announced to the world, a process had been set in motion which no work of literature would reverse.

If his readers were not persuaded to think twice before heading to Australia, Gerstäcker's book nonetheless has left an important legacy. For its readers then and later, *Australien* painted a vivid picture of a part of the world that was not well known or understood. That was especially useful for those who contemplated travel, business or migration, but it had its appeal also for those whose wanderings were confined to their armchairs. Gerstäcker's *Australien* offered them drama, humour, suspense, excitement and a heightened sense of the exotic. Yet amid the exotic – and perhaps this feature lay at the core of Gerstäcker's genius – there was also and always the reassuringly familiar.

Afterword: Friedrich Gerstäcker's Australia

Whether he was describing the Australian bush or the jungles of Brazil, a small piece of Germany was never far away. No other author united the familiar and the exotic as successfully as Gerstäcker did. His prolific output was devoured by a legion of devoted readers.

The passing of time, alas, has not been kind to Friedrich Gerstäcker. Even in his native Germany he is no longer the household name he once was. In Australia Gerstäcker never attained the status of his countryman Ludwig Leichhardt, whose mysterious disappearance might have cut short his quest to understand a continent and its people, but it at least guaranteed him a prominent place in folklore. Gerstäcker, in contrast, finished his grand narrative, but then slipped quietly into obscurity.

Nonetheless, in this 21st century, and with the 200th anniversary of Gerstäcker's birth, his *Australien* bears revisiting. For readers of English, this translation offers a first chance to read the work of an author who was blessed with the skills to delight, to instruct, and above all to allow us to view a piece of Australia's history through fresh eyes.

Notes

1. Sydney

1. Opposition to the transportation of convicts to the Australian penal colonies had been growing since the 1830s and was particularly strong among Sydney's middle and working classes. In 1850, the year before Gerstäcker's visit, the Australasian Anti-Transportation League was formed with the aim of bringing a total cessation of transportation. Convict transports to New South Wales had already ceased at this time, but they continued to Tasmania and to Western Australia. In early April 1851, shortly after Gerstäcker's arrival in Australia, a petition was sent to Queen Victoria requesting there be no renewal of convict transportation to New South Wales.
2. Looting which occurred after a fire in San Francisco in June 1851 had led to multiple arrests, including of a number of men from Sydney. Among those hanged in the wake of these events was a former New South Wales convict, John Jenkins.
3. Augustus Dreutler was a German businessman in Sydney. In the year of Gerstäcker's visit he was also formally appointed Consul at Sydney for the Free Hanseatic City of Lübeck.
4. Gerstäcker was eager to visit that colony because large numbers of Germans had already settled there. Although he had not yet been to South Australia, in 1849 he had published a guide on emigration to South Australia based on the writings of others. See the Afterword to this volume.
5. The use of the word 'Indians' in referring to indigenous Australians is not just an echo of Gerstäcker's previous, extensive experience in the Americas but is also an adoption of the language of his day in Australia as well. At other times he also uses '*Wilde*' – translated here as 'savages' – '*Schwarze*' – translated as 'blacks' – and '*Eingeborene*', which is translated here as 'Aborigines'.
6. The *Speziestaler*, or *Speziesthaler*, was a silver coin widely used in German-speaking Europe before the introduction of the Mark in 1871.

7   Gout.
8   In the German currency of the time there were 24 *Reichsgroschen* to a *Thaler*.
9   Wilhelm Hötzer, who became known in Australia as William Hetzer, and his wife Thekla arrived in Sydney in 1850 and set up a photographic studio in Hunter Street, then in George Street.
10 Wilhelm Kirchner, who was born in Frankfurt in 1814 and had lived for a time in Manchester, moved to Sydney in 1839, where he set up a merchant firm and married an Australian woman. From the mid-1840s he began to submit proposals for solving the colony's labour shortage by subsidised German immigration and was appointed immigration agent for Sydney in 1847. On his initiative a series of 'bounty ships' sailed to Sydney, in most cases from Hamburg, carrying German emigrants. When Gerstäcker met him, Kirchner was formally the 'Sydney Consul for Hamburg and Prussia'. By 1852 some 2000 Germans had made their way to Sydney in schemes organised by Kirchner.
11 The French navigator Jean François de Galaup, comte de Lapérouse, who commanded the exploratory vessels *L'Astrolabe* and *La Boussole*, arrived off Botany Bay on 24 January 1788, just as Arthur Phillip was shifting the British penal colony to nearby Sydney Cove in Port Jackson. After his departure in early March Lapérouse and his men mysteriously disappeared. Much later it was established that both vessels were shipwrecked on the Pacific Island of Vanikoro.
12 Gerstäcker shares many of the prejudices of his day regarding both the appearance and behaviour of indigenous Australians. Only after extending his experience of Australia beyond Sydney was he to become aware that the prejudices of the white settlers rested on shaky foundations.
13 The Hunter Valley's potential for viticulture had recently been recognised, as had the benefits of bringing to the region German setters with appropriate experience. In 1849, 104 German families disembarked in Sydney and immediately took up residence in the Hunter Valley, the Illawarra south of Sydney, and in the Camden district to the south-west.
14 James King, a merchant and businessman, had arrived in New South Wales from England in 1827. In about 1835 he settled at Irrawang, where he manufactured pottery and played a leading role in the development of the wine industry. He and other producers in the region brought German vine dressers to Australia, three of whom reached Irrawang in 1848. In the year before Gerstäcker's visit King won a gold medal of the Horticultural Society of Sydney for his wines.
15 *Equisetum arvense*.
16 Richard Cobden was a British liberal who tirelessly advocated free trade. On the question of education, however, Cobden saw an important role for the state and

campaigned for the introduction of a national system of free, secular schools funded through local taxation.

17   Born in the Prussian province of Brandenburg in 1813, Ludwig Leichhardt arrived in Australia in 1842 with the intention of undertaking exploration. He completed an expedition from Moreton Bay to Port Essington in 1844–45 but then famously and mysteriously disappeared during his effort to traverse the continent in 1848.

18   Sir Charles FitzRoy was the tenth governor of the colony of New South Wales and from the beginning of 1851 was also 'Governor-General of all Her Majesty's Australian possession'.

19   Gerstäcker presumably means pounds.

2.   By Mail Coach from Sydney to Albury

1   When the explorers William Hovell and Hamilton Hume reached the Murray near Albury in 1824, they named it the Hume in honour of the explorer's father. Six years later, when Charles Sturt entered the Murray after travelling down the Murrumbidgee, he named it the Murray after the British Secretary of State for War and the Colonies, Sir George Murray, not realising it was the river already named by Hovell and Hume further upstream.

2   Imeo or Eimeo is the old name for Mo'orea, a French Polynesian island near Tahiti.

3   It was a widely held notion among Europeans that Australian Aborigines killed in order to extract and consume the 'kidney fat' of their victims. An early example is to be found in George French Angas' *Savage Life and Scenes in Australia and New Zealand* (London: Smith, Elder and Co., 1846), in which the author describes a visit to a station near Lake Alexandrina: 'A case had recently occurred in which some of the Tattayarra tribes had come down to the lake and taken away several black children for the purpose of devouring them. It is not uncommon for the natives of this district to take out the fat from the kidneys of an individual of another tribe whilst he is living, should he happen to be amongst them! If they catch him asleep, they generally avail themselves of the opportunity, and turning him over, cut out his fat; and the unfortunate victim lingers from two to eight days after this inhuman treatment. The fat thus procured they regard as a charm: they say it has the power of preserving them from spirits; and when their bodies are anointed with it they imagine they can fight more courageously.' (pp. 122–23) Even in the early twentieth century ethnographers continued to make such claims. Alfred Howitt, for example, in *The Native Tribes of South East Australia* (London: Macmillan,1904) claims that Aborigines consumed the kidney fat of both enemies and fellow tribesmen for magical reasons. Gerstäcker returns to this theme in Chapter 8 below.

4   John Roper was an English-born civil servant and explorer who, as Gerstäcker notes, had taken part in Ludwig Leichhardt's expedition from the Darling

Downs to Port Essington 1844–45. The Roper River in the Northern Territory is named after him. From 1847 to 1853 Roper was clerk of petty sessions at Albury and for a time postmaster and registrar of the Court of Requests.

5   In an article published on page 3 of the 25 June 1851 edition of the *South Australian Register*, Gerstäcker names his companion as C. Simon.

6   Possibly a reference to Billabong Creek, which flows into the Murray River system via the Edward River at Moulamein, a considerable distance upstream from Albury.

7   Gerstäcker's own note: The Bunyip is that hitherto legendary Australian monster that only the blacks claim to have seen here and there, especially in the Murrumbidgee and Murray rivers and the neighbouring lakes, and about which they tell dreadful stories.

8   In 1830 Charles Sturt had sailed down the Murray from the confluence of the Murrumbidgee to the mouth of the Murray; the stretch upstream from the Murrumbidgee confluence to Albury was thus *aqua incognita* for Europeans. In the year after Gerstäcker's travels in Australia, 1852, Francis Cadell sailed the river downstream from Swan Hill in a canvas boat.

3. A Canoe Excursion on the Hume

1   The Fourche la Fave is a tributary of the Arkansas River in western Arkansas.

2   In 1840 the American Albert Koch discovered the remains of a mastodon in Missouri and placed the assembled skeleton on display.

3   The Hydrarchos was a mythical sea serpent.

4. March through the Murray Valley

1   The Edward or Kyalite River is an anabranch of the Murray in the Riverina District of south-western New South Wales.

2   The Moulamein, derived from a local Aboriginal word meaning 'the meeting of the waters'.

3   It is unclear to which group Gerstäcker is referring here; possibly it is the Wergaia people of the Wimmera region of north-western Victoria.

4   Gerstäcker seems here to be confusing the boomerang and the woomera, which are quite different weapons, the latter being the throwing-stick as described above.

5   As earlier Gerstäcker indicates his awareness of the Australian travels of his countryman Ludwig Leichhardt and of the latter's work *Journal of an Overland Expedition in Australia, from Moreton Bay to Port Essington, a Distance of Upwards of 3000 Miles, During the Years 1844 and 1845* (London: T. and W. Boone, 1847).

6   Today the Edward River, but on Gerstäcker's 1848 map the section of the Edward River from the confluence with the Wakool to the confluence with the Murray.

5. March through the Murray Valley (continued)

1. The 'bunyip' went under different names in Aboriginal mythology and is sometimes translated as 'devil' or 'evil-spirit'. It was said to inhabit riverbeds, creeks, swamps and waterholes. In Gerstäcker's time it was still widely believed by white settlers that the bunyip was some kind of unknown Australian animal awaiting formal discovery.

2. Located north of the Murray River some 60 kilometres downstream from the confluence of the Darling and the Murray, Lake Victoria, in Gerstäcker's day not yet dammed, was a natural freshwater lake whose size depended hugely on the rainfall in any given year.

3. In fact Rufus River, so named by Charles Sturt in 1830, and running between Lake Victoria and the Murray. After Sturt's explorations 'overlanders' took sheep and cattle between New South Wales and South Australia through this district, provoking the 'Rufus River Massacre', at a site where the overlanders' road crossed the river, on 17 August 1841. At least 30 indigenous people were killed.

4. Lake Bonney in South Australia's Riverland is named after one of the first Europeans to see it, Charles Bonney. In 1838 Bonney, an 'overlander', was droving livestock from New South Wales to South Australia when he came across a large expanse of water. Barmera is on the shore of the lake, which is connected to the Murray by a creek.

5. A gunyah or humpy is a small, provisional shelter made from bark or branches.

6. The Rufus River massacre of 1841 was the nadir in relations between Aborigines and overlanders in the region. An inquiry held in Adelaide in the wake of the killings recommended establishing a police presence to avoid further violent encounters. Edward Eyre was appointed Resident Magistrate and Protector of Aborigines on the Murray, and police stations were established at Moorundie, Ral Ral (near Renmark) and Chowilla. It is true that attacks on overlanding parties had ceased by the time of Gerstäcker's travels in 1851, but this had less to do with the 'friendliness' of the Aborigines than with a forceful assertion of European power to guarantee the security of overlanders.

7. The 'bottomland' is the low land running beside a watercourse.

8. The lake was named Alexandrina after Princess Alexandrina, the niece of William IV, who on ascending the throne became Queen Victoria. Thoughts of changing the name to Lake Victoria were raised but not realised.

9. Several years later, in 1855, the Austrian-born artist Eugene von Guérard sketched tribes from Lake Victoria and Lake Bonney camped in Adelaide. It was a custom over many years for European authorities in Adelaide to distribute blankets and provisions to Aboriginal people who had made their way to Adelaide to receive them.

6. The Adelaide District

1. Norton Summit, located some 12 kilometres east of Adelaide in the Adelaide Hills, was named after Robert Norton, who had arrived in South Australia in 1836. The public house visited by Gerstäcker was not identical with the current Scenic Hotel, which was built in the 1870s.
2. Gold was discovered at the Ophir Diggings north-east of Orange in February of 1851; the discovery was then proclaimed by Edward Hargraves in April, word not reaching Gerstäcker until he arrived in South Australia.
3. Karl Moor is a character in Friedrich Schiller's 1781 play *Die Räuber* (*The Robbers*), from which this line is cited.
4. Probably a reference to the copper mine at Montacute.
5. George Fife Angas, who in Britain had done much to advance the cause of establishing a colony in South Australia, had himself arrived in Adelaide at the beginning of 1851. He had invested great energy in promoting German immigration, in particular the immigration of the German Lutherans led by Pastor August Kavel.
6. Angas Park, named after George Fife Angas, was the original name for the Barossa Valley township of Nuriootpa.
7. Hans Hermann Behr was a German doctor, entomologist and botanist who spent time in South Australia in 1844–45 and then again in 1848–49. Clearly Gerstäcker had become acquainted with Dr Behr in San Francisco before making the journey across the Pacific to Australia.
8. In naming Lyndoch in 1837, Colonel William Light mis-spelt the name of his friend Lord Lynedoch, who was his captain in the Battle of Barrosa in 1811. It was the mis-spelling of this Spanish location that gave the Barossa Valley its name.
9. *Die Fahnenwacht* (*The Standard Bearer*) is a piece of music by the German composer Peter Joseph von Lindpaintner.
10. Christian Ludwig Meyer was the Consul of the Kingdom of Hanover to South Australia. His partner in the firm Noltenius, Meyer and Co. was Bernhard August Noltenius. One of the achievements of the company was to bring large numbers of miners from the Harz district in the Kingdom of Hanover to work in the fledgling South Australian mining industry. Noltenius's older brother Heinrich was also a well-known Adelaide businessman.
11. Actually Schomburgk. Otto Schomburgk was one of three German brothers who emigrated to Adelaide and distinguished themselves in many ways. Otto arrived on *Princess Louise* in August 1849 with Richard Moritz Schomburgk, who later became Director of the Botanic Garden. The two brothers took up land at Buchsfelde near Gawler – named after the geologist Leopold von Buch. Like Buch, the Schomburgks were friends of Alexander von Humboldt, who helped finance their emigration. Gerstäcker would have been sympathetic

with the brothers' politics, since all three men supported the liberal agenda of the 1848 revolution; the Schomburgks' emigration after the failure of the revolution was politically motivated. A man of many talents and great energy, Otto Schomburgk ran a medical practice and co-founded the *Südaustralische Zeitung*. Another brother, Julius Ludwig Schomburgk, emigrated to Adelaide later and became chief designer for noted Adelaide silversmith J.M. Wendt.

12 Carl Wilhelm Ludwig Mücke – or Muecke – also emigrated to South Australia on the *Princess Louise*, his political hopes dashed by the failed revolution of 1848. Apart from his excursion into newspaper publishing, as Gerstäcker describes here, Muecke farmed and worked as a pastor, following a much more liberal interpretation of the scriptures than the 'Old Lutherans' such as August Kavel. After Muecke Gustav Dröge (or Droege) took on the newspaper, which had first appeared in 1850 under the title *Deutsche Zeitung für Südaustralien*.

13 Rudolf Eimer was a wealthy businessman who established the *Adelaider Deutsche Zeitung*.

14 Wilhelm Eggers, formerly of the *South Australian Register*.

15 The *Spenersche Zeitung* was an influential Berlin newspaper.

16 Not until 1856 did the first steam train run between Adelaide and Port Adelaide.

17 The Burra Burra copper mine 150 kilometres north of Adelaide was established in 1848 and attracted miners from the United Kingdom and Germany. At the time Gerstäcker was in South Australia the set of townships was known collectively as 'The Burra'; its reported population of about 5000 made it the seventh largest town in Australia and the largest inland settlement.

18 Osmond Gilles, a fluent speaker of German, had made a career as a merchant in Hamburg from 1816 to 1833. Mining was just one of a remarkably wide range of commercial and other interests.

19 The schoolmaster H. von Schleinitz, who had arrived in Adelaide in late 1849, established a German School in Freeman Street (now Gawler Place) shortly before Gerstäcker's visit.

20 The parliament at this time before the colony's self-government (achieved in 1857) was the Legislative Council, which in 1851 was enlarged to 24 members, a third of whom were chosen by the Governor, two-thirds elected by adult males who owned land or paid rent in the colony. In the campaign for the 1851 elections, which were staged in early July, the issue of state aid for churches played a prominent role.

21 The text here is taken directly from the *South Australian Register*, not Gerstäcker's translation into German.

22 William Giles was colonial manager of the South Australian Company and a busy lay preacher, while also a fierce opponent of the separation of church and

state. He was beaten when he stood for Port Adelaide on that ticket, but then he stood for Yatala and won narrowly.

23 The English-born comic actor George Coppin had lived and worked in Adelaide since 1846, taking over the New Queen's Theatre, until in 1848 he passed the running of it to John Lazar. The Edinburgh-born actor Lazar went on to become Mayor of Adelaide from 1855 to 1858.

24 Sir Henry Edward Fox Young was the fifth Governor of South Australia, from 1848 to 1854. In the year he met Gerstäcker, Young offered a prize of £2000 for the first person to travel up the Murray to the confluence with the Darling – a prize claimed in 1853 by Francis Cadell in a paddle-steamer, having earlier explored the river in a canvas boat.

25 The Indian-born Charles Sturt had explored extensively in South Australia and would have been interested to learn of Gerstäcker's travels on and along the Murray. Sturt had been Colonial Secretary in South Australia since 1849 and remained in that position until the end of 1851.

26 An article by Gerstäcker indeed was published on page 2 of the *South Australian Register* on 26 June 1851 under the heading 'Steam Navigation of the Murray'. In it Gerstäcker stated his unambiguous view: 'my thoughts have been strongly engaged in favour of the possibility of its being navigated, and I am most willing to give my individual and unbiased opinions.' Even allowing for the very real problems posed by snags, steam navigation, Gerstäcker wrote, 'would create an entirely new zeal in the population of the surrounding districts'.

27 Matthew Moorhouse had arrived in Adelaide in June 1839 to take up the position of first permanent protector of Aborigines in the colony; with it came a broad brief to safeguard Aboriginal interests. Though Moorhouse had a strong philosophical commitment to his role, his efforts did not always bring the results he desired, as the conditions in which indigenous people lived deteriorated.

28 Pastor Eduard Meyer of Bethany, who had previously been a missionary at Encounter Bay, worked with Moorhouse and also lived alongside him.

29 The founding of the school Gerstäcker alludes to here was a sign of Moorhouse's belief in the importance of Aboriginal education, but in time the school closed.

30 Poonindie mission was established outside Port Lincoln in 1850. Its founder, the Adelaide Archdeacon Matthew Hale, conceived of it as a 'training institution' for young Aborigines. The first students included those who had attended the school in Adelaide. After the Adelaide school's closure in 1852 indigenous people from all over South Australia were sent to Poonindie.

31 William Henry Charnock, who arrived in Adelaide in 1849, was a shipping agent who promoted the establishment of River Murray trade.

32 Carl Sutter settled with his family at Macclesfield, south-east of Adelaide.

33 German-born Johann Augustus (later John) Sutter was a pioneering settler in California even before the gold rushes. He was known as Captain Sutter because of a period of service in the Swiss army.
34 Mount Barker.

7. Tanunda

1 Gawler.
2 James Chambers arrived in South Australia in 1837. With horses bought from Van Diemen's Land he was probably the first to open a livery stable in Adelaide, enabling him to take mail contracts and to run passenger services. With the money he gained in this way he later developed substantial pastoral and mining interests in the colony.
3 Located some 70 kilometres north-east of Adelaide, Tanunda was settled by Germans; the Aboriginal name means 'waterhole'.
4 The nearby village of Langmeil was settled by German 'Old Lutherans' led by Pastor August Kavel. That group had originally settled in Klemzig just east of Adelaide, but then relocated into the Barossa Valley.
5 Gerstäcker has the congregations confused here: Kavel was in charge of the congregation at Langmeil, the original village later becoming part of the township of Tanunda, and of Lights Pass. The Tanunda congregation was formed in 1850 by an independent group of Lutherans, who called it Tabor after the mountain referred to in the Old Testament. For a brief period the pastor was the Reverend Adalbert Kappler of Adelaide, until he was succeeded by Dr Carl F.W. Mücke. That congregation had no connection with Kavel in nearby Langmeil. The majority of the Hahndorf congregation had by 1848 seceded to Pastor Gotthard Fritzsche from Lobethal, though a Kavelite remnant remained. Fritzsche had led his flock to establish communities in Lobethal in the Adelaide Hills and in Bethanien – later Bethany – close to Tanunda.
6 The grain of truth in Gerstäcker's story is that Kavel and his followers were indeed 'chiliasts', who interpreted certain passages in the biblical Book of Revelations literally and believed that at the end of the world the Messiah would come to reign on earth with the faithful for a thousand years, the 'Millennium'. Between 1848 and 1851 Kavel had published several pamphlets on this subject, but none of them contain any such prediction or betray even a hint of the numerological pre-occupations that underpin all such predictions – which are normally also made public in order to warn the unbelieving world of its impending doom. In an anti-Catholic letter to the *Observer* in April 1849, Kavel outlined his chiliastic beliefs but declared: 'I hope I shall have quitted this life when these things shall happen, though they are approaching very swiftly, for I do not feel strong enough to enter through such fiery trials into the millennium.' The New Testament Christians 1500 years earlier had also believed that the day was 'approaching very swiftly'.

Notes

7   William Miller (1782–1849), one of the founders of the Adventist Church, believed that the end of the world and the return of Christ would occur in 1843. He and his followers, the 'Millerites', consequently experienced a 'Great Disappointment'.

8   Here Gerstäcker's geographical confusion becomes apparent: Langmeil, the area around the Langmeil Church and Billy-Goat Square in Tanunda, was by the time of his visit already part of Tanunda or immediately adjacent to it, while the village two miles away is Bethany (then Bethanien). That would make the location of the mythical event described here Mengler's Hill on the Tanunda Creek – not Kaiser Stuhl, as the more absurd folk variants of the story have it.

9   That is, the Bethany congregation chose H.A.E. (Eduard) Meyer as its pastor. Meyer had earlier run a mission to the indigenous population of the Encounter Bay area.

10   Again, the grain of truth in Gerstäcker's misinterpretation of South Australian Lutheran history is the fact that Kavel's chiliasm did contribute to the split within the Lutheran church, although it was not the immediate trigger. The split occurred not as a result of the mythical event Gerstäcker recounts here, but had taken place five years earlier, in 1846. The Bethany congregation (which Gerstäcker always mistakenly calls Langmeil) had never been part of Kavel's flock but had been founded by Pastor Fritzsche and had always belonged to his parish, together with Lobethal. Gerstäcker seems to be totally unaware of Fritzsche's existence, since it seems he had no interest at all in the equally German community of the Adelaide Hills. It is also true that Fritzsche and his followers were from the start (even in Prussia) anti-chiliasts, although in South Australia Kavel and Fritzsche had reached a gentlemen's agreement to avoid the subject, as it was creating tensions among the laity. Once the split had occurred at the Bethany Synod in August 1846, that agreement no longer applied, and the two parties had embarked on a public pamphlet war. Meyer, a close colleague of Fritzsche, had been called as pastor by Bethany as early as 1848. Gerstäcker's main informant was presumably Muecke, who had not witnessed any of those events, as he had arrived in the colony only in mid-1849.

11   Although Gerstäcker virtually admits here that the story is a fabrication, that has not prevented it from becoming a persistent rural myth or even being cited as historical 'evidence', although Gerstäcker is unable to state accurately either when or where it 'occurred'.

12   Bethany.

13   Gerstäcker's use of the ecclesiastical term 'ordination' rather than the expected secular term 'licensed' suggests he was aware of the current controversy regarding the Marriage Act: although South Australia in theory had no established church, Anglican clergy were licensed to perform marriages by virtue of their ordination alone; the clergy of other denominations had to apply for licenses to perform the same rites. The validity of Kavel's first marriage in

1840 was challenged in the press on the grounds that the missionary Christian Teichelmann was not licensed to perform marriages in South Australia.

14   The Donatists were a Christian sect in Roman North Africa in the fourth and fifth centuries. They believed themselves, and not the Catholic Church, to be the 'true Church'. The Novatians were similarly a Christian sect who held the firm view that those whose Christianity had lapsed, even under intense pressure from secular forces, should be refused readmission to communion.

15   This is from the *Kirchenordnung der evangelisch-lutherischen Gemeinen zu Hahndorf, Langmeil und Lightspass in Süd-Australien* (Church Constitution of the Evangelical Lutheran Congregations at Hahndorf, Langmeil, and Lights Pass in South Australia), printed by Carl Kornhardt in Tanunda in 1851. Translation by Dr F.J.H. Blaess in *The Apostolic Church Constitution*, published in *Australian Theological Review* 1964, pp. 133–48. Lutheran Archives, Kavel-Fritzsche Synod File, Apostolic Constitution Folder.

16   As always, when Gerstäcker says Langmeil he means Bethany (Bethanien), where in 1851 Pastor Meyer was elected as President of the congregations of Lobethal, Blumberg, Bethanien, Rosenthal, Hoffnungsthal and Trinity in Adelaide. That body also adopted a constitution in 1851, which did retain much of Kavel's constitution but dedicated three paragraphs to its reasons for not including the 'committal to Satan' outlined in point 3 of Article 10 above. Blaess (see note 15 above) presents the two constitutions side-by-side.

17   As mentioned in note 9 above, H.A.E. Meyer for a time had run a mission to the indigenous population at Encounter Bay.

18   H.A.E. Meyer, *Vocabulary of the Language Spoken by the Aborigines of the Southern and Eastern Portions of the Settled Districts of South Australia, Preceded by a Grammar*, Adelaide: James Allen, 1843; H.A.E. Meyer, *Manners and Customs of the Aborigines of the Encounter Bay Tribe, South Australia*, Adelaide: George Dehane, 1846.

19   Johann Friedrich August Fiedler, the Klemzig-born son-in-law of Pastor Kavel, is particularly well known for planting Shiraz vines near Bethany Creek in 1847. To this day they are still producing grapes for commercial use.

20   Julius Pabst was a German doctor with a successful practice in Tanunda.

21   George Fife Angas, a businessman and banker, established the South Australian Company in England and played a crucial role in facilitating the emigration to South Australia of Germans – among them Pastor Kavel and his flock – escaping religious persecution in Prussia. As Gerstäcker well knew, the Germans whom Angas had helped had to repay him with interest the money he had lent them. Eventually, shortly before Gerstäcker's visit, Angas moved to South Australia, settled on a property at Angaston, and was elected as a member of the Legislative Council for the Barossa district.

22   Actually Schomburgk.

23 As indicated in Chapter 6 above, both Richard and Otto emigrated in 1849 aboard the *Princess Louise*; another brother, Julius, followed later.
24 Christian Leopold von Buch was a German geologist and paleontologist who had studied with Alexander von Humboldt in the School of Mining in Saxon Freiberg. Buch had given generous assistance to the Schomburgk brothers in leaving Germany.
25 This is a reference to the liberal revolution of 1848, which Gerstäcker himself had supported, but which was brutally crushed by conservative forces the following year. Both Schomburgks had left Germany after the failed revolution, so that Buchsfelde became something of a haven for so-called '48ers'. It is not clear here who the 'other German' is, except that he was one of those who were deeply disillusioned by Germany's thwarted attempt at democracy.
26 Australian slang for a serving of alcohol.

8. The Natives of Australia

1 As mentioned in Chapter 4 above (footnote 3), the myth that Aborigines extracted kidney fat from their slain enemies was widespread. One possible source of Gerstäcker's treatise on the topic here is Edward John Eyre, whose observations of Aboriginal life and customs were recorded in the last section of his two-volume *Journals of Expeditions of Discovery into Central Australia, and Overland from Adelaide to King George's Sound, in the Years 1840–1; Sent by the Colonists of South Australia, with the Sanction and Support of the Government: Including an Account of the Manners and Customs of the Aborigines and the State of Their Relations with Europeans*, London: T. and W. Boone, 1845 (hereafter *Journals of Expeditions*). On the issue of kidney fat Eyre wrote, 'It is a common practice among many of the tribes to grease their weapons and implements with human fat, taken from the omentum, either of enemies who have been killed, or of relations who have died. Spears, and other offensive arms, are supposed to possess additional powers if thus treated; and nets and other implements for procuring game are imagined to become much more effectual in ensnaring prey.' Eyre, *Journals of Expeditions*, pp. 314–15.
2 Luzon is the largest island in the Philippines.
3 As mentioned above in Chapter 6, footnote 26, Moorhouse had arrived in South Australia in 1839 to take up his appointment as Protector of Aborigines.
4 Here again Gerstäcker mis-spells Lake Bonney.
5 Moorundie, the first place on the Murray River in South Australia to be settled by Europeans. Edward John Eyre lived there from 1841 to 1844, having been appointed resident magistrate and protector of Aborigines. Gerstäcker made use of Eyre's ethnographic observations in the second volume of Eyre's *Journals of Expeditions*. Eyre for his part, and by his own acknowledgement, drew heavily on the journals of Matthew Moorhouse.

6   That is, the journal of Matthew Moorhouse, to which Moorhouse gave Gerstäcker access.
7   As indicated above, Moorhouse was appointed Protector of Aborigines. What follows appears to be a selection of extracts from Moorhouse's journal.
8   Possibly Mount Terrible.
9   'Ramong' is another name for Ramindjeri.
10 The information in this paragraph is drawn from Matthew Moorhouse's Report of January 14, 1840, published in *British Parliamentary Papers*, Colonies Australia, Vol. 7, Shannon, Ireland: Irish University Press, 1969, p. 324.
11 Moorhouse's Report of 27 July published in *British Parliamentary Papers* mentions this incident at Horrock's station. Gerstäcker's mis-spelling ('Honock' rather that 'Horrock') suggests he was using Moorhouse's hand-written report.
12 In his 1840 report Moorhouse had written, 'They are supplied with biscuits, rice, or sugar for attending, and as soon as they can read and pronounce accurately words of four syllables, they have a dress or blanket given to them. [...] That we may secure their regular attendance, we propose to supply them with as good food as they can obtain in Adelaide; and our project is to prepare them a soup with fresh meat and peas – a dish for which they have great partiality.' Moorhouse, Report of 14 January 1840, *British Parliamentary Papers*, Vol. 7, p. 325.
13 These figures are from Moorhouse, Report of 20 February 1841, *British Parliamentary Papers*, Vol. 7, p. 356.
14 Robert Gouger initially held the position of colonial secretary for South Australia and later became colonial treasurer until his resignation in 1844.
15 This incident is recounted in Eyre, *An Account of the Manners and Customs*, p. 388.
16 This is almost certainly a reference to what is more commonly known now as the 'Rufus River Massacre', in which on 27 August 1841 a party of Europeans clashed violently with Aborigines at Rufus River, between Lake Bonney and the Murray, causing an unknown number of deaths.
17 Figures are from the report presented to the Adelaide Statistical Society by Moorhouse and the missionary Christian Teichelmann in December 1841. The report, which was published in two South Australian newspapers in January 1842, was republished in 1990 by Robert Foster. See Matthew Moorhouse and Christian Teichelmann, 'Transactions of the Statistical Society. Report on the Aborigines of South Australia', ed. Robert Foster, *Journal of the Anthropological Society of South Australia*, 28, 1 (1990), pp. 40–53. See also the Moorhouse Report of 20 February 1841, *British Parliamentary Papers*, Vol. 7, p. 326.
18 Eyre had written, 'The diseases to which the natives are subject, are with the exception of those induced by artificial living, as gout, rheumatism, &c. very similar to those which afflict Europeans, the principal being the result of

inflammation, acute, or chronic, arising from exposure to the cold, and which affects most generally the bronchiae, the lungs, and the pleura. [...]. A disease very similar to the small-pox, and leaving similar marks upon the face, appears formerly to have been prevalent. Eyre, *Journals of Expeditions*, p. 379.

19 These figures from Eyre, *Journals of Expeditions*, pp. 417–18.
20 Moorundie.
21 Queen Victoria's birthday was 24 May.
22 The above figures are from Moorhouse's 'Annual Report of the Aborigines Department for the Year ending 30th September 1843', pp. 59–60; also Eyre, *Journals of Expeditions*, pp. 371–73.
23 This observation is made also by Eyre, *Journals of Expeditions*, pp. 361–62.
24 The marriage of Thomas Adams and the Kaurna woman Kudnarto was the first in South Australia between a black woman and a white man.
25 Kudnarto was the first indigenous person to take up a land grant.

9. The Manners and Customs of the South Australian Tribes

1 Possibly Glenelg-Sturt River and Hurtle Vale. The unusual transcription of Glenelg suggests Gerstäcker was working with a hand-written manuscript. Hurtle Vale was never formally adopted as a geographical name, but it encompassed an area including Happy Valley, O'Halloran Hill, Trott Park, Reynella, Hallett Cove and Morphett Vale.
2 Alternative spellings of Noarlunga and Myponga.
3 Moorhouse, Report of 27 July 1840, *British Parliamentary Papers*, Vol. 7, p. 355: 'A more extended knowledge of the language has introduced us to a more general acquaintance with the manners and customs of these peoples. We find – what Europeans thought the Aborigines of Australasia did not possess – territorial rights, families owning and holding certain districts of land which pass from father to son, never to daughters, with as much regularity as property in our own country – they go further than this: occasionally one family will barter their territory for a district belonging to another family, as in the case of King John, who formerly belonged to the districts of Adelaide, Glenelg, Sturt River, and Hurtle Vale, and he exchanged them for Ugaldinga and Maitpunga plains. One circumstance regarding property is peculiar; some own large districts of land, while others have none at all. We do not know how it was originally obtained; how it happens that some have, whilst others have not.'
4 Moorhouse writes, 'The implements are equal in simplicity to the clothing. Those of the men consist of the winda (largest spear), from eight to twelve feet in length, with a point plain, or barbed with flint or glass, or sometimes having hooks cut out on it, and is thrown by the hand a distance of five or ten yards; the kaiya (smaller spear), from five to six feet in length, occasionally barbed with glass, consisting of two parts, the pointed part made of heavy material, as the tea tree, and the posterior part, about two or three feet in length, of grass-tree

or reed, fixed to the first by gum and tendons of animals; the weapon is thrown by the midla (propelling stick) a distance of 60 or 80 yards with considerable precision.' See Moorhouse, 'Transactions', p. 42.

5   This section on needles and skin is drawn largely from Moorhouse's 'Transactions', pp. 42–43.
6   This paragraph is based on Moorhouse's 'Annual Report', p. 54.
7   This observation is drawn from Moorhouse's 'Annual Report', p. 55.
8   The following section dealing with Aboriginal social life is based largely on descriptions in Moorhouse's 'Transactions', pp. 43–44 and Eyre, *Journals of Expeditions*, pp. 218, 225–26.
9   This information is drawn from Eyre, *Journals of Expeditions of Discovery*, p. 322
10 This section on names, including the names themselves (though with spelling variations), is based on Eyre, *Journals of Expeditions*, pp. 324–26.
11 Eyre writes, 'In their domestic relations with one another polygamy is practiced in its fullest extent. [...] The females, and especially the young one are kept principally among the old men, who barter away their daughters, sisters, or nieces, in exchange for wives for themselves or their sons. [...] Female children are betrothed usually from early infancy [...] the girls generally go to live with their husbands about the age of twelve, and sometimes before that. Relatives nearer than cousins are not allowed to marry, and this alliance does not generally take place.' Eyre, *Journals of Expeditions*, pp. 318–19.
12 The section following below on life-stages, ceremonies and circumcision borrows heavily from Eyre, whose account in turn seems to be based on the findings of Moorhouse. See Eyre, *Journals of Expeditions*, pp. 333–36, and Moorhouse, 'Transactions', p. 44, and 'Annual Report', pp. 56–57.
13 The section beginning here dealing with religious beliefs draws from Moorhouse, 'Transactions', pp. 44–45; also 'Annual Report', p. 59, and Eyre, *Journals of Expeditions of Discovery*, pp. 355–60.
14 That is, from the Lake Bonney district.
15 This is based on a passage in Moorhouse, 'Annual Report', p. 59; Moorhouse gives the creature the name 'Kuinyo'.
16 Gerstäcker's section on medicine here is similar to Moorhouse in 'Transactions', p. 45 and 'Annual Report', p. 59; also Eyre, *Journals of Expeditions of Discovery*, pp. 360–61.
17 The description of burial rites is based on Moorhouse's 'Annual Report', p. 57 and Eyre, *Journals of Expeditions*, pp. 343–45. The paragraph on mourning is similar to passages in Moorhouse's 'Annual Report', pp. 58–59, and Eyre, *An Account of the Manners and Customs*, pp. 353–54.
18 Lake Bonney.
19 Heinrich August Eduard Meyer (mentioned in Chapter 7) of the Dresden Mission Society performed missionary work at Encounter Bay for eight years to

1848 and was then pastor of the Bethany congregation in the Barossa Valley. He is the author of *Vocabulary of the Language Spoken by the Aborigines of the Southern and Eastern Portions of the Settled Districts of South Australia, Preceded by a Grammar Showing the Construction of the Language as far as at Present Known*, Adelaide: James Allen, 1843, and *Manners and Customs of the Aborigines of the Encounter Bay Tribe*, Adelaide: George Dehane, 1846. Clamor Wilhelm Schürmann, also of the Dresden Mission Society, initially worked in Adelaide and then went to Port Lincoln as Deputy Protector of Aborigines. For a time he joined Meyer at Encounter Bay but in 1848 returned to Port Lincoln, where he started an Aboriginal school. After its closure he moved to Victoria in 1853.

20   Meyer. The section that follows here dealing with sorcery is drawn largely from Meyer, *Manners and Customs of the Encounter Bay Tribe*, pp. 8–9.
21   This section on the disposal of the dead is drawn from Meyer, *Manners and Customs of the Encounter Bay Tribe*, pp. 10–11.
22   This section is based on Meyer, *Manners and Customs of the Encounter Bay Tribe*, pp. 11–12.
23   This story of the origins of the stars is based on Meyer, *Manners and Customs of the Encounter Bay Tribe*, p. 12.
24   This paragraph is based on Meyer, *Manners and Customs of the Encounter Bay Tribe*, pp. 12–13.
25   This telling of the stories of the cause of rain and the origins of languages based on Meyer, *Manners and Customs of the Encounter Bay Tribe*, pp. 14–15.
26   Lake Bonney.
27   Corroboree.

10. Sydney in August 1851

1   The *Wilhelmine* was a Hamburg-registered barque of 408 tons. She sailed from Adelaide on 20 July and reached Sydney on 1 August.
2   Troy weight is a system of weights for precious metals and gemstones.
3   The Ophir Diggings, located at the confluence of Summer Hill Creek and Lewis Ponds Creek north-east of Orange, produced payable gold in February 1851 and triggered the gold rush in New South Wales.
4   *Sydney Morning Herald*.
5   Also known as the Marine Railway, and cheaper than a Dry Dock, the Patent Slip was an inclined plane built on land but extending into the water. Vessels could be hauled out of the water on a cradle for repair.
6   The Turon River north of Lithgow flows into the Macquarie River.
7   The diggings known as 'World's End' or 'Meroo' were on Meroo Creek, about 30 kilometres south of Mudgee.
8   Actually Hargraves. The English-born Edward Hargraves, like Gerstäcker, had spent some time on the goldfields of California. Back in New South Wales, and

with the help of others, Hargraves found gold in February 1851. After claiming a government reward and advertising his success in the area he named Ophir, he did much to promote the gold rush that ensued.

9   In 1851 the first such committee, the San Francisco Vigilance Committee, was formed by a group of citizens to curb the illegal activities of gangs known as 'hounds' or 'regulators'.

10 Schmidt.

11 There were several disastrous conflagrations in San Francisco in the period 1849–51. The reference here is likely to be to a fire which took place on 3 June 1851, which led to the arrest of a number of people believed to be arsonists, as well as to popular demands to hang them. The Committee of Vigilance of San Francisco undertook to bring the arsonists to justice. One man hanged as a result of the committee's efforts was the ex-convict from Sydney John Jenkins, who was found guilty of theft and hanged the same night. Among the other four hanged and the 30 or so banished were reportedly a number of others from New South Wales or other British colonies.

12 Gerstäcker's own footnote: It might interest the reader to see a certificate for the members of the California Vigilance Committee. These certificates were printed with the heading: 'Committee of Vigilance. Fiat justitia ruat coelum.' To the left in a cross of oak-leaves are the words, 'Be just and fear not', and to the right, 'Self preservation the first law of nature'. A coat of arms in the middle shows a sword and scales across a row of stars, with an eye superimposed as a sign of the Union, separated from a bundle of fasces with an axe protruding from it. Under this is written, 'This is to certify that Mr ___ is a member of the Committee of Vigilance of the city of San Francisco, organised on 9 June 1851. For the mutual protection of life and property, endangered by the general insufficiency of the laws and their maladministration.' I.E. Woodworth, President. Isaak Bluxome, Secretary.

13 Michael William Balfe was an Irish composer, best known for his opera *The Bohemian Girl*.

14 As noted in Chapter 1, Sir Charles Augustus FitzRoy was Governor of New South Wales and, from January 1850, 'Governor-General of all Her Majesty's Australian possession', a title which later became 'Governor-General of Australia'. 'Steward' should be 'Stewart'.

15 It is not known with certainty who composed the anthem. Joseph Haydn probably borrowed the tune after hearing it in London.

16 Sara Flower was an English-born contralto singer who had a successful musical career in London before moving to Australia for unknown reasons in late 1849. She was arguably Australia's first diva.

17 Carl Maria von Weber's *Der Freischütz*, usually translated as *The Marksman*, is considered by many to be the first important German romantic opera. The plot, set near the end of the Thirty Years War, is based on a German folk legend.

It was first performed in Berlin in 1821. Gerstäcker had a great fondness for opera, in large part because both his parents were opera singers. He had a special interest in this opera, because his father had played the role of Max at its premiere in Dresden.
18   Samiel is a mythical figure, sometimes regarded as an angel of death, who appears in *Der Freischütz* as a black huntsman.
19   A scene in *Der Freischütz*.
20   At the time of Gerstäcker's visit to Australia the first efforts were being made to establish the fate of Ludwig Leichhardt's transcontinental expedition, which by 1851 would have run out of supplies. Then and over the following years multiple expeditions, both official and unofficial, were mounted to follow in Leichhardt's footsteps and establish the cause of his disappearance – all of them in vain.
21   As explained in Chapter 1, the photographer Wilhelm Hötzer – known in Australia as William Hetzer – and his wife Thekla had emigrated from Germany in 1850.
22   Augustus Dreutler, a German merchant, as mentioned in Chapter 1.
23   Gerstäcker's *Narrative of a Journey Round the World* (1853) contains a dedication to 'His dear little friend, Sarah Mary Rickards, of Sidney'.

11. Voyage through Torres Strait

1   The *Sarah* was an emigrant ship which had arrived in Sydney from England in early June 1851.
2   Raine Island is a coral cay on the outer edges of the Great Barrier Reef, some 620 kilometres north-north-west of Cairns.
3   Ashmore Reef is at the eastern end of the Torres Strait; it should not be confused with Ashmore Reef off the north-western coast of Australia.
4   Sir Charles Hardy's Island was named by James Cook in 1770.
5   These are all part of the East Islands group about 100 kilometres north of Cape Grenville.
6   The rubble cays which are the Cairncross Islands are part of an inshore patch reef, the islands connected by sand spits.
7   Possibly a manta ray.
8   The bonito is a tuna-like fish found in many parts of the world. The Australian bonito, the sarda australis or horse mackerel, is found in the waters of eastern Australia.
9   Mount Adolphus Island, also known as Mori Island, is dominated by the flat-topped Mount Adolphus. The island is about 4.5 kilometres long by two kilometres wide and is located about ten kilometres from the mainland.
10   This comment offers an insight into Gerstäcker's politics. The red, black and gold tricolour was the flag of the German liberals during the failed revolutions

of 1848–49. It did not become the flag of a united Germany until the founding of the Weimar Republic in 1919.

11 Wednesday Island is also known today as Maururra, and is another of the roughly 270 islands of the Torres Strait.

12 Booby Island is 30 kilometres west of Thursday Island. It is well-known today for its lighthouse, which however did not exist in Gerstäcker's time.

13 Gerstäcker here mis-spells the name of Johannes Elias Teijsmann, curator of the Bogor (in those days Buitenzorg) Botanical Gardens in Java from 1830 to 1869.

Afterword: Friedrich Gerstäcker's Australia

1 For a brief overview in English see especially Leslie Bodi, 'Gerstaecker, Friedrich (1816–1872)', Australian Dictionary of Biography, National Centre of Biography, Australian National University, http://adb.anu.edu.au/biography/gerstaecker-friedrich-3604/text5593, accessed 15 January 2014. A full-length biography in German is Thomas Ostwald, *Friedrich Gerstäcker – Leben und Werk. Biographie eines Ruhelosen*, Braunschweig: Friedrich-Gerstäcker-Gesellschaft, 2007.

2 Reichsministerium des Handels an den Herrn Friedrich Gerstäcker, 2 March 1849, Stadtarchiv Braunschweig, G IX 23, 38a.

3 Initially his accounts would be published as a supplement to the *Allgemeine Augsburger Zeitung*. Cotta granted him 400 Taler to supplement the 500 he was to receive from the government. See Gisela Heathcote, 'Friedrich Gerstäcker zum 100. Todestage. Australienreise 1851: Das Australienbild seiner Zeit und sein Werk als Dokument nach 120 Jahren', *Beiträge zur Friedrich Gerstäcker-Forschung*, 1 (1981), pp. 3, 18.

4 Under the title *Omoo oder Abenteuer im stillen Ocean*, Leipzig: Verlag Gustav Mayer, 1847.

5 'Overland News', *South Australian Register*, 31 May 1851, p. 3.

6 See Heathcote, 'Friedrich Gerstäcker zum 100. Todestage', p. 3.

7 Friedrich Gerstäcker, 'The Navigation of the Murray', *South Australian Register*, 26 June 1851, p. 2. His views were published under the heading 'Steam Navigation on the Murray River' in the *Sydney Morning Herald*, 15 July 1851, p. 3 and in *The Courier* (Hobart) 6 August 1851.

8 The other volumes in the series as published by the J.G. Cottascher Verlag in Stuttgart follow the course of his travels. The first three volumes, published in 1853, are *Südamerika, Californien* and *Die Südsee-Inseln*. Both *Australien* and *Java* were published in 1854. Nonetheless, the appearance of five large volumes within two years gives some indication of how quickly Gerstäcker worked.

9 The full title is: *Narrative of a Journey Round the World. Comprising a Winter Passage Across the Andes to Chili; with a Visit to the Gold-Regions of California and Australia, the South Sea Islands, Java*, etc., New York: Harper and Brothers, 1853.

It was published concurrently under the same title by Hurst and Blackett in London.

10   The collection of Gerstäcker's complete oeuvre, of which his works relating to Australia are just a small part, were published posthumously as 43 volumes by the Jena publisher Costenoble as *Gesammelte Schriften* in the period 1872 to 1879, yet the collection is incomplete. For a detailed bibliography of Gerstäcker's massive literary output see Manfred R.W. Garzmann, Thomas Ostwald and Wolf-Dieter Schuegraf (eds), *Gerstäcker-Verzeichnis. Erstausgaben, Gesammelte Werke und Sekundärliteratur mit Nachweis im Stadarchiv und in der Stadtbibliothek Braunschweig*, Brunswick: n.p. 1986. See also the website: http://de.wikisource.org/wiki/Friedrich_Gerst%C3%A4cker For studies of the works relating to Australia see especially Alan Corkhill, *Antipodean Encounters: Australia and the German Literary Imagination, 1754–1918*, Bern: Peter Lang, 1990, 80–95, and Matthias Morgenroth, *Nachrichten aus dem Land der Gegenfüssler*, Tübingen, Stauffenberg, 2001.

11   On these two fictional works see especially Alan Corkhill, 'Space, Place and Identity in the Australian Fiction of Friedrich Gerstäcker', *Limbus. Australisches Jahrbuch für germanistische Literatur- und Kulturwissenschaft*, 6 (2013), 141–55.

12   *Nationalverein für deutsche Auswanderung*. See Ostwald, *Friedrich Gerstäcker*, p. 88.

13   Ostwald, *Friedrich Gerstäcker*, p. 102.

14   Friedrich Gerstäcker, *Nord- und Süd-Australien. Ein Handbuch für Auswanderer. Frei nach englischen Werken von Dav. Mackenzie, J.C. Byrne, G.F. Davidson, C. Rowcroft und G.B. Wilkinson, bearbeitet von Friedrich Gerstäcker*, Dresden and Leipzig, Arnoldsche Buchhandlung, 1849.

15   J.K. Hasskarl, *Australien und seine Kolonien*, Elberfeld: Julius Bädeker, 1849; Ludwig Krahmer, *Die deutsche Auswanderung mit besonderer Rücksicht auf Australien*, Berlin: Ferdinand Reichardt, 1849; J.P.D. Dieseldorff, *Wegweiser nach Südaustralien*, Hamburg: Kittler, 1849; Georg Doeger, *Der Auswanderer nach Südaustralien*, Tangermünde, Verlag der G. Doeger'schen Buchhandlung, 1849; Dr Ebel, *Über Australien. Von Privatdocumenten*, Königsberg: n.p., 1849; Eugen Laun, *Führer und Rathgeber für Auswanderer nach Australien und Port Adelaide*, Bremen: A.D. Geisler, 1849.

16   See for example Wilhelm Kirchner, *Australien und seine Vortheile für Auswanderer*, H.L. Brönner, Frankfurt a.M., 1850; Rudolf Reimer, *Süd-Australien. Ein Beitrag zur deutschen Auswanderungsfrage*, Berlin: D. Reimer, 1851; Albert Heising, *Die Deutschen in Australien*, Berlin: J.A. Wohlemuth, 1853; W. Schulze (ed.), *Reise- und Lebensbilder aus Neuholland, Neuseeland und Californien*, Magdeburg: Bensch, 1853; E. Bieber, *Praktischer Rathgeber und Reisehandbuch für deutsche Auswanderer nach Australien*, Potsdam: C. Schmoock-Smok, 1854. An unusual case is that of Gustav Listemann, who emigrated to Adelaide in 1849 and soon returned to Germany to write a damning account of the colony. See G. Listemann, *Meine*

Auswanderung nach Südaustralien und Rückkehr zum Vaterland. Ein Wort zur Warnung und Belehrung für alle Auswanderungslustigen, Berlin: A.W. Hayn, 1851.
17 Gerstäcker, *Nord- und Südaustralien*, title page.
18 David Mackenzie, *The Emigrant's Guide; or Ten Years' Practical Experience in Australia*, London: W.S. Orr, 1844.
19 Shelagh Spencer, 'Joseph Byrne and his Immigration Scheme', http://shelaghspencer.com/josephbyrne/
20 G.F. Davidson, *Trade and Travel in the Far East; or recollections of twenty-one years passed in Java, Singapore, Australia and China*, London: Madden and Malcolm, 1846.
21 Rowcroft was the author of the fictional *Tales of the Colonies, or, the Adventures of an Emigrant, Edited by a late Colonial Magistrate* (3 vols. London: Saunders and Otley, 1843) which might have influenced Gerstäcker because of its lengthy preface explaining the advantages of taking up land in the colonies.
22 Charles Rowcroft, transl. Friedrich Gerstäcker, *Die Abenteuer eines Auswanderers. Erzählungen aus den Colonien von Van Diemensland*, Leipzig: Otto Wigand, 1845; Charles Rowcroft, transl. Friedrich Gerstäcker, *Die Buschrähndscher*, Leipzig: Otto Wigand, 1853.
23 *South Australia, Its Advantages and Its Resources: being a description of that colony and a manual of information for emigrants*, London: John Murray, 1848; *The Working Man's Handbook to South Australia, With Advice to the Farmer, and Detailed Information for the Several Classes of Labourers and Artisans*, London: John Murray, 1849. The first of these had been translated and published in German under the title *Handbuch für Auswanderer nach Südaustralien*, Leipzig: Verlag der Dyk'schen Buchhandlung, 1849.
24 August Klaehn to Eduard Delius, 9 January 1848, in Gerstäcker, *Nord- und Süd-Australien. Ein Handbuch für Auswanderer*, p. 179.
25 Edward John Eyre, *Journals of Expeditions of Discovery into Central Australia, and Overland from Adelaide to King George's Sound, in the Years 1840–1; Sent by the Colonists of South Australia, with the Sanction and Support of the Government: Including an Account of the Manners and Customs of the Aborigines and the State of Their Relations with Europeans*, 2 Vols., London: T. and W. Boone, 1845.
26 Geoffrey Dutton, 'Eyre, Edward John (1815–1901)', Australian Dictionary of Biography, National Centre of Biography, Australian National University, http://adb.anu.edu.au/biography/eyre-edward-john-2032/text2507, published in hardcopy 1966, accessed online 16 October 2014.
27 The report, which was published in two South Australian newspapers in January 1842, was republished in 1990 by the Adelaide historian Robert Foster. Matthew Moorhouse and Christian Teichelmann, 'Transactions of the Statistical Society. Report on the Aborigines of South Australia', ed. Robert Foster, *Journal of the Anthropological Society of South Australia*, 28, 1 (1990), 40–53

28 Heinrich August Eduard Meyer, *Vocabulary of the language spoken by the Aborigines of the southern and eastern portions of the settled districts of South Australia, preceded by a Grammar showing the construction of the language as far as at present known*, Adelaide: James Allen, 1843.

29 Heinrich August Eduard Meyer, *Manners and customs of the aborigines of the Encounter Bay tribe*, Adelaide: George Dehane, 1846.

30 Published in Berlin by Verlag von Justus Albert Wohlgemuth. We know that Gerstäcker became familiar with this book because he mentions it in the foreword to the translation and abbreviation of Charles Mundy's *Wanderungen in Australien und Vandiemensland*, Leipzig: Carl B. Lorck, 1856, ix. Mundy's original was *Our Antipodes, or Residence and Rambles in the Australian Colonies; with a Glimpse of the Gold Fields*, London: Richard Bentley, 1852.

31 Mrs Robert Lee (that is, Sarah Bowditch Lee, née Wallis), *Adventures in Australia, or, the Wanderings of Captain Spencer in the Bush and the Wilds; Containing Accurate Descriptions of the Habits of the Natives, and the Natural Productions and Features of the Country*, London: Grant and Smith, 1851. The note in Gerstäcker's journal is observed by his biographer Thomas Ostwald, *Friedrich Gerstäcker*, p. 178.

32 Friedrich Gerstäcker, letter to 'Tumgumlong', 23.8.1851, *Braunschweiger Stadtarchiv* GIX 23.21a.

Acknowledgements

First and foremost, my gratitude goes to those who combined their linguistic skills with their creative talents to produce a lively English rendition of Friedrich Gerstäcker's wonderful travelogue, true to the word and spirit of its author. Without the dedicated labours of Thomas Kruckemeyer, Judith Wilson, Aileen Ohlendorf, Harald Ohlendorf, Lois Zweck and Storm Graham, this book would never have seen the light of day.

These collective efforts were supported by generous grants from History SA and the School of History and International Relations at Flinders University. The patience of those benefactors through a lengthy gestation has been exemplary. I hope that they now believe their forbearance and munificence to have been suitably rewarded.

Gerstäcker's original text has not only been translated here but has also been supplemented with notes and an afterword to familiarise the modern Australian reader with the circumstances in which Gerstäcker lived, travelled and wrote. I am particularly indebted to the insights into these matters provided by Judith Wilson and Lois Zweck, who graciously went far beyond the call of their translating duties.

For his assistance in various matters, above all with the provision of Gerstäcker's map, I am grateful to Thomas Ostwald, Germany's foremost expert in all things relating to Friedrich Gerstäcker. Similarly the Gerstäcker Museum in Braunschweig – commonly known in the Anglosphere as Brunswick – proved an invaluable source of knowledge and assistance, as did

Acknowledgements

Braunschweig's Stadtarchiv. When he was not travelling, Gerstäcker spent a good part of his life in Braunschweig, where he is also buried. I hope that in a small way this book helps to keep alive the name of Friedrich Gerstäcker in that charming town he chose to call home and in the wider world – his other home.

Finally, I thank and commend Wakefield Press for its commitment to publishing this work and, in doing so, deepening our knowledge of South Australia's uniquely German past.

Peter Monteath

Index

A

Aboriginals, *see* Indigenous Australians.

Adelaide   4, 6, 7, 12, 30, 46, 60, 119, 121, 129, 130–35, 141–49, 150, 152, 168, 188, 191, 199, 200, 264–66, 270, 272

Albury   31, 41, 42–43, 44, 45, 46, 47, 50, 60, 66, 88, 278

Angas, George Fife   124, 127, 164, 281, 286

Angas Park   124, 125, 281

Anti-Transportation movement   4, 201, 276

B

Barossa Valley   264, 265, 271, 273, 281

Bathurst   123, 203, 204, 207, 208, 209, 218–19, 266

Behr, Hans Hermann   129, 281

Billy the Bull   65, 68–69

Black Police   66–67

Blacks, Black fellows, *see* Indigenous Australians.

Booby Island   255–57, 294

Boomerang   74–75, 84, 86, 101, 106, 279

Botanic Gardens (Sydney)   9–10

Botany Bay   13–15

Buch, Leopold von   165, 281

Buchsfelde   165, 265, 281

bunyip   97, 102, 107, 279, 280

Burra (Burra Burra Mine)   135, 282

C

Cairncross Islands   243, 246–47, 249, 250, 253, 255, 293

California   122, 123, 132, 209, 211, 213, 214, 217–18, 219, 222, 273

Chinese   27, 153, 176, 224

Cobden, Richard   28, 277–78,

cockatoos   14, 23, 64, 80, 100, 101, 110, 182, 191, 247

Cockburn Islands   241, 242

convicts ('government people')   3, 4, 267, 276

coral   237–38

Cotta (German publisher)   ix, x, 263

Index

D

Darling River 52, 89, 98, 101, 278
dingo 77–78, 98, 117–119
Dreutler, Augustus 5, 13, 24, 232, 276, 293
Dröge, Gustav 133, 282
drought 29, 47

E

education, *see* Schools
Edward River 61, 63, 64, 65, 75, 115, 279
Eggers, Wilhelm 133, 282
elections 139–41, 282
emu 76
Encounter Bay 115, 172, 190, 194, 196
Eyre, Edward John 272, 280, 287, 288–89, 290

F

Fiedler, August 162, 286
FitzRoy, Charles 29, 223, 278, 292
Flower, Sara 224, 292
Frankfurt Parliament 262, 268

G

Gawler (Gawlertown) 129, 130, 150, 152, 168, 265, 281
Germans 26, 27, 41, 46, 124–29, 130, 132–3, 160, 165, 166, 265, 269, 277
Gerstäcker, Friedrich 261–75
Gilles, Osmond 136, 282
gold 122–23, 168, 199, 203, 204, 210–214, 228, 230, 266, 269, 273, 274, 281, 291–92
Goulbourn 37, 38, 39, 123
Great Barrier Reef 236–241, 249

Gundagai 37, 40, 44

H

Hahndorf 148, 153, 154, 284
Hardys Island 241, 242
Hargraves, Edward 212, 281, 291–92
Harris, Mister/Captain 220–21, 223
Hötzer, Wilhelm 13, 232, 277, 293
Hume River 48, 49–60, 61, 278
Hunter Valley 22–28, 270, 277

I

Indians, *see* Indigenous Australians)
Indigenous Australians ('Black fellows', 'blacks', 'Australian savages', Aborigines), 1, 12, 43, 44–45, 54, 60. 63,64, 66, 67, 68, 72–76, 79–80, 82–87, 89, 94–95, 96–7, 101–104, 105–114, 116, 142–48, 163, 169–98, 244, 249–55, 268, 276
Irrawang 24, 27, 28, 277

K

kangaroos 12, 14, 72, 76, 90, 119–120, 119, 179
Kavel, August 133, 153–57, 281, 284, 285–86
'Kidney fat' myth 65, 73, 84, 87, 102, 170, 189, 268, 278, 287
King, James 24, 25, 277
Kirchner, Wilhelm 13, 24, 30, 277, 295

L

Lake Alexandrina 115, 172, 175, 278, 280
Lake Bonney (Bonin, Boni) 107, 171, 189, 197, 280
Lake Victoria 101, 102, 114, 115, 189, 280

301

Langmeil 153, 154, 158, 284, 285, 286

Lapérouse, Jean François de Galaup, Comte de 14, 277

Leichhardt, Ludwig 29, 45, 75, 89, 230, 275, 278, 279, 293

Liedertafel 134

Logan River 75, 77

Lyndoch Valley 129–30, 281

M

Macclesfield 148–49

mallee bush 71–73, 81, 89–90, 91, 92, 101, 104, 109, 116, 119, 198

May, Karl 267–68

Meyer (Meier), Heinrich August Eduard 142, 154, 158, 190, 273, 283, 285, 286, 290–91,

Melbourne 4, 42, 58, 60, 69, 88

Mississippi 10, 23, 54, 100, 222, 262

Moorhouse, Matthew 142, 148, 171, 272, 283, 287, 288, 289–90,

Moulemein (Mouleman) River 65, 279

Mount Adolphus Island 249, 253, 293

Mount Barker (Barkershill) 148

Mount Lofty 148–49

Mozart 59

Mücke, Carl Wilhelm Ludwig 133, 154, 159, 282, 285

Murray (River) 6, 7, 12, 20, 22, 38, 42, 43, 45, 48, 49–119, 121, 123, 130, 135, 142, 143, 147, 148, 170, 171, 172, 173, 174, 175, 176, 179, 180, 182, 185, 186, 187, 189, 190, 212, 254, 261, 264–65, 268, 270, 272, 278, 279, 287, 288, 294

Murrumbidgee 40, 42, 52, 61, 83, 87, 101, 142, 189, 265, 278, 279

N

Newcastle 23

Noltenius, Bernhad August 130, 148, 281

Northwest Bend 61, 115, 116, 172

Norton Summit (Norton's place) 121, 124, 128, 281

O

Ophir Diggings 122, 203, 281, 291, 292

P

Parramatta 34, 205

platypus 1, 80

Port Adelaide 134, 141, 199–200

Port Lincoln 174, 176, 190, 283, 291

R

Raines Island 239, 241

Raymond Terrace 24, 28

Roper, John 45, 278–79,

Royal Mail 31, 35, 36, 41, 43, 123, 204, 209

Rufus Creek 104, 173, 189, 280, 288

S

San Francisco 129, 131, 218, 222, 230, 276, 281, 292

Savages, *see* Indigenous Australians

schools 136–39, 142–148

Schleinitz, H. von 136, 282

Schomburgk (Schomburg), Otto 133, 165-7, 265, 281, 282, 287

Schomburgk (Schomburg), Richard 165-7, 265, 281, 282, 287

Sturt, Charles 142, 265, 278, 279, 280, 283

Index

Sydney 1–5, 9, 13, 15, 19–22, 24, 28, 29–30, 31, 34, 36, 37, 43, 46, 66, 83, 88, 94, 135, 145, 167, 168, 199, 201–205, 212, 215, 216, 218, 219–20, 223, 228–230, 232, 235, 261, 263, 266, 267, 269, 270, 271, 276, 277, 291, 292, 293

T

Tanunda 125, 128–30, 133, 136, 138, 142, 149, 150. 153–55, 158, 159–65, 168, 199, 284, 285

Teichelmann, Christian 272, 273, 286, 288, 296

theatre 15–19

Timor 258–59,

Torres Strait 75, 233, 236–57, 266, 273, 293, 294

Turon River 209, 210–211, 216, 217, 218, 291

W

Wakool 75, 279

Woolshed 60, 61

Y

Yass 31, 39, 123

Wakefield Press is an independent publishing and
distribution company based in Adelaide, South Australia.
We love good stories and publish beautiful books.
To see our full range of books, please visit our website at
www.wakefieldpress.com.au
where all titles are available for purchase.

Find us!

Twitter: www.twitter.com/wakefieldpress
Facebook: www.facebook.com/wakefield.press
Instagram: instagram.com/wakefieldpress

www.ingramcontent.com/pod-product-compliance
Lightning Source LLC
Chambersburg PA
CBHW032056230426
43662CB00035B/441